90 0804227 1

D1765192

Sociological Cultural Studies

Also by Gregor McLennan

MARXISM AND THE METHODOLOGIES OF HISTORY
MARXISM, PLURALISM AND BEYOND
PLURALISM
EXPLORING SOCIETY (*with A. Ryan and P. Spoonley*)

Sociological Cultural Studies

Reflexivity and Positivity in the Human Sciences

Gregor McLennan
University of Bristol

First published 2006 by
PALGRAVE MACMILLAN
Houndmills, Basingstoke, Hampshire RG21 6XS and
175 Fifth Avenue, New York, N.Y. 10010
Companies and representatives throughout the world

PALGRAVE MACMILLAN is the global academic imprint of the Palgrave Macmillan division of St. Martin's Press, LLC and of Palgrave Macmillan Ltd. Macmillan® is a registered trademark in the United States, United Kingdom and other countries. Palgrave is a registered trademark in the European Union and other countries.

ISBN-13: 978-0-230-00885-4 hardback
ISBN-10: 0-230-00885-2 hardback

This book is printed on paper suitable for recycling and made from fully managed and sustained forest sources.

A catalogue record for this book is available from the British Library.

Library of Congress Cataloging-in-Publication Data
McLennan, Gregor.
    Sociological cultural studies:reflexivity and positivity in the human sciences/Gregor McLennan.
       p.   cm.
    Includes bibliographical references and index.
    ISBN 0–230–00885–2 (cloth)
    1. Culture—Study and teaching.   2. Sociology—Philosophy.
    3. Sociology—Methodology.   I. Title.
    HM623.M385 2006
    306.01—dc22   2006049466

10   9   8   7   6   5   4   3   2   1
15   14   13   12   11   10   09   08   07   06

Printed and bound in Great Britain by
Antony Rowe Ltd, Chippenham and Eastbourne

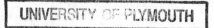

Contents

Acknowledgements

I am particularly grateful to Stuart Hall, Tom Osborne, John Holmwood, Steve Kemp, Maureen O'Malley, Nicos Mouzelis, Angela McRobbie, Michele Barrett and Brennon Wood for their part in the dialogues (real or imagined) that have helped me formulate my thoughts on sociology and cultural studies over the years. I also want to express loving thanks to Suzanne Battleday for her fantastic support during the writing of this book and in many other ways.

Chapters 4, 5, and 7 are revised versions of previously published journal articles. I am therefore grateful to Sage Publications Ltd for permission to draw upon the following:

'Sociology's Eurocentrism and the "Rise of the West" Revisited', *European Journal of Social Theory*, Vol. 3, No. 3, 2000.

'Sociology, Eurocentrism and Postcolonial Theory', *European Journal of Social Theory*, Vol. 6, No. 1, 2003.

'The "New American Cultural Sociology": An Appraisal', *Theory, Culture & Society*, Vol. 22, No. 6, 2005.

Introduction

Over the past 20 years or so, within radical intellectual and pedagogical circles, a widespread presumption could readily be encountered: that sociology as a progressive project had been decisively challenged, perhaps even supplanted, by newer critical perspectives. These 'successor discourses' – cultural studies, (post)feminist studies, the 'new' social theory, multiculturalism, postcolonialism, post-Marxist discourse theory, queer theory and others besides – whilst by no means identical to one another, have been systematically cross-referenced in the literature and show many family resemblances at the theoretical level. Most generally, what is shared is the view that there is sufficient enough validity in the postmodern and cultural 'turns' to render the traditional social science disciplines, but perhaps especially sociology, profoundly problematical. This common perception has not proved completely agreeable to those working within the sociological mainstream. Some sociologists instinctively regard the new discourses as lightweight and diversionary, while many others feel, rather indignantly, that they have helped *transform* their discipline to include just those questions and impulses that the challengers say are conspicuous by their absence. With the academic consolidation of the successor discourses, a tendency to divide into clear and opposed camps was pronounced, each finding it convenient to portray the other as nothing less than the reigning academic establishment, the assumed superiority of which was buttressed on all sides by insider practices.

Yet things did not continue in quite that sectarian direction, so that today these characterizations, if they ever did fit, no longer hold. Indeed, since the mid-1990s there have been definite signs of a constructive, if still uneasy, relationship between sociology and cultural studies, the latter being the post-sociological formation that has lasted longest, and the one that can be regarded in some respects as the convenor of the other successor discourses. As cultural studies stabilized, many sociologists began to jostle for position in the queue to claim that they have *always* supported cultural studies, and practised it *within* the older discipline. Prominent cultural studies practitioners, for their part, became alarmed at the lack of basic sociological grounding in the newer tradition's exploration of social novelty and textual effect.

These moves to clarify and resolve the tangled relationship between cultural studies and sociology were effective up to a point, but no single, sustained treatment of the principal theoretical issues that stand on the interface between the two ensued. That is what I seek to provide in the present book, and I conduct my discussions of the different aspects of their relationship in the form of a general argument: that cultural studies researchers and theorists need to reclaim their own investment in the very *idea of sociology*. In recommending this idea of sociology, I should make clear, I am not necessarily seeking to uphold the *discipline* of sociology as such, nor would I deny that the periodic assaults launched by successor discourses on sociology's heartlands have been difficult to ward off. This book is not, therefore, one of those periodic, straight-ahead defences of 'the discipline' (Kilminster 1999, Goldthorpe 2000, Turner and Rojek 2001). But I do want to say that even if the corridors of university Departments of Sociology were to lie deserted and forlorn, the idea of sociology would continue, whether thinly or well disguised as something else. The thought is that any compelling overall vision of the humanities and social sciences has to have this idea of sociology, or some surrogate for it, at its heart, and so the book is written in the belief that even if sociology and cultural studies are not identical, they are continuous and overlapping discourses governed by the same logic of enquiry.

Andrew Abbott (2001) has suggested that the process of growth, clash and split that characterizes intellectual formations, like many other social and material processes, is essentially *fractal* in nature. This means that even when we find new disciplines and sub-disciplines emerging, often in an atmosphere of bitter opposition and revolutionary change, the binary structure present in the superseded context gets replicated, albeit in a new guise, in the subsequent settlement. What this means for us is that if the idea of sociology refers to the way in which we seek to validly characterize social formations as being of a certain systemic, objective *type*, the effects and signs of which can be identified across a range of empirical particulars, then we could expect to find this way of thinking *reinvented* in cultural studies, even when it is assumed to have broken decisively with disciplinary sociology. The conceptual matrix of sociology would be likely to re-emerge with special force whenever cultural studies theorists believe that, in their own backyard, tendencies towards ultra-discursivity, fragmentation, and subjectivism go too far. Feeling the urge, militantly at times, to break free of the hold of this generic idea of sociology, cultural studies theorists have not finally managed – because they *cannot* manage – without it.

The book pursues this overarching dialectic through topics and arguments in the field of general theoretical 'methodology' in the Neo-Kantian sense (I am not sure if it is 'philosophy of social science' as such). I proceed on the presumption that in spite of many creative moves in the programme of cultural studies, discussion around methodological questions in that conceptual sense has typically lacked depth and detail, a judgement that tends to be echoed when cultural studies practitioners themselves take the longer view of progress in their area (Johnson *et al.* 2004: 3). In that regard, the forms in which sociological theory is imbibed and debated give the latter a relative advantage. One of sociological theory's strengths is its greater *analytical* clarity: cultural studies theorizing has, in my view, *suffered*, rather than gained overall from being cast stylistically in poststructuralist ways. Another methodological strength within sociological discourse is the abiding concern with the task of *explanation*, even if this mode of understanding is perennially found to be hazy at the edges, and even if classification, 'thick description', evocative and evaluative summations, are fully acceptable as vital modes of understanding. Lastly, the inculcation of an investigative ethos of *positivity*, without neglecting the requirement of reflexivity, has stood the sociological imagination in good stead, especially when moods of *ultra*-reflexivity become excessive, as arguably they have in recent times.

The book develops these guiding threads through three main sectors of argument. One concerns the whole business of disciplinarity, interdisciplinarity and post-disciplinarity. The temptation is to say that these are 'merely' academic matters, and therefore of little real importance. But these days, academic training is the *sine qua non* of a large range of employment, and increasing numbers enter and exit higher education receptive to ways of thinking about themselves, and the world around them, that have been derived from their teachers and peers. So what the 'disciplines' are, and what spirit of inquiry or world-view they inculcate, makes a significant difference to the state of the citizenry. That aside, issues of disciplinarity are of considerable import in how we review the state of social understanding in general. Are the academic disciplines, as it were, merely constructed? Are they just ideological fig leaves for the social interests of their practitioners and subcultures? And is post-disciplinarity, right across the board, a viable and progressive professional prospect? In presenting and tackling issues of disciplinarity, I have to declare my commitment to the old-fashioned notion of the 'human sciences' as a continuous body of ideas reflection and research, in which imaginative and ideological motivation effectively *combine with*, rather than undermine, adherence to 'scientific rigour'. Although this book does not develop that platform to any great extent, the general ethos of the book carries it, and it is actively in play in Chapters 2, 3, 7 and 9.

For all their interest, however, issues of academic disciplinarity lack full-bloodedness, and so a second stumbling block to any integrative strategy for sociology and cultural studies brings more directly into play our deeper political and cultural sensibilities. This is the very firm adoption within cultural studies of an explicitly *postcolonialist* stance. Whilst this move is, without doubt, culturally and politically significant in itself, and whilst it has created hugely enhanced awareness of *Eurocentric* assumptions and practices within the mainstream academic disciplines, it is too readily taken for granted that once the 'taint' of Eurocentrism has been spotted, 'Western' discourses of all sorts are condemned to be forever contaminated. A number of concomitant assumptions are then also held to be self-evident: that what Eurocentrism refers to is necessarily bad; that postcolonial cultural studies avoids these traits; that the theorists in the postcolonial canon must be accepted as being of almost unarguable stature; and that the kind of intellectual politics that goes along with these shifts in theoretical register has to be couched as *multiculturalism*, albeit of a 'critical' sort. In Chapters 4, 5 and 6, I take issue with all the links in this chain of association, partly because they go beyond what any fine-tuned analysis can support, and partly because they undermine the kind of radical secular humanism that remains the most powerful source for Left cultural politics, long-term.

The third theme that is regularly marshalled against sociology, and in support of successor discourses, is that of *postpositivism*. Even if it is accepted that sociology has not exactly been a Board member of the positivist club, there is widespread agreement that its habitual anguishing over the goal of objectivity in methods and substantive conclusions make it an uncomfortable denizen of the postpositivist community. From this observation, it is all too quickly concluded that the idea of sociology is *incompatible* with the complex, pluralistic and reflexive temperament that dominates contemporary meta-theory, and that these intellectual inclinations very obviously represent signal improvements on their implied contrary mindsets. As with postcolonialism, my approach to this issue is not to question the value, or indeed the validity, of postpositivism as a meta-theoretical stance. But I do seek to demonstrate, in Chapters 1, 8 and 9, that a fair amount of (paradoxically) unreflexive and simplistic argument goes on in its name. And I want to suggest that we need to pay due respect to the intellectual moods of objectivism, monism and positivity, for assuredly their time will come again.

Those, then, are the main themes and sequences of the book. I anchor my general inclinations in critical discussion of texts and authors that seem to me somehow exemplary or representative of the specific issues under examination. These readings and dialogues are by no means exhaustive, of course; what they seek to offer is a good enough diagnostic register of debate. Their purpose is to establish a careful but not pedantic style of thinking about the key issues that sociology, cultural studies and other human science discourses share, and to encourage us to press on towards a common, principled approach to them.

Part of the ethos of 'positivity' that I am recommending is a recovery of the hope that we can grow out of the (in)famous picture of social science and cultural studies as intrinsically and inescapably 'multi-paradigmatic', forever in disagreement over fundamental presuppositions. Without wanting to deny that substantive and ideological dispute is bound to continue in various ways, the prospect of a kind of 'reflective equilibrium' around philosophical methodology seems to me attainable, and worth explicitly pursuing, not least as part of the battle against the kind of intellectual *instrumentalism* that seems abundant today. If intellectuals of the social-theoretical type ever were the peremptory 'legislators' in Zygmunt Bauman's (1987) model, or even his more modest hermeneutic 'interpreters', then these models no longer seem to prevail. Instead, facilitative 'mediators' and make-do 'vehicular' ideas are the order of the day (McLennan and Osborne 2003, Osborne 2004). No doubt this intellectual style has its uses, but it is not satisfactory. One of the reasons that 'the idea of sociology' still has force is that it returns us to the promise, and the business, of continually reconstructed totalizations.

1
Postpositivism and the Idea of Sociology

If a strong whiff of suspicion characterized the response of many practising sociologists to the whole question of postmodernism and the
cultural turn, this may have been because the very *idea of sociology*
appeared to be under threat. We can elaborate this generic, often tacit
idea of sociology by saying that it has to do with the viability of notions
of structured social totalities, and the possibility of making authoritative
distinctions between the objects of social enquiry and the frameworks
of discourse available to configure them. Our motivation for sustaining
such an idea ultimately stems from our nature as social beings making
our practical, collective way in the world; and as part of *that*, we routinely
seek to increase our knowledge of a historical and natural context that is
considerably larger than ourselves, but to which we have many points of
access. When that project of cumulative partial understanding is rigorously conducted and transmitted, both empirically and theoretically, we
call it 'science'. And the traditional argument is that there is no reason
why sociology – here standing as proxy for the promise of the social
sciences as a whole – should not be considered 'scientific' in that sense.

To supporters and critics alike, this familiar guiding image implies
an approach to the study of social life that is realist, objectivist,
naturalistic and structuralist. Undoubtedly, there are many ways in
which these terms could be defined and combined. However, within
the successor discourses, many of those influenced by poststructuralist
thought suspect that *any* positive definition, and *any* combination, is
unsustainable. Harbouring outmoded positivistic aspirations, these four
props for the idea of sociology have surely been dismantled and laid
to rest by the postpositivist movement in philosophy. In this chapter,
I show why postpositivism does *not* jeopardize the traditional image
of sociology, a conviction that guides the arguments in later chapters.

That said, under postpositivist tenets, a significant *deflation* of realist, objectivist, naturalist and structuralist themes has certainly occurred. My discussion of these matters, inevitably, takes a very truncated form for our purposes. Its upshot is that whilst the four meta-theoretical supports for the idea of sociology remain compelling, they are best regarded as *analytical values* rather than strict *criteria of judgement* or *methodological rules*.

Realism

Realism, scientific realism, critical realism: these labels within social science meta-theory were from the time of their reinvention by Roy Bhaskar (1978, 1979) couched as definitively postpositivist in remit. Pitched directly against an empiricist epistemology according to which universal generalizations are derived from constantly conjoined observable events, realism developed a rich picture of the realm of the generative mechanisms and potentials that both under-girded and explained the surface world of observable appearances and contingent actualities. However, as poststructuralist modes of theorizing in the successor discourses took hold, realism itself became widely regarded as 'essentialist' in its quest to uncover the core nature of (social) reality. Realism was questioned for positing causal powers as crucial factors having shape and force *outside* the way in which, in circumstances of profound cultural variety, we construct and construe what is 'real' in our projects and contexts.

Constructivist and discursivist approaches to social knowledge have operated separately from mainstream philosophy of science, and the fact that the latter has been effectively postpositivist for some forty years still hardly registers. But across these traditions, and within modest forms of realism itself (Outhwaite 1987, Sayer 2000a, Woodiwiss 2001), three problems have emerged to confront full-blown realism of the Bhaskarian sort. The first concerns the frequent insistence that realism is an *ontological* doctrine that, when elaborated, resolves *epistemological* difficulties. These difficulties are basically to do with the continual threat of *scepticism* as to the reliability and objectivity of even our best current accounts of the world. Realists re-figure this classical issue by showing that the less-than-assured reliability of knowledge based on observation/appearance is only to be *expected* because the world is stratified into three levels of being (the real/deep, the actual, and the empirical). The deepest of these levels is populated by a large number of (sometimes cross-cutting) causal powers and tendencies that are only ever partially realized at the latter two levels. Realists think that this situation should lead to epistemological *optimism* rather than skepticism, as long as we concentrate on retrodictive explanation rather than prediction, and on the power of abstraction rather than the seductions of observation. Under these guidelines, we can productively, if never completely, reveal the complex structure of nature's and society's open worlds. In the 'harder' natural sciences, this task is rendered easier by the partial system-closure that experimentation contrives. In social science, experimental closure not being possible, an iterative spiral of abstraction, critique and evidential assessment is thought to take us a long way towards cognitive adequacy.

Now the reason that this line of thinking is problematical is that committed realists are reluctant to accept that it stands chiefly as a valuable *heuristic*. Realists who follow Bhaskar accept his view that a *transcendental* argument can be performed that takes us securely from the existence and success of scientific enquiry to the underlying structure of reality in general, our view of which then becomes thicker and stronger than anything available to epistemological empiricism. But it is hard to see how such special assurance can be given, at least in purely philosophical terms (Kemp 2005). Realists, after all, allow that our best current knowledge is *fallible* and that scientific accounts of the fundamental forces and constituents of reality have constantly changed, sometimes quite dramatically, over time. Realists also accept that our knowledge of the world is essentially *perspectival*, born of the fact that as a species we are but a small part of a changing wider world, and that each person or scientific community or social group occupies a necessarily limited niche within it. How, then, *can* our ontological understanding in terms of powers, mechanisms and structures be qualitatively different from, and more philosophically dependable than, whatever good science tells us are the sorts of things and qualities that might well, but do not necessarily, exist?

With ontology brought back on a par with epistemology and the best scientific bets of the day, realists might be advised to exercise greater caution before promulgating their favoured – somewhat tumescent – depictions of the ultimate structure of the world. This is not least because the principal argument used by advocates of realism tends to be one that starts out from the *success* of science. If the success of science is not to be a fluke, the argument goes, then the world must be as realists say. But what do we mean by 'success' here? Realists are not exclusively pragmatists, so success must include something like truth or truth-likeness. Yet it is precisely truth and truth-likeness that cannot be vouchsafed, even in the best science, simply because whatever science today says the world is truly like, science tomorrow significantly modifies. The issue does not end there, because further options arise in the postpositivist philosophy of science in which assorted realists still take on assorted non-realists. But the point is that little of that subsequent debate on the 'pessimistic meta-induction' just outlined involves the kind of rift between ontology and epistemology that social science realists tend to demand.

The second set of problems for realism relates to its claim to provide a distinctively *critical* meta-theoretical outlook. The line is that because realism has identified the three ontological strata, it possesses the analytical leverage to assign particular facts, relations and powers to their appropriate level. Realists can thus assess, through their methods of conceptualization and retrodiction, how some things (and beliefs about those things) belong in the superficial domain of *the empirical*, an essentially 'ideological' state of cognition, whilst other relations (and theories of those relations) can justifiably be allocated to the 'deep' generative level.

There are a number of difficulties with this presumption, however. One is that we cannot know *a priori* whether something is part of a deep structure or is part of the structure of appearance. Another snag is that even after the substantive investigation that might give us clues here has been conducted, we can seldom be sure *which* identified mechanism (or combination of mechanisms) is causally or functionally decisive for a given social outcome. This is because mechanisms in the (unclose-able) system of society are always multiple, only partly realized and mutually counteracting or even mutually cancelling. And that is all before we consider whether our own social interests and ideological inclinations might be being in some way projected on to our claims about the state of the world 'in itself'.

All this means that the strong link between cognitive and *normative* commitment that critical realism promises to forge turns out to be quite fragile, in ways that can be illustrated from recent realist textbooks. One problem is that critical realism cannot presuppose, from 'on high' as it were, that theories couched in realist discourse will either be *adequate* to their object of enquiry or politically *progressive*. Thus, when Higgs *et al.* insist that only by adopting a critical realist theory of class 'can we hope to understand . . . class inequalities in health' because only 'realist social theories can theorize class relations as affecting health through mechanisms at various levels' (2004: 101, 106), one cannot help thinking that the effort to show that Marxist class theory has the required realist *form* actually detracts from the task of demonstrating its *substantive* adequacy.

Another difficulty is that various 'deep' causal explanations that might have unfortunate *ideological implications* cannot be simply ruled out as non-realist. For instance, Carter and New (2004: 10–11) accept, on the one hand, that the 'biopsychiatric account of women's depression . . . is realist enough', yet, on the other hand, 'sociologists have not been satisfied' with this because the mechanisms registered in that account are chiefly chemical and neurological. What is therefore needed is a properly realist 'stratified model of co-acting mechanisms'. This response works, in its way, for sociologists, but the conceptual issue has not been resolved. After all, when the social constructedness of patriarchy or sex is being asserted, sociologists are seldom quite so keen to bring in the full range of underlying mechanisms for gender difference, including biological factors. In any case, limited or even reductionist accounts are not necessarily illegitimate or un-realist, because *no* specific theory or theoretical combination can exhaust the full list of potentially relevant 'co-acting mechanisms'. The rather incongruous welcome that realists have recently given the revival of religion (Bhaskar 2000, Archer *et al.* 2004) might be explicable in those terms: causal processes of a spiritual sort occasionally burst through to 'co-act' with mechanisms of a more material sort.

Then there is the tendency amongst realists to insist that arguments that are formally non-realist, but politically progressive, are *really* realist, deep down. When this association becomes pre-emptive, realism itself appears basically *un*critical: its very *rhetoric* (the undeniability of 'reality') serves to curtail intellectual exploration in order to enter a moralistic blame game (Edwards *et al.* 1995, McLennan 2001). For example, the 'discourse-theoretical' positions of Laclau and Mouffe (1985) on radical democracy and social structure, seem in some obvious way to be 'on the Left'. But realists are continually exhorting such theorists to 'ontologize their discourse' (Joseph and Roberts 2004: 3). And they also like to track down the *source* of such reality-denials – Jacques Derrida is usually in the frame – and re-position that source as being, if not exactly realist, then not exactly *irrealist* either (Joseph and Roberts 2004: 14). The sheer defensiveness in play here gets in the way of fresh and creative thinking.

The third key area of problems for critical realism, prompted by doubts in the first two sectors, concerns the basic question of what *kind* of realism is at issue, and what we are supposed to be realist *about*. Psillos has usefully divided realism's 'philosophical package' into three parts (Psillos 1999: xix). Metaphysical realism holds that the world has a definite and concept-independent nature; semantic realism holds that theoretical terms in particular accounts of the world have putative factual reference; and epistemological realism is the view that successful theories can be taken to be approximately true of the world. But if there is undoubted coherence across the realist package, it also seems possible to decide on its merits in a piecemeal way, and lately, social realists have wondered whether the metaphysical part of realism is not rather excessive. A fall-back position is available, however: perhaps the metaphysical part of realism is nothing more – and nothing less – than what has been dubbed the 'natural ontological attitude' (Fine 1984), referring to our firm but relatively unreflective conviction that the material world exists independently of our particular conceptions of it, and that it contains various kinds of entities with specific characteristics. Overviews of critical realism often begin with something as straightforward, and in its way compelling, as this (Sayer 2000a: 2, Joseph and Roberts 2004: 2).

The point about the natural ontological attitude, however, is that few non-realist philosophers seek to quibble with it, in its appropriate place. Just to take the most debated non-realist philosopher of science in recent years, Bas van Fraassen (1980) only resists realism in relation to the existence of theoretical posits in science. Otherwise he is, to all intents and purposes, as realist as makes little difference. In the semantic domain, a sophisticated rerun of an ancient distinction has emerged over those properties of phenomena that are to be taken as intrinsic and independent, and those that seem at least partly 'projected' by our theorized responses to experience. In accordance with that distinction, our theories are considered either 'truth-tracking' or 'response-dependent' (Norris 2002). But once again, whilst realism in its more technical implications still seems to be a pertinent issue in these debates, few of the participants challenge the kind of realism captured in the natural ontological attitude. That being the case, it remains questionable whether fine-grained expressions of ontological or epistemological realism are strictly required to motivate a basic kind of opposition to anti-realism in social discourse.

If developing realism *is* to remain a priority in social science philosophy, then one task might be to explore analogues and extensions of the several brands and theorists of realism that populate the philosophy of science – causal-mechanical realism, inferential realism, perspectival realism, structural realism, realism as unification, realism as intervention and others besides. And we could try to devise societal equivalents or extensions of the various candidates for what it is that we are to be realists *about* – whether it be entities, behaviours, relations, structural forms, laws, theories, mature theories, mature predictive theories, or the web of science in general (Ladyman 2002: Ch. 8). This is perhaps only to say that critical realists have a tendency to exaggerate the extent to which such disputation can be easily *resolved* and readily brought to bear upon problems of *substantive* social research and ideological affiliation. Despite the fact that, by 2005, no fewer than 28 titles had been published in Routledge's series of texts on realism, the prevailing sentiment, and a somewhat bland one, is that critical realism is not a homogeneous doctrine, but an open and evolving tradition, one that embraces 'many different perspectives and developments' (Danermark *et al.* 2002: 1).

To sum up: the mistake is to think that realism supplies clear and superior *criteria* for selecting and appraising theories and research strategies within specific domains. This does not render realism indefensible; rather, it re-positions realism as offering a powerful heuristic understanding of the *goals* of investigation. Realism in that sense represents a kind of 'default position' (Bird 1998: 142) that we can work around, its viability needing to be established in terms of our best inferential practices rather than through assertions about the truth of science or the ultimate nature of the world. The main task then becomes countering the local excesses of anti-realism, not giving a seamlessly realist account of everything.

Objectivism

Objectivism is not the same as realism, but they form a basic alliance, and similar sorts of arguments arise. To take an objectivist attitude to understanding is to hold that although we may initially approach things and relations through a transitory, limited and biased perspective, our considered views (a) are not (always) to be regarded as entirely relative or subjective, and (b) can be made less relative or subjective through greater basic knowledge, sustained debate and self-criticism. A widespread negative reason for being hesitant about objectivism is fear of being caught in possession of the 'God's-eye' view of things, a crime that is made (too) much of in textbook presentations of post-structuralism. A more positive factor is the popularity, under the influence of Habermas above all, of notions of *inter-subjectivity*. As with the 'natural ontological attitude' in the realism debates, inter-subjectivity offers a convenient meeting point for (mild) objectivists and (minimal) subjectivists, suggesting that if the 'God's-eye' version of objectivity cannot be attained, at least an 'anthropological' version is viable (Bevir 1998: 109, 125). After all, we know that deeply held beliefs sometimes change through dialogue, dispute and further consensus, resulting in definite epistemic gain. Minimal subjectivists can go along with this too, construing any inter-subjective consensus of this sort as a new type of *collective* subjectivity, with 'absolute' objectivity not necessarily more nearly approached.

As with the realism question, this matter cannot be definitively settled, but we need to remember that references to 'objectivity', more than references to 'reality', pertain to the *modality* of our thinking and to our processes of learning and exchange. Put that way, objectivism is even more closely bound up with countering the deficits of subjectivism than realism is with combating anti-realism. But still, the suggestion that objectivism is strictly 'anthropological' is unwarranted, except tautologically. Whilst our considered views clearly always remain *ours* in some constitutive sense, and although our knowledge of the world is typically both *aspectival* and *corrigible*, it seems perverse to keep tagging strongly reasoned and well-evidenced claims, ones that are also subjected to inter-subjective critical scrutiny, with the qualification that they are valid only 'from our point of view'. In the first place, *within* our point of view, we do seek to generate *unconditional* claims about the aspect in question. To refer such objectivizing tendencies within lower-order discourses up to meta-level relativities (for example those of the overarching values of the group, culture or species) does not render them any less unqualified, or any more subjective, as truth-claims. And if we can genuinely *see* that the web of our claims might only be spun within particular horizons and conditions of life, then that proposition too becomes an unconditional hypothesis about 'our relation to the world' (Nagel 1997: 92). Sometimes, then, it is just not appropriate to say that our claims make sense only 'from our point of view' because the added phrase can often best be read as a specification of *the respect* in which our views hold objectively.

Social theorists are unlikely to be so confident about the connection between objectivity and *rationality* as the philosopher I just cited, Thomas Nagel. But Nagel follows the examples of Popper and Davidson in effectively undermining the deterministic picture we have, especially in the social disciplines, of being *trapped* or even *imprisoned* by our prevailing 'frameworks', 'perspectives' or 'conceptual schemes' – this image being the source of much of the social-theoretical doubting of rationality. Nagel argues that reason emerges through processes of dialogue, dilemmas and contradictions, and these factors routinely, not exceptionally, ensure that whatever grip our personal and theoretical blind-spots and visualities have on us, they can be prised open. Of course, critical social theorists are habitually wary of the many ways in which local identities and advantages are *rationalized* in universalist and rationalist terms, to specific ideological effect. But if those 'exposures' are not themselves offered and taken as rational and objective, then no epistemic gain, and no political progress, can be forthcoming.

This insight allows us to address an unsatisfactory ambiguity in one of the favoured formulae of realist social theory, which states that whilst epistemic relativism must be accepted alongside ontological realism, *judgemental* relativism can still be resisted. In Sayer's version (2000a: 47), epistemological relativism refers to the fact that we only apprehend the world 'in terms of available descriptions and discourses', yet, in spite of this, we proceed to 'decide that some accounts are better than others'. But this is a rather odd reading of both relativism and judgement. We can certainly grant that knowledge only comes under available descriptions, but if different available descriptions directly clash in relevant respects, at least in terms of their truth claims, and we go on to make decisive judgements between them, then we are withdrawing from epistemological relativism, not endorsing it. What this realist embrace of 'relativism' is really drawing attention to is that human knowledge is epistemically *constrained* and inevitably partial, one dimension of which partiality is sociological: our angle on reality is significantly shaped by our forms of social organization and conflict. However, this is still not epistemological relativism *stricto sensu* because if we take our judgements seriously, no two descriptions that clash directly in relevant respects can be agreed to be equally, because differently, valid. Perhaps, then, it might be better to turn the phrase around and say that we can be judgemental relativists without being epistemological relativists.

Naturalism

The combination of realism and objectivism is often seen as constituting an undesirable 'scientistic' or 'naturalistic' approach to human enquiry (Sorell 1991). Much of course depends on just what the image of science here involves. 'Naturalism' usually refers to the aspiration of social thought to fall into line behind the (largely positivist) models and methods once thought characteristic of the natural sciences, and to share the latter's (strongly) realist and objectivist ethos. But this model no longer obtains, postpositivist thinking about the procedures and status of scientific knowledge having greatly broadened out to include social, pyschological and rhetorical components, and many degrees of certitude, invention, and speculation. Calls for the methodological unity of the sciences, in any narrow sense, have consequently faded away, and it is more readily accepted now that the influence and 'privilege' of natural science *vis-a-vis* social science can at least at times, and in principle, run in the other direction.

We might even say that scientism, reconceived in postpositivist terms, appears once again to be *attractive* to the social disciplines. A blithely 'anti-science' stance often seems just dogmatic and ignorant, wilfully overlooking the painstaking evidential *work* and inspired *imaginings* that good science routinely involves. 'Naturalism' as a guide to social inquiry has thus lost some of its forced and slavish connotations. One interesting aspect of this rediscovered naturalism in social research is the way in which erstwhile social theorists (for example in the sociology of science/knowledge, and in cultural studies itself) have re-labelled themselves as 'modest empiricists', newly sensitized to the need for *some* kind of distinction between careful observation/witnessing and full-on value advocacy (Haraway 1996b, Woolgar 2002). Another aspect of naturalism is carried by the argument that even critical realism went too far in postulating fundamental *differences* between the logic of inference in the natural and in the social sciences. Realists tended to state categorically that because empirical *regularities* in social life do not occur, social science knowledge is almost entirely dependent upon rigorous conceptual *abstraction* alone. But this seriously underestimates the ability of social science to encounter, discover and even *produce* 'quasi-regularities', materials which constitute the state of the evidence to which competing conceptual frameworks must be adequate, and which they must seek to explain in novel and productive ways (Kemp and Holmwood 2003).

A third dimension of reinvigorated naturalism is the persistence and reformulation of *evolutionary* approaches to social structure, and indeed evolutionary approaches to epistemic change itself. Arguments against the teleology and determinism that evolutionary explanation is supposed to need frequently emphasize the essential *contingency* of social relations and events. But the traditional stand-off between evolutionary-teleological and contingent-causal styles of reasoning is just no longer sustainable. The whole of human life, it can immediately be acknowledged, is 'contingent': its course is not predetermined, or cosmically 'necessary', and it has no 'natural' end-point or *telos*. Moreover, the causal sequences which produce one concatenation of circumstances out of another are undeniably complex, multiple and specific. But none of this rules out a *determinate logic of change* in human history, any more than the absence of determinism in innumerable situations of individual human action rules out the latter's supervenience on structural patterns of social relations. There are two steps in the case for an evolutionary perspective in sociology.

The first is made when we realize that if sociology's goal is the analysis of the 'construction and transformation of social orders' (Mouzelis 1991), then a project of that sort is not viable without a developmental theory of societal types, and causal and functional investigation into the way that each comes into being and passes away. One way of denying the relevance of evolutionary conceptions is to insist that historical and contemporary societies need not be analysed in a typological way at all. The response to this must be that sociology simply cannot proceed without, at all levels, encoding individual events and existents (including people) into some kind of classificatory matrix.

Another familiar protest is that we should not be wasting time with macro-sociological schemas, but instead should be busying ourselves with documenting the specific conditions and experiences of particular social groups. But this expression of investigative *preference* raises no point of *principle* because the very act of naming the particular groups to be studied – peasants, landless labourers, the *petit bourgeoisie*, housewives, professionals, subcultures, the working class and so on – inevitably carries the freight of more general societal characterizations.

A more interesting debate arises as to whether it is right to call the identification of developmental processes in terms of societal forms and stages 'evolutionary' at all. For example, Michael Mann's important work in historical sociology (1986, 1993) is fuelled by his conviction that we must get away from searching for necessary causal connections and adaptive sequences in a linear and totalizing way, partly because the whole notion of 'society' needs to be replaced by that of 'overlapping networks'. The analysis of social orders, in that case, whilst still classificatory, would be largely descriptive and oriented more stringently to contingency. But this modest depiction does scant justice to Mann's own work, which impresses by the consistency with which the author names a *limited number* of salient overlapping networks, traces their trajectory in terms of the *societal dimension* thought to be most critical to their competitive success ('power'), and evaluates them according to the specific *selection mechanism* ('organizational outflanking') that seems to govern whether they fail or succeed in reproducing/transforming themselves.

We may be stronger or weaker in our evolutionary leanings, and there is still considerable uncertainty about what exactly explanation in terms of *social* evolution involves. In particular, the issue of how far social evolutionary explanation must cite, or derive analogies from, *biological* models of development is constantly a moot point (Lopreato and Crippen 1999). At the very least, social scientists should insist on the 'relative autonomy' of their objects of enquiry and patterns of causality, and be vigilant in exposing the presence of ideological residues within the conceptual schemes of the natural sciences themselves. We can then point legitimately to the specificity and complexity of the mechanisms of selection, adaptation, scarcity, competition, survival and transform-ation within social relations over time, and we may want to devise terminology that might avoid any kind of imitation of biology. But the tendency of some social scientists to dismiss *any* kind of naturalism just because various reactionary stories have been constructed in that way is indefensible. If, for example, Daniel Dennett (2006) is felt to be mistaken in his attempt to explain the contemporary revival of religion in terms of the reproduction of 'memes', then this is because there might be better *social* explanations available, not because Dennett has had the affrontery to bring evolutionary reasoning to bear on this precious and contingent human proclivity. Whether our 'better' social explanation will be evolu-tionary in the strict sense or just somewhat naturalistic (being couched, say, in terms of species, societal or individual 'needs') is an important question. As a minimum, people in sociology and cultural studies should accept that social beings are *also* natural beings, and cease denying that natural factors can legitimately enter into the understanding of societal development and identity. In this regard, not only has Benton's (1991) call for a *rapprochement* between sociology and biology still properly to be taken up, but more attention needs to be given to the substantial articulations of *non*-teleological, *non*-deterministic evolutionary social theory that are available (Runciman 1989a, Sanderson 1995).

Structuralism

The idea of sociology that I favour posits the social world as comprising various groups of people, things, relations and roles, existing in complex and changing, but determinate, relationships with each other. At any point in social history, including the present, these relationships can be configured into more or less 'typical' material and cultural forms, whose emergence, dispositions and constraints *structure* the concrete forms of life that exhibit them. Three things quickly become apparent here. One is that this specification of social structure involves an 'integ-rative pluralist' approach to realist understanding: we get to grips with phenomena and the processes that generate them by making their (genuine) differences visible within the horizon of some larger shared generative properties or levels of existence. The second is that, contrary to ordinary ways of talking about 'society' and 'societies', these latter entities are, strictly speaking, *constituted* by the social structure(s) they are deemed to possess. Relatedly, as Luhmann reminds us (1995: 345), social change can only be intelligibly comprehended *in terms of* structures. Third, this process of constitution is thoroughly and necessarily abstract, since social structure refers to the logic of only *some* social relations out of many, and only some *aspects* of empirical social interaction, the latter being almost too inexhaustible to specify in its concrete richness. An unavoidable 'gap' then opens up between, on the one hand, statements of the logic of the system and concrete particulars on the other, a gap that stands as the source of all the familiar temptations of 'closure' in cultural and social theory, from outright discursive constructivism to sheer empiricist particularism.

Two sorts of considerations militate against reviving the notions of structure and structuralism, even in the broad form that I am recommending. One is the belief that structuralist thinking was rendered altogether inoperable by Derrida in his famous critique. The other obstacle is more substantive, suggesting that there is something about the contemporary *knowledge-based economy* that has rendered structural theorizing redundant. The deconstruction of 'structure' can be approached initially by seeing that there are different ways of conceptualizing social structure, with no ready-made way of guaranteeing their correctness, or of rendering them entirely compatible. Lopez and Scott (2000) thus usefully distinguish between 'institutional' conceptions of structure, focusing on norms and roles; 'relational' conceptions that highlight the organization and appropriation of resources and logistics; and strategies designed to foreground the 'embodied' aspect of social structuration. Lopez has gone on to illustrate how individual *theorists* engage in 'writing structure', emphasizing the 'language-borne' character of all schemes for identifying just what the essential structure of society is. He emphasizes that when we observe Durkheim or Parsons or Althusser theorizing structure, we find a great deal of metaphorical and ideological creativity and variation. Because of this, they cannot be taken as 'mirroring' the real structures that are supposedly being elucidated (Lopez 2003: 152).

If such considerations acutely point up the provisionality and metaphor-laden character of theorizing social structure, perhaps the general idea of structure itself is too unstable and misleading to be retained at all? Derrida pursued this in his essay 'Structure, Sign, and Play', in *Writing and Difference*. Derrida's train of thought begins by noting that the idea of a centre-less structure is incoherent. Yet countless 'classical' efforts have failed to show how it is that structure's centre, its governing principles, can be *both* present 'at' the centre (of the structured totality that it governs) and yet also present 'outside' the centre (across the outposts of the totality as a whole). And one mighty term has followed another – substance, existence, God, man, class – in an attempt to find the *content* that will solve the formal problem of a centre-less centre. Every new philosophy that tackles this problem, Derrida says, through mobilizing *difference*, represents only a 'substitution', a *repetition*.

In the movement specifically labelled 'structuralism', Derrida goes on, the centre was elevated out of any particular substantive site and into the medium of abstract relationality itself. Only by being repositioned as a 'non-locus' could *everything else* find its locus in the system. Nothing other than *language itself*, with its rules of form, its infinite modes of substitutability and derivation, could act as the structure of last resort. Thus, in Levi-Strauss's version, the structuralist analytical apparatus itself was enthroned as the form of forms, the 'tertiary mythology' within which all lower-level mythologies could be convened and rendered equivalent, in spite of all their concrete differences.

Derrida had no time for the kind of 'empiricist' objection to all this which denies abstract structural colonization on the grounds that something rich and concrete is always going to be 'left out' of consideration – 'spurious infinity', he dubs this. But he did think that the structuralist imaginary is vitiated by the infinity of endless 'play' constituted by the centre's simultaneous internality and externality. How, he asks, can the structured totality be ascertained as 'all there is' without continually invoking, indeed constituting, a fatal *remainder*, a surplus that falls right outside the structural centre's remit? The antinomy of structuralism is that it is caught forever in this coherence-in-contradiction. Such theoretically recurrent impossibility can only be understood, he says, as having the 'force of a desire' (Derrida 2002: 352).

I am freely interpreting Derrida here, as anyone must. But it seems to me that he is not in the end doing anything as decisive as demolishing structuralism, or condemning it as 'totalitarian', as his translator Alan Bass reported so influentially. Indeed, there is even a certain 'play' in interpreting just *what* it is that Derrida ultimately wants to say about structuralism. Is he posing it, negatively, as essentially inadequate because it is over-structured, or is he elucidating, in structural fashion, the nature of the play between necessity and exceptionality that structuralism must always combine? This appears not to be decidable.

However, that final explanatory reference by Derrida himself to the 'force of desire' that stands as simultaneously governing (present within) structuralist discourse, yet which is also absent from its content and manifestations, is clearly itself a quintessentially structuralist figure.

This impasse leaves us free to revive the useful 'generative' or 'genetic' variants of structuralism that dropped out of sight as a result of the post-structuralist critique. Piaget (1971) in particular offered a productive account, anticipating aspects of present-day complexity theory in the social sciences. For Piaget, structures are 'virtual' – they are relations, and relations of relations. This means that their existence cannot be other than abstractly identified. But for Piaget, this has nothing to do with the static or logicist conception of structure articulated by Levi-Strauss – 'the doctrine of the primacy of structure' *per se* (Piaget 1971: 106). Rather, Piaget conceives structures as coming into being over time out of formative elements or previous structural relations, then developing and consolidating new governing principles of their own. Structures thus possess definite *emergent* qualities: they become more than the sum of their parts, and they react back on their formative contexts. They do exhibit the indispensable systemic property of *self-regulation*, but they *generate*, over time, various internal and external effects, some of which then come to threaten the stability of the structure itself. For Piaget, in other words, structures are transformational totalizations, not eternally self-regulating ones.

No doubt this sort of specification of structuralism is rather ideal-typical, but it immediately helps unlock a number of problems. For example, 'social structure' has long been directly pitched against human or individual 'agency' in a contest about what is supposed to have primacy in social life, or in terms of whether social life can be said meaningfully to *be* 'structured'. But these are *not* rival concepts for the same conceptual space, as increasing numbers of sociologists are pointing out (Holmwood 1996, King 2004, Stones 2005). Structures themselves possess generative qualities, which can be understood as forms of 'agency' and self-regulation, just as collectives, groups, and individuals – the items that prototypically exercise human agency – are themselves complex structures, composed of complex structures. Of course, human agents cannot be 'reduced' to their component formative elements, or entirely 'subsumed' within the higher-level structural whole that they help enable, but that is true of all complex structures.

Second, it becomes feasible to think of Scott and Lopez's institutional, relational, and embodied structures as different locutions for, or different aspects of, the same structural process. As for Lopez's anxiety about reconciling realism with the subjective vagaries involved in 'writing structure', this can be relieved by remembering that structural relations cannot be 'visualized' as such, nor therefore 'mirrored' as a photograph images a scene. A degree of play between our formulations of structure and what these are taken to encode, and between contending structural accounts too, is therefore unavoidable. But this only shakes our realist understanding of the work of knowledge if what we seek is an impossible *ontological guarantee* for 'inference to the best explanation' (Lipton 2004). We can therefore respect Piaget's preference for what he calls 'methodological' structuralism over the variety he describes as 'ultimate'. Where the latter posits an ideal 'structure of all structures', the former leads us to focus on *which* structures are there, and whether they are *strong* or *weak* structures (Piaget 1971: 140–2). Whether these two 'moments' of structural analysis are quite so separate as Piaget thinks is in my view doubtful, but the distinction has pragmatic value.

The other main obstacle to structural understanding that I mentioned earlier is the claim that in post-industrial 'knowledge societies', previous structural ensembles of positions and constraints no longer obtain. Rather, social being is *self*-generated, either in terms of autonomous individual creativity, or through some combined power of general knowledge and ideas-driven social movements. For Nico Stehr (2001: ix, 20), it is not only our economy but also our 'reality' as a whole that 'we arrange and produce... on the basis of our knowledge', so that knowledge becomes 'the constitutive identity-defining mechanism of modern society'. Such statements sometimes appear to be announcing, absurdly, the *disappearance* of material objects and processes, but this should be taken as a purely rhetorical flourish. Another familiar refrain is that in a world of incessant images and ideas, the old recipes for 'ideology critique' cease to work.

In that vein, Scott Lash argues that instead of focusing on the rightness or wrongness of beliefs around informationalism, we need to pay attention, phenomenologically, to its radiance, practices and technologies. If there *is* a characteristic 'structure' within this all-consuming informational inside, it is one of systematic *de-structuring*, Lash suggests. Social relations in this situation are 'less a question of sociality than informationality' (2002: 75). Our collective experience is now one of continual flow and immanence. We are in a world of endless speed, compressed communication, 'the byte' and its multiple users. Not only has universal 'intellection', in this picture, had its day, even 'discourse' stands as something of a reification, and 'reflexivity' is 'more like reflex than reflection'. Consequently, critique itself becomes *part of* 'infotization', with the consequence that 'social theory becomes media theory', neither explaining nor interpreting the media, but instead 'resembling' it. To structuralist diehards, this may not seem entirely satisfactory, but 'it is our fate' (Lash 2002: x, 76–7).

The basic problem with this argument, apart from its racy extravagance, is that it falls headlong into 'the myth of the framework' that I referred to before, giving no credibility at all to Lash's hope that if our fate *is* to be media insiders, we should at least try to be 'critical' insiders. All we are left with, rather, is dialogic infotized sensationism. The logic of Stehr's anti-structuralism is quite the opposite, we might note. If there is no material externality, then there is no trapped, phenomenalist *internality* either: we can freely and knowledgeably construct the world that we individually and collectively wish for, and this includes being as critical of speedy informationalism as we like.

Two main points can be made against knowledge society 'autonomism'. One is that human knowledge is a constant driver within any set of productive forces. Thus, what Manuel Castells (1996: 17) describes as the peculiarity of 'knowledge acting upon knowledge' in the network society applies to all human history, and Charles Leadbeater's (1999: 10) proposition that only now do we seek consciously to produce *more value with less material* on the basis of new-found principles, has applied to all scientific-technological innovation since the eighteenth century.

The second point is that despite their best efforts, knowledge society theorists retain structuralist, and sometimes even materialist, notions in the background. Resorting to a version of the base/superstructure model, Castells describes informationalism not as 'a new social structure' in itself, but as the particular cultural form taken by *capitalism* (Castells 1996: 2, 372–5). Alain Touraine (1995: 361) strongly champions the ethical ideal of a structure-evading Subject, but allows that this is 'inconceivable in the absence of social relations and especially of the power than transforms instrumental rationality into a system of order that seeks more and more power'. And Stehr elaborates knowledge society as a 'structural and cultural configuration', one that displays distinct conditions of distribution, participation, stratification, and interactive density (Stehr 2001: 18–19, and *passim*).

Postpositivism and the 'new' social theory

I have made a case for the continuing value of the four theoretical 'props' of the idea of sociology. My argument is that if postpositivism, with its more inclusive matrices of understanding and appraisal, rules out dogmatic expressions of realism, objectivism, naturalism and structuralism, these explanatory coordinates can still be well sustained. But even this sort of claim is sometimes regarded as excessively 'foundationalist', that is to say, insufficiently postpositivist. I want to counter that suggestion, and round off the chapter, by looking at one prototypical version of it, namely Steven Seidman and Jeffrey Alexander's (2001) attempt to draw cultural studies authors into their presentation of the 'new social theory'.

Seidman and Alexander introduce the 'new social theory' by observing, uncontentiously, that much current social theory is post-disciplinary, normatively orientated and anti-foundationalist in spirit. Moreover, given the greater emphasis today on post-disciplinarity and normative thinking, we can wholly agree that it is no accident, and no bad thing, that formations such as cultural studies and postcolonialism have come to the forefront of intellectual life, largely by unsettling older discourses like sociology. On this basis, Seidman and Alexander claim to be witnessing, and assisting, a veritable 'sea change' in the nature and task of social theory.

But in what sense exactly is the new social theory definitively anti-foundationalist? Seidman and Alexander position post-foundationalism as resting on a rejection of 'scientism', that is to say, the conviction that social science knowledge can 'parallel in precision and objectivity the frameworks of the hard sciences' (Seidman and Alexander 2001: 1). Now, if such a parallel is thought to 'provide logical chains of propositions and models that can be empirically tested and elaborated' into positivistic general laws, then it is indeed widely agreed that such a goal for social theory is inappropriate. However, a precipitous slide then takes place, whereby the abandonment of scientism equates to the rejection of *any* 'scientific explanatory framework' whatever, and what we are left with as the modality of social theory is the construction of 'credible or persuasive arguments' *rather than* 'research testing theory' or the ambition of developing a 'specifically social science' (2001: 2). Against this, it can be insisted that few serious postpositivist philosophers would maintain that science as such is being abandoned in the process of loosening up the benchmarks of explanatory adequacy. Rather, the conception of science itself is being re-thought and broadened out. Even if we accept that 'credible and persuasive argument' is particularly significant in the social and cultural disciplines, the suggestion that contestability operates *in the place of* systematic empirical and quasi-objective reasoning is wrong. This is because what counts as credible and persuasive necessarily involves a painstaking assessment of *truth and validity*. This can never be a definitive matter, perhaps; but the same goes for natural science too.

Anti-foundationalism is further interpreted as the abandonment of attempts to 'establish the most basic general ideas about society that would then guide social analysis' (2001: 2). Again, this seems an illegitimate extension of an uncontroversial proposition: that social scientific theory and research practice are fallible and contestable. Following up, Seidman and Alexander single out some 'new' theorists for purposes of anti-foundationalist praise. Thus, Stuart Hall is said to argue 'that culture is the ensemble of meanings, beliefs, values, norms and rituals that structure a society', while Frederic Jameson's basic position is given as 'arguing that genres are a response to the fragmentation of modern capitalist life'. 'Rather than providing an authentic meaning', Jameson explains, they express 'the suppressed hope of the political unconscious' (Seidman and Alexander 2001: 8). But a moment's thought shows that what is on offer in these theoretical statements from Hall and Jameson is *precisely* some kind of attempt to establish 'basic ideas' about society that would then usefully serve to 'guide social analysis'. Their innovations would hardly command our interest or allegiance otherwise.

Finally, Seidman and Alexander's characterization of postpositivism gives emphasis to the greater concern with *normativity* within contemporary commentary: our greater readiness to situate theorizing in, and limit its relevance to, the specific moral and social contexts in which they arise. Theorists who explicitly accept this limitation are then regarded as somehow having more integrity and interest than those who do not. For example, Seidman and Alexander put Marx in the latter category, Marx supposedly being the kind of earlier foundationalist author who sought to establish materialism 'as the only sound basis for a non-ideological, objective sociology' (2001: 1). This is entirely debatable. Even if there is a sense in which Marx was scientistic, it is utterly implausible to claim that his project involved the suppression of values and normativity. So, when Habermas is portrayed as having 'fully abandoned the final romantic vestiges of neo-Marxism' in order to advocate 'democratization rather than socialism' (2001: 4), this will hardly do as a case of how foundationalist theory has yielded to anti-foundational normativity. Rather, it is a case of replacing *one kind of* foundationalist normativity by another, one with which the commentators clearly have greater sympathy.

This leads to the general point, somehow missed by Seidman and Alexander, that normative (or structural) theorizing of any power will always be susceptible to foundationalism. To say that certain kinds of norms (concepts) trump others, and to try to demonstrate that those norms (concepts) are more attuned to what is central in society, is to hope that they will prove 'persuasive' *just to the extent* that they are (approximately) true and valid. Perhaps it is because they are implicitly aware of these problems that Seidman and Alexander emphasize that normativity under postmodern conditions increasingly takes the form of theoretical *pragmatism* (2001: 3). However, despite widespread reference to the virtues of 'ethical' pragmatism, 'strategic essentialism' and the like, it is extremely difficult to rise from pragmatic denials of foundationalism towards passionate advocacy of specific new norms, values and theories. Pragmatism may well be an appropriate mindset for those who believe, as Seidman and Alexander do, that we have gone beyond any need for 'ideology critique' (2001: 6). But it is hard to see how any powerful expression of social theory, 'new' or otherwise, can get started if one accepts from the outset that social and political thinking is necessarily fragmented and merely opinionated, lacking any potential for objectivity.

2
Cultural Studies//Sociology

In this chapter, I develop an accounts of the *rhetorical scenarios* that have governed debate between cultural studies and sociology over the years. These are presented more as theoretical attitudes and writing styles rather than as explicit *models* as such. And whilst they follow, roughly, a timeline from the 1970s to the present day, they are not intended to mark precise chronological *phases*, as the overlapping dates of various references will reveal. I begin with an account of the discourse on sociology that prevailed at the Birmingham Centre for Contemporary Cultural Studies (CCCS) before it was reconfigured as a full academic department in the 1980s. I take my time here because I am not aware that the writings on sociology at Birmingham have been detailed even in this summative way. The second scenario – 'postmodern conjuncturalism' – takes cultural studies' academic 'coming of age' (Inglis 1993: ix) as its premise, and part of its wider agenda is to *displace* the sociological imaginary from any ostensible role in the definition of the field. This attitude lends itself to a third strategy – 'sociological revenge' – in which the tables are turned entirely. Towards the close of the 1990s, the 'cultural turn' was widely adopted as a new synthesizing moment, and it stands as the fourth configuration in the sequence. I take issue with these constructions as I go along, but two overarching and problematical features stand out. One is that, whilst nowadays we are well attuned to the role of rhetoric and discourse in the construction of all identities (including disciplinary ones), *over*-rhetorical and *self-absorbed* constructions are invariably unconvincing. Another common deficit is that the focus tends to fall on the question of disciplinary homes, fields, or turns rather than on the things that should really count, namely substantive understanding and general explanation.

In the first decade of the twenty-first century, a mood of 'pragmatic reflexivity' has spread, in which the obsession with finally settling issues of disciplinarity and intellectual superiority has faded. Both sociology and cultural studies are characterized by considerable diversity and openness, and along with those features comes *anxiety*, alongside *excitement*, about endless diversity and theoretical indeterminacy. In Whiggish fashion, I take this latest scenario to represent definite progress, but it is still not the best of all possible worlds because obvious difficulties remain. One is that intense conflict between defenders of cultural studies and sociology can readily re-surface, just like before. Another problem is that reflexivity and pragmatism, in spite of their intermediate virtues, do not offer fully productive resolutions.

'Birmingham'

In a series of statements that set the parameters for the 1970s Birmingham mode, Stuart Hall affirmed the need for sociology to break with orthodox sociology. In keeping with Hall's inclusive cast of thought, these formulations were by no means *rejectionist*, though there were reasons to be polemical. On the anecdotal level, the perception was that the local Birmingham sociologists felt annoyed to be upstaged by the newcomer down the corridor, and made their hostility felt in a 'blistering attack' (Hall 1980: 21). More generally, much Centre thinking at that time revolved around themes circulating in *New Left Review* (NLR), central to which was Perry Anderson's depiction of the British intellectual scene in 'Components of the National Culture'. According to Anderson, Britain alone among modern European nations failed to produce a classical sociology, leaving an 'absent centre' in social theory and research, a gap that came to be filled only rather pathetically by British sociology's reformist derivative of empiricism and functionalism (Anderson 1969: 221–2). Robin Blackburn went on to complete the *NLR* rout by positioning leading British sociologists Goldthorpe and Lockwood on the list of straight bourgeois ideologists (Blackburn 1969).

Hall's approach was more carefully modulated. In one of the early Centre 'mapping the field' essays, written chiefly by Hall (CCCS 1973), a 'sociology of literature' line is firmly endorsed in an effort to combat textualist cultural criticism. In another of his signature overviews, Hall (1978: 9–14) develops a similar attitude of 'sublation' rather than 'supercession' to figures in the sociology of knowledge. By turns, the valuable contributions of Durkheim and Weber, then Mannheim, Merton, and social constructionism/phenomenology, are acknowledged, even if they are ultimately trumped by a 'complex Marxist' account of ideology. But the customary division between Marxism and sociology is narrowed in Hall's treatment, which notes not only the close connections amongst Lukacs, Weber, Simmel and Mannheim, but Merton's acknowledgement as far back as 1949 that it was Marxism that formed the 'storm centre' of the sociology of knowledge(Hall 1978: 28).

So when it came to defining the posture of cultural studies in general (Hall 1980: 20–5), it was envisaged as 'posing sociological questions against sociology itself'. Birmingham cultural studies did not seek to emulate sociology, yet it was undoubtedly sociological 'in a loose sense'. Homing in on 'lived practices, belief systems and institutions, some part of the subject matter of sociology... fell within our scope', Hall observed. Significant aspects of conventional sociology were undoubtedly to be opposed, notably complacent models of the pluralist society and the lifeless 'mass society' model of culture, a bogey figure that motivated a wide range of Centre work on the press and television. But the problem was held to reside in the 'dominant structural-functionalist models' rather than sociology as such, and Hall espied signs in the latter of 'a parallel movement of recovery' of questions of agency, culture and resistance. That sociology was to be given due as well as critical attention was underlined in the syllabus of the MA theory courses taught by Hall from 1975, which featured not only Marx, but Durkheim and Weber too; not only Lukacs and Althusser but also Schutz, Berger and Luckmann and Garfinkel. Looking back from the vantage point of 1980, Hall pointed out that the 'disarray' of mainstream sociology had become quite evident, but commented that this was a 'creative disintegration'. He had by this time become Professor of Sociology, albeit in a profoundly interdisciplinary institution, the Open University, and the 1981 British Sociological Association volume on 'practice and progress' in the discipline contained keynote contributions by both Hall and Richard Johnson, another pillar of the Birmingam Centre (Abrams 1981: 1, 3).

In terms of particular substantive areas, various critiques of sociology appeared in the volumes of the Birmingham Centre's work published between 1976 and 1982. The most intimate encounter took place within the 'subcultures' strand of work, especially in *Resistance Through Rituals*. Substantively, the lead essay in that collection cleared the ground for the new approach to subcultures by identifying and critiquing a veritable 'sociological trinity' of ideas about social change in post-War Britain: affluence, consensus and embourgeoisement (Clarke *et al.* 1976: 21–8).

Methodologically, the volume represents an extensive engagement with symbolic interactionism, labelling theory and generally 'appreciative' brands of sociological ethnography (Pearson and Twohig 1976: 120, Grimshaw *et al.* 1980: 73). In one sense, this whole dimension of the Birmingham work was heavily reliant on previous traditions of sociological ethnography, and the Centre's publications during these years included numerous external contributors, including some based in sociology departments. The attitude could not, therefore, be one of straightforward dismissal. Thus, Stan Cohen's embodiment of the dilemma of the radical sociologist – finding ways of 'staying in without selling out' – was admired, and the position of the sociology of deviance genre was approvingly clarified as being a deviant one relative to the sociological mainstream (Roberts 1976: 250, 243).

Ultimately, however, naturalistic participant observation was considered positivistic, in that the values, theories, purposes and expertise of the researcher had to be somehow suppressed, sociology fearing the 'distortion of the field' and the 'contamination' of the object by the subjectivity of the researcher (Willis 1980: 90). If the risk of distorting sociology itself was at the back of the mind – 'it may well be that my critique traduces certain texts in the ethnographic tradition' (Willis 1980: 89) – in the end even someone like Howard Becker is accused of developing 'sociological imperialism' to the point where it drops us into 'a depoliticised and de-moralised phenomenological never-never land' (Pearson and Twohig 1976: 124–5).

Stepping up the corrective tone, sociological participant observation was castigated for its 'mystified consciousness of its own practice' (Butters 1976: 263). But if the true theoretical problem seemed clear enough – 'to find a way of documenting the ideological practices of youth culture (etc.) which leads to an understanding of contradiction in which they have their determination, while simultaneously opening a road to the identification of the processes of historical movement in which this effectivity is only a conjunctural moment' (Butters 1976: 271–2) – exactly *how to proceed* empirically was not so easy. Paul Willis (1980: 91) felt that there must be *something* in the notion of methodological distance between researcher and researched, otherwise we would never be 'surprised' by our enquiries – a standard nostrum within sociology teaching. And as testimony to the difficulty of integrating the right kind of (structural) theorization with the evocation of real lives, Willis's own *Learning to Labour* (1977) was definitively split between one part couched in theoretical terms and the part that acts as vehicle for readable ethnographic representation. Conceived in neo-Gramscian terms, Willis's work subsequently became widely taken up by specialists not only in the sociology of education, but in the upper reaches of sociological theory too (Giddens 1984: 289ff.).

Other Birmingham groups defined their concerns in part by encapsulating what the sociologists on their patch had to say, then by, emphatically, undermining their accounts. Across these engagements – in the areas of working-class culture, community studies, education, 'race relations' – sociology is presented as producing abstract dichotomous categories. These begin life as ideal types that seek to approximate the contours of lived, structured experience, but they quickly turn into reified contrastive variables, the operationalization of which generates the kind of data that masks rather than illuminates the underlying and dynamic real relations. In this vein, a series of classificatory schemes are identified and countered: Parkin's division of working-class value-systems into dominant, subordinate and radical types (Brook and Finn 1978: 135); the *Affluent Worker* studies' scheme of solidaristic *versus* instrumental attitudes (Critcher 1979: 32); educational sociology's reification of the distinction between 'disadvantaged' and non-disadvantaged children (CCCS 1981: 133–5); and the race relations sociologists' contrast between the 'weak family culture' of first- and second-generation West Indian youth and the 'strong family culture' which supports Asian 'acculturation' (Lawrence 1982: 100).

In all these instances, the problem is that sociological empiricism remains solely on the surface of social analysis, 'hypertypifying' real experience without properly theorizing it (Brook and Finn 1978: 139, Critcher 1979: 14, Lawrence 1982: 95). 'General sociology' was found to be inadequate because 'its main categories were (and are) descriptive, even methodological: they are designed to enable certain calculations to be made; they do not deliver explanations' (CCCS 1981: 136–7). This leads to a fatal slippage whereby sociologists tend to take *cultural attitudes*, rather than *material realities*, as their lens for understanding social structure. Race relations sociologists, for instance, translated class and other material determinants of Black experience into diversionary questions of 'self-esteem' and 'cultural communication' (Lawrence 1982: 100, 114); Lockwood organized his whole enquiry around working-class 'images of society' (Brook and Finn 1978); educational sociologists registered differences in cultural resources in terms of 'aggregates of attitudes' (CCCS 1981: 140); and working-class culture was assumed to be knowable from home-based attitude surveys rather than life- and work-centred ethnographies (Critcher 1979: 31).

The 'unasked or partially asked questions' that invalidated sociology concerned 'the nature of the society as a whole', especially its *class* nature, and about 'specifically cultural processes' (CCCS 1981: 136). And sociology's inability to ask these questions ultimately derived from two things: the petit bourgeois–class interests and liberal ideology of professional sociologists, and the nature of sociology itself as a reformist project. Given their preoccupation with multiple perspectives, good sociologists could readily *entertain* Marxism, but they could not follow its political imperatives. With this in mind, Critcher (1979: 28–33) found the *Affluent Worker* studies 'meticulous, sophisticated, substantial', and even glimpsed a 'skeletal' Marxism in them, but this was of a 'confused' sort. The Education Group noticed a significant attempt at structural analysis in the 'old' sociology of education, but this 'was not related to the class organization of the society as a whole' (1979: 138). The sociologists of race were acknowledged as recognizing 'class differences', but not 'class determinations' (Lawrence 1982: 123), and therefore could be said to be espousing merely 'sociologistic pseudo-Marxism' (Gilroy 1982: 281). Sociologists of community, finally, are praised for contesting the 'post-industrial society' thesis, but like the others they simply did not go far enough (Brook and Finn 1978: 127). Ultimately, sociology is condemned as 'reformist and repressive' (Brook and Finn 1978: 130), with 'white sociology' in particular leaving itself open to being 'incorporated into existing state ideologies' (Lawrence 1982: 133–4). Its problem is that, being progressive in *intention*, sociology eschews social transformation in favour of mere understanding, unable finally to break out of its 'self-enclosed discipline', and residually prone to 'pathologizing' working-class and black people (Critcher 1979: 34, CCCS 1981: 141, Lawrence 1982: *passim*).

From that review, it would clearly be false to argue that these Birmingham writings are 'sociological' in any literal sense. As the anti-racist scholarship in the Centre particularly brought out, if existing sociology was being critiqued, this was not simply because 'we happen to disagree with their "theories"' (Lawrence 1982: 134). There was a fundamental political charge here that could not be captured just in terms of gaining a better *perspective* as such. Nevertheless, because of this activist purpose, and partly because most of these authors were postgraduate students taking on established academics, they took their sociological opponents very seriously.

Moreover, in analytical terms, the pattern of assessment that I have identified would nowadays immediately be recognized as 'sociologistic'. Each critique depicted some standard approach in the field, and exposed it as being superficially empiricist, revealing sociology's 'inability to understand society as a total structure' (Brook and Finn 1978: 130). This is precisely the way of thinking that was soon to look dubiously 'essentialist' in subsequent incarnations of cultural studies. Within sociology over the generations, and unquestionably in most of the social science disciplines today, a central meta-theoretical issue arises about how exactly to square a holistic societal understanding with intermediate complexity and pluralism. No one at Birmingham was unexercised by this issue, though ranks were closed from time to time in relation to non-Marxist frameworks like those within sociology. Internally, however, things were rather different, not least because culture and subculture themselves could have little 'relative autonomy' if any strenuously reductionist Marxism was adopted.

Then, crucially, there was the issue of how to put *gender* and *race*, together with their corollaries subjectivity and experience and their different communities and solidarities, into the theoretical mix. Not that this was 'merely' a theoretical matter, as the remarkable political, substantive and theoretical essays in *Women Take Issue* made very clear. The masculinism of the Centre's own post-sociological ethnography had already been flagged up in *Resistance Through Rituals* (McRobbie and Garber 1976), and the issue was thus simultaneously about how the Centre's prevailing male Leftism as well as its theoretical structuralism could respond to *this* kind of challenging plurality. Yet it was not as though the point of view of the totality was lost in the challenging perspective itself; rather it was a matter of the right way to articulate structures of gender and subjectivity 'with the structured relations of production and reproduction' (Bland *et al.* 1978a: 48, 1978b: 173). This volume, its priority being quite different and more urgent, was one of the few Centre collections never even to mention sociology. And yet in a way, sociological re-imaginings enter most fully on to the scene precisely when political challenge is most acutely felt. We have already noted this in relation to the Centre Race and Politics Group's engagement with sociology. But no more than in the case of feminism was their sense of the social totality straightforwardly Marxist or reductionist. Paul Gilroy (1982: 282) offered a particularly telling resume of the 'correspondences, connections, ruptures and breaks between capital, patriarchy and their racial structures', all the ingredients that were thought to make up 'a view of the social formation as a contradictory but complex unity'. In the terms of my Chapter 1, this governing conception, together with the Women's Studies Group's call for 'critiques of existing understandings, the discovery of new material and new questions, and the development

of a theoretical understanding of women's subordination under capitalism' (Editorial Group 1978: 15) involve a deeply sociological reworking
of the object of enquiry at the very moment that they signal something
different again.

'Postmodern conjuncturalism'

That a decisive break with disciplinary sociology was needed, just to get
off the ground, became a settled part of the story of cultural studies as
it established a global academic identity. This claim of 'succession', that
cultural studies was in a key sense both coming *after* and paradigmatic-
ally *displacing* sociology, became a consolidated theme within textbook
introductions in the late 1980s and early 1990s (Brantlinger 1990: 61,
Turner 1990: 112, Grossberg *et al.* 1992: 1–2, Inglis 1993: 20). We can see
its starkest logic by looking at two Australian versions. In one of these,
Simon During (1993: 1) points up the right way to approach culture
by warning of how *not* to do it: 'sociologically, for instance'. This is
because sociology proceeds 'by "objectively" describing its institutions
as if they belonged to a large, regulated system'. The full-blown version
of displacement runs like this:

> The international dissemination of cultural studies can be compared
> with that of one of its predecessors: sociology. As a modern discip-
> line, sociology has always presented itself as a universal body of
> knowledge. Its object of study is 'society' in general. 'Society' oper-
> ates in sociological discourse as a hegemonic, all-inclusive, singular
> term, denoting a comprehensive, integrated totality. Driven by a
> functionalist problematic, this discourse accords a space for internal
> differences – for example, of class, gender and race – only in terms
> of (the problems of) inclusion and integration rather than in terms
> of the radicalization of difference. What constitutes the conceptual
> limits of a 'society' are rarely discussed; where limits are recognized,
> a society is generally defined as coterminous with the geographical
> territory of the nation-state: 'American society', 'Japanese society',
> 'French 'society', and so on. However, all these national particulars
> can be specified and described in terms of the presumably universal
> concepts and theories of a presumably generally-applicable sociolo-
> gical master narrative. In this way, sociology manages to construct
> a world of separate, clearly demarcated 'societies' whose differences
> can be contained as mere variations of the same. The 'society' serving
> as a universal model, of course, at least as American functionalist

sociology would have it, is American society – both descriptively and prescriptively. (Stratton and Ang 1996: 364)

The writing here is very much aimed at the already converted, because the contrast it sketches is scarcely credible otherwise. Stratton and Ang seem to be altogether unaware of the many 'unorthodox' trends in sociology, or the atmosphere of profound disciplinary 'crisis' that has afflicted it for at least a quarter century (Lemert 1995). And like the protagonist in a morality play, cultural studies is positioned as possessing none of the vices that are built into the depiction of sociology: cultural studies could not possibly be either 'modern' or a 'discipline'; it has no master narrative to keep it in order; it pays more than lip service to difference; it is radically free of integrationist motifs; it avoids the realism and scientism which constitutes 'society' as the general object of enquiry; its particularism does not fall into the trap of unproblematically reproducing the mental space which corresponds to the nation state; it is not driven by any kind of functionalist questing; it does not bolster American (or any other) political ideology; and it has never faked attempts to separate out descriptive content from preferred ideological effect.

It is especially remarkable that these authors fail to see that their critique exemplifies the very structural *form* that it condemns in sociological discourse. Thus, the latter is conceived as an empirical phenomenon, 'knowable' by the superior cultural studies critic. Sociology is presented in its essential sameness rather than by way of its contingent, sometimes radical, differences. Its universalizing formal structure is connotatively demarcated as error, and the successor paradigm as true insight. Sociology is portrayed as having an ideological function in bolstering the material interests of modern capitalist society, but for this claim to hold, we must take that social totality to be some kind of integral phenomenon and object of knowledge, something that the critical statement, at first glance, casts profound suspicion upon. This statement of cultural studies succession, in other words, follows an entirely 'modernist' template, one that is shared by much sociological thinking. In fact, sociologists of a more reflexive inclination would be the first to point out that the problem with this mode is that it is essentially *monologic*, making 'effective dialogue unattainable' (Mulkay 1985: 101).

After the 1980s, cultural studies saw a steady shift in allegiance 'from Marx to Foucault' (Barrett 1991). If Birmingham engaged with sociology on the basis of a 'break into complex Marxism', then a rush out of complex Marxism became evident as cultural studies took off worldwide. The 'politics of difference' was in command and considerable puzzlement was aired (sometimes celebrated, sometimes regretted) about the kind of sociologistic critique that remained implicit but strong in previous Leftist thought. For some, it was the 'sociological pull' of previous cultural studies that needed to be eradicated (Grossberg 1993: 60), to the point where the very notion of 'society' came to be placed, in the jargon of the time, under erasure (During 1993: 13).

With the modernist mode of thought being figured as the principal defect in disciplines like sociology, new labels for the alternative imaginary were needed, such as 'postmodernist conjuncturalism' (Grossberg 1993: 40) and the 'French model' (During 1993: 13). For Grossberg, an altogether new kind of Deleuzian paradigm had to be embraced, in which rationalist modes of social explanation would give way to 'rhizomatic and affective theorizing', in which the notion of the 'social' subject is replaced by a 'nomadic' subject, 'reshaped as a mobile situated set of vectors in a fluid context' (1993: 61). For During, cultural studies would need to emphasize the 'variety of styles of belonging' and accept that 'the individual's relation to the fields continually incorporates and shifts under the impact of contingent givens' (1993: 12).

However, postmodern conjuncturalism had considerable difficulty getting rid of structural and causal reasoning. For example, having told us that society is radically decentred, that meta-discourses have been negated and that cultural forms are fragmented and indeterminate, During explained that all this was part of 'the globalization and consequent concentration of media/cultural production over the past decades' (During 1993: 15–16), an explanatory move that is wholly dependent upon rationalist understanding and social realism. Attention consequently shifted to the problem of *universalism* in sociological reasoning, partly because that trope could be more readily associated with the cultural hegemony of Western liberal values. Typically, though, the conjuncturalist critique of universalism never came to grips in any precise way with the range of possible meanings of universalism, or why any of them was so unacceptable. Even when sociological generalizations are framed as covering 'society as a whole', for example, they are not truly universal as such, but rather pertain to the particular time horizon of the emergence and development of human history. Moreover, most sociological theories do not in any case apply to anything so wide as that, but rather to definite epochs and regions within it, notably 'modernity' in the 'West'. Not only is it not obvious why these large-scale but specific coordinates, suitably formulated, are illegitimate horizons of enquiry, postmodernists themselves clearly had to aspire to just that level of universalism to be able to sustain the proposition that the 'project' of modernism was in process of being replaced by something else equally global and epochal.

Another way of taking universalism is as the idea that however *particular* things are, some kind of general truth can be glimpsed about the pattern and nature of the most specific relations and events. Grossberg perhaps had this meaning in mind when he insisted that 'history is always the production of struggles which empower and disempower different practices and social positions in different ways', or in his assertion that 'power is the enablement of participatory practices within specific relations' (1993: 61–2). The point here might be that practices and empowerings are always constituted in and through struggles that are radically particular, constituted by sheerly different subjectivities and purposes, thus allowing no common horizon whatsoever. But such assertions of radical contingency and of the constitutively split character of social understanding in some perpetual present are themselves couched as *unbounded* generalizations about the nature of historical being, and so are universal to that extent.

Efforts to embed within cultural studies a rhizomatic style of thought, and resistance to generality, went hand in hand with presentations of cultural studies as an *anti*-discipline (Grossberg *et al.* 1992: 2). This new discursive space was regularly pronounced to be open, inclusive, experimental and pluralistic, but postmodern conjuncturalism was anything but welcoming to discursive outsiders. In the texts and on the conference circuit – from the stellar plenary sessions to postgraduate student reports, everything had to be framed in terms of such mantras as 'striated and smooth spaces', the 'impossibility of translation', and 'storying the other'. This kind of remorseless generality, moulded incongruously out of homages to contingency and indeterminacy, still appeals to some commentators even now. For example, one New Zealand writer tells us to follow Deleuze's advice that we should 'start in the middle of things'. This entails that, when we want to understand New Zealand's contemporary makeover as the land of *The Lord of the Rings*, we are 'not looking for coherence', for fear of rendering messy things too neat and static (Jutel 2004: 55.) Gollum would surely approve. Elsewhere, in a text invitingly titled *The Basics*, Jeff Lewis follows up a patently ill-informed character assassination of sociology (2003: 72–3) with a statement of the 'transculturalism' that he hopes will stand as the rearticulated theoretical core of cultural studies. This refers to the 'desire to interrogate the forming processes of meaning-making and the instabilities which characterize their operation'. And what it entails is that 'transculturalism acknowledges in the contemporary context that cultural contiguity is inevitable'. Indeed, 'transculturalism offers no guarantees'; it is 'a theory of perpetual exchange'. Saving the reader the trouble of responding to this drivel, the author helpfully adds that 'transculturalism is deeply suspicious of itself' (2003: 437–8).

'Sociological revenge'

Let us take a step back again. The development of cultural studies to the point where all structural and realist assumptions were declared either void or optional caused perturbation amongst those with lingering allegiances to conventional forms of inquiry. For them, the celebration of discursive cultural analysis represented not the supersession of disciplinary traditionalism, but the comeback of literary textualism as the first parent of cultural studies, something that was reflected in some of the primers of the time (Brantlinger 1990). Another fear was that its radical pluralism would turn cultural studies into a ghastly mish-mash, fears that were fuelled by the appearance of increasingly vacuous introductions (Inglis 1993). For some, the solution to this degeneration was not so much to turn to sociology, nor to hark back to Birmingham, but to ensure that the multi-disciplinary character of cultural studies was genuinely sustained. Angela McRobbie (1992, 1997) and David Morley (1997) in particular drew attention to the dearth of grounded, ethnographic and sociological projects in cultural studies, 1990s-style.

McRobbie did not feel that getting 'back to reality' meant losing touch with everyday tastes and cultures, but others were much more suspicious of 'eclectic populism'. Kellner (1995: 39–42) defended an 'insurgent' cultural studies against the 'fetishism' of consumerist analysis, while Agger (1992: 76) argued that the new 'culturalism' had 'betrayed' the best interdisciplinary traditions. Agger rescued a degree of sociological realism by insisting that issues of culture and conflict are eminently *empirical* (1992: 10) and he proposed to reinvigorate this sociological element by maintaining that cultural studies 'must be connected to, and must further develop, social theory that explains the circuitries of cultural production, distribution and reception in both ideological and political-economy terms' (1992: 113). Similar lines in the sand were drawn firmly by Jim McGuigan (1992) and a range of feisty contributors to the highly charged collection *Cultural Studies in Question* (Ferguson and Golding 1997). There, sociology seemed to merge with political economy as the guardian of the vital dimension that was thought to have disappeared. If that kind of association would once have been deemed very unlikely, what was emerging with clarity was that cultural studies' *problem* with sociology was partly of its own making, and that it had to take some responsibility for regaining a more productive approach (Wood 1998).

Within sociology itself, at this time, especially in the USA, many who had seemed perfectly at home in their sociological credentials started to gravitate rather dizzily towards cultural studies, its edgy image proving particularly attractive to those working in the sociology of culture and symbolic interactionism (Alexander and Seidman 1990, Becker and McCall 1990, Munch and Smelser 1992). Much of this work took a frankly idealist slant. Crane, for example, sought to revive the sociology of culture by taking out the element of social realism, on the grounds that 'struggles over meaning constitute the reality' (Crane 1994: 100). And Denzin recommended a 'merger' between cultural studies and symbolic interactionism, one that involved an effort to undercut the 'great myth of late capitalism, that there is after all, a real world out there' (Denzin 1992: 169). This 'new sociology of interpretation' was not very consistent, however, since no sooner were such constructionist notions loudly trumpeted than realist sentiments bounced back. Thus Denzin states, 'social actors define for themselves the conditions in which they live', yet our accounts of such definitions must be 'anchored in the bedrock worlds of material existence that shape human consciousness' (1992: 118, 167).

These (mixed) responses to, and within, postmodern conjuncturalism revived the productive side of the tension between sociology and cultural studies, and testified to their mutual porosity. But could it not be said at this stage that sociology had simply been *wronged* by cultural studies, and was it not sociology's *own* healthy pluralism that cultural studies *aficionados* wished now to emulate, where once they had sought to decimate it? Along those lines, Chris Rojek engaged with cultural studies thinking in the field of sport and leisure. He argued that in spite of *theoretical* recognition of the 'vital interplay' between work and leisure, this was 'remorselessly denied when the theory is applied to concrete empirical processes' (Rojek 1985: 134). And referencing his own pluralistic attempt to build bridges between figurational sociology and cultural studies, he accused the guardians of Birmingham-ism of dogmatically refusing to grasp this olive branch, thus exposing the claimed 'openness' of cultural studies as a fraud (Rojek 1992).

In a more general critique, David Harris had little difficulty accepting the value of Birmingham/Gramscian cultural studies – as long as it was regarded as 'one option rather than the only option' (Harris 1992: 165).

In relation to empirical exploration, 'sociology and other bourgeois disciplines could claim to have had a more open relation to empirical evidence', and meanwhile, there were more substantial theoretical overlaps between cultural studies positions and the likes of Giddens, Weberian sociologists of culture, and sociologically committed feminists than cultural studies researchers were ever willing to admit. That being so, perhaps the 'revolutionary fantasies of "breaking" [with sociology] should have been resisted from the outset' (Harris 1992: 195–6).

The resurgent sociologists delighted in claiming that, having once been deep critic of surface empiricism, cultural studies had turned into its handmaiden, content with descriptive impressionism. As for its much-paraded moral and political commitment, Keith Tester (1994: 3, 4, 10) went as far as to say that 'cultural studies is a discourse that is morally cretinous because it is the bastard child of the media it claims to expose'.

Once a critical force, it had become 'facile and useless . . . about nothing other than cultural studies itself'. Sociology, by contrast, could be praised because it 'holds out the possibility of a lively study of culture which is informed by a seriousness of moral and cultural purpose'. This is possible because 'if it is worth doing sociology is not happy just to describe and explore what exists. Sociology ought to be driven by a sense of moral commitment and by a moral outrage at what presently passes as the good life.'

In appraising these expressions of 'sociological revenge', it is notable how this scenario exactly reverses the series of binary contrasts that we saw working polemically for cultural studies. Tester's statements in particular amount to a spectacular show of force. But the spectacle is just that: a set-piece staging, conducted in a tone of high dudgeon and theorized in a strangely counterfactual register. Thus, 'sociology holds out the possibility of a lively study of culture . . . if it is worth doing, sociology is not happy just to . . . sociology might do this because, unlike cultural studies . . .' and 'this book is written as if sociology is . . .' (Tester, 1994: 4). The wholesome sociological alternative to cultural studies is, patently, an idealized 'imagined community', fully believable only in the 'as if' mode.

The reality of sociology's engagement with culture, in the mainstream at least, afforded little ammunition for Tester's case, especially in the USA, where difficulties were being experienced in devising durable alternatives to the clunky duality that presents the 'social system' exchanging with the 'cultural system'. Elder statesman Neil Smelser asked whether culture should be treated as a coherent totality, or if it did not instead represent the kind of congeries of phenomena that needs to be rigorously *disaggregated*. Smelser's fear of generalized realism led him to think that culture should *not* be seen as the result of some independent social patterning. Rather, it is 'the product of our imposed categorization' (Smelser 1992: 17, 20). Contrary to portrayals of reductionist sociology in cultural studies, the profound neo-Kantianism of the sociological tradition is in evidence here, to the embarrassment of both postmodern conjuncturalism, which it rather resembles, *and* sociological revenge, from which it can draw only cold comfort.

'The cultural turn'

A more synthetic way of conceiving the relationship between cultural studies and sociology was developed under the aegis of 'the cultural turn'. This idea signals a growing appreciation of the centrality of culture across a range of (inter)disciplines, and suggests that a new kind of common ground had opened up. Thus, sociologist Jeffrey Alexander volunteered to take sociology boldly into the 'thicket' of cultural studies so that the 'return of culture' can be properly addressed (Alexander 1988: 93, 91). Similarly, David Chaney talked about the cultural turn as representing a 'fundamental movement or era' that would bring together cultural sociology and cultural studies (Chaney 1994: 2). Finally, Hall's Open University team explicitly deployed the flag of the cultural turn to summarize significant epistemological and substantive changes in the human sciences as a whole (Du Gay 1997: 1–2, Hall, 1997b: 208).

The central focus of a sociologically inflected cultural studies, in this scenario, is the dialectic between forms of *representation* and other practices. Any sharp sociology/cultural studies split is avoided by ensuring that the typically textualist interest in representations is balanced with the more materialist emphasis on institutions and practices. The stimulus generated by this new agenda became apparent in the range of fruitful investigations triggered by the theorists cited: Alexander's enthusiasm for symbolic expressions of the modern sacred in political events such as Watergate; Chaney's suggestion that 'lifestyle' imagery is the open-ended language of identity today; and Hall *et al.*'s series of 'case studies' in cultural studies, ranging from the Sony Walkman to the contemporary panoply of (multi)cultural otherness.

However encompassing these expositions of the cultural turn were, they were framed around the continuing role of 'conventional sociology' as the rhetorical 'other' of cultural turn studies. According to Chaney, the cultural turn initially expressed a development *within* sociology, though it came to 'transcend conventional sociology' (1994: 43), whilst

Alexander championed (the later) Durkheim because neither Marx nor Parsons, nor their various offspring, were thought to supply the 'opening to cultural studies that sociology needs' (Alexander 1989: 169). Hall *et al.*, by contrast, registered how various classics, including those undervalued by Alexander, might be enlisted to *support* the cultural turn (Du Gay 1997: 18). But on the whole, it was resolved that conventional sociology should be seen as standing for *resistance* to the cultural turn. Thus for Hall and Du Gay, the conventional sociological approach to culture treats it as subordinate, superficial, ephemeral, and reducible to something more *material* (Du Gay 1997: 2, 3, 13, Hall 1997a: 5–6). Remarkably, both Marxism and the sociological mainstream are intended to fall into that category. At one point, Hall hesitated over this massive statement of equivalence (Hall 1997b: 225), but only for a moment. Even allowing for the fact that these presentations were constructed with students principally in mind, it is unfortunate that these texts work chiefly in terms of their sense of urgency, the imperative they convey that it is simply time to 'move on'. If we do not make the cultural turn soon, it is implied, the leading people will be round the corner and out of reach, and we will be left floundering in the past.

The theoretical nub of the debate is the contraposition of a definition of culture as *constitutive* of social relations as against one in which culture is depicted as a specific sphere or component of the wider social totality. Chaney reveals the 'anti-sociologistic' core of the first option when he accepts that the cultural turn represents both 'triumphant culturalism' in popular culture, and strenuous reflexivity within cultural analysis. Simply put, he argues, there is no 'outside' of culture. Here, both sociology and cultural studies are folded into a certain vision of *anthropology*, governed by one 'founding principle' only: that 'culture is reflexive in the sense that it is displayed and sustained through everyday occasions of its being invoked' (Chaney 1994: 211).

Hall's navigation of the issue can be regarded either as finely negotiated or notably strained. The required association between conventional sociology and reductionist materialism (Marxism) is certainly dubious, and it becomes hard to decide how to take the proposition that culture 'has a constitutive position today in all aspects of social life' (Hall 1997b: 208, 220). One reading is that instead of treating culture, wherever and whenever we find it, as explicable in terms of its relation with other social things, we must take it as self-explanatory, and in *that* sense 'constitutive'. This seems unsatisfactory because it is just what Chaney and other cultural sociologists assert in their most idealist moods. A second take would be to say that culture is *more* constitutive today than it has been in the past. But if culture is constitutive now, surely it was always so? Or, if there are respects in which substantive aspects of culture are more important today, these can only be explicated in terms of their relationship to the total social context, in which case no novel *methodological* moves seem to be involved. With those sorts of complications hovering unresolved, Hall, and Chaney too, back off somewhat. We are dealing, after all, not with a full-scale 'paradigm shift', but with a change of emphasis only (Chaney 1994: 2, Hall 1997b: 220). The point is to recover some neglected elements in modern thought rather than making a 'total break' with it (Hall 1997b: 223). In the end it is not the case that 'everything is cultural', only that every social practice has cultural or discursive conditions of existence (1997b: 226), the kind of summation that allows sociologists and materialists either to reclaim their stake in the cultural turn or to wonder what precisely has been turned into what, and by how many degrees.

'Pragmatic Reflexity'

The current situation is one in which all the previous scenarios recruit willing representatives, with no one mood dominating. Partly because sociology has endlessly debated its identity in the thirty-five years since Gouldner announced its 'coming crisis', and others declared it to be destined to remain a pre- or multi-paradigmatic discipline, it is cultural studies, of the two, that now appears to be in greater disarray. While it was still relatively novel, uncertainty about cultural studies' identity was a secondary matter, and a definite 'pull'. Now that, like sociology, cultural studies is fully ensconced in the mainstream teaching, research, funding and career structures, this lack of a clear self-conception has become much more problematical. It leads the current generation of teachers to talk in terms of cultural studies' own 'paradigm crisis' (Storey 2001: 171), and to consider the prospect of 'cultural studies *after* the cultural studies paradigm' (Baetens 2005, emphasis added). Introductory texts now have to cover so many origins, formations, founding and current theorists, overarching meta-themes, particular substantive areas and competing perspectives, not forgetting all the quasi-political movements that cultural studies feels obliged to be engaging with/in, that their authors remark on the lack of 'obvious cohesion and unity' in their discipline (White and Schwock 2006: 1). And whilst they want to add that 'inconsistencies keep the discipline fresh, energize it' (During 2005: 214), this rider now lacks full conviction.

In that context, the original designation for cultural studies – *inter*-disciplinarity – has seemed worth reinstating, especially for those with roots in Birmingham (Johnson 1997, Morley 2000: 245). But the trouble is that the whole academic scene has changed, so that in the social disciplines, probably only *economists* are comfortable with a strictly disciplinary identity. When sociologists attempt to rise to that level, usually by taking 'the social' as their global object of enquiry, they are dismissed by internal and external specialists for being hopelessly vague, or for resurrecting the mirage of a meta-discipline. Those who make a pitch for seeing *cultural studies* in a similar way, that is, as 'a discipline of the disciplines' (Willis 2003: xxi), might therefore do well to reconsider. As for 'traditional' disciplines like history and geography, the former has for decades been embroiled in issues about where its guiding theoretical threads are to be taken from, if not from elsewhere and outside, whilst textbooks in human geography are virtually indistinguishable from those of cultural studies itself. Even 'space', geography's customary trademark, reappears these days as a core theme within cultural studies (Barker 2003: Part 4, During 2005: Part 3). Meanwhile, delegates of what once seemed unarguably *topic areas* – social policy, media studies, education and the like – today confidently assert that their field is simultaneously *both* disciplinary *and* interdisciplinary.

If the idea of disciplinary stabilization remains problematical for cultural studies, it is not as though the kind of *instability* prized by postmodern conjuncturalism is any longer compelling – just try for size cultural studies as 'a happening that escapes the homogenizing influence of narrative' (Belghazi 1995: 172). Nor, as During (2005: 8) remarks, does the 'nominalist' assumption that 'cultural studies is what cultural studies does' bespeak intellectual integrity either. Across the last decade, therefore, the textbooks display a spread of descriptors, none of which fully satisfy: discipline, quasi-discipline, anti-discipline, interdisciplinary space, inter-discursive space, plural field, fluid project, ambiguous border zone, the specialism of non-speciality, the current that washes the shores of the islands of discipline. We are regularly told, of course, that cultural studies is above all an 'exciting' thing to be doing, and that its very nature is to be more 'engaged' and more 'critical' in relation to the contemporary world than other disciplines, but this is becoming hard to substantiate. There is no reason why those in, say, geography or sociology should be deemed to be *un*engaged or *un*critical, and such is the breadth and pluralism of cultural studies, within a context of principally *academic* politics, that it is no longer clear what kind of *politics* it represents. In an ironic onslaught, Francis Mulhern (2000) has accused cultural studies of habitually *misrecognizing* itself in that regard. Far from representing a genuine politics of opposition and resistance, Mulhern argues, cultural studies has come to inhabit the very *form*, if not exactly the content, of the principle of 'metaculture'. This is the attempt, exemplified by Arnold, Leavis and others, to construct a vision of the social as fundamentally cultural in constitution, the truth of which lies in the grasp only of a select group of guardians. Metaculture's quest authoritatively to fix and articulate cultural *value*, Mulhern insists, is profoundly depoliticizing, and he classifies cultural studies as meta-cultural in this sense because of its in-house way of assuming that to be political is to talk cultural politics.

Clearly this matter, like the debate around cultural populism, is both specific to cultural studies and likely to remain contentious for some time, and to that extent cultural studies will retain its distinctiveness amongst the disciplines and spaces. But its security of position as a uniquely fresh and disruptive intellectual presence is in question. To make amends, some urge cultural studies to resume the 'forgotten engagement with Marxism' (Smith 2000: 77), whilst others emphasize the major opportunity that cultural studies has before it to become properly professional, by developing its implications for *cultural policy* into an unapologetic 'reformer's science' (Bennett 1998). Indeed, if the Leftist *heritage* of cultural studies is something to be taught and accepted as a matter of fact, there are many today who think that its typical way of enquiring into the way that 'cultural forms have supported social divisions and exclusions' (During 2005: 36) is entirely compatible with 'reflexive liberalism' (Barker 2003: 433).

With this kind of breadth and complexity in play – at the most basic level these things are simply functions of longevity – newer groups of marginalized scholars and activists prefer to set up their own quasi-disciplines rather than affiliate directly with cultural studies. Disability studies writers, for example, make no bones about the limitations of *sociological objectivism* in relation to their own 'emancipatory' agenda (Shakespeare 2002). But they do not run to cultural studies for solace. What they want, along with some of the tools and perspectives borrowed from sociology itself, is their own 'standpoint epistemology', something that cultural studies, in all its sophistication, can no longer contemplate without qualms. Queer theory is a more promising candidate for convergence because its authors tend to reproduce all the extravagant terminology of postmodern conjuncturalism, in return for which cultural studies can share the disruptive aura of all-purpose outing and anti-normalization. Still, 'critical introductions' to queer theory can proceed without a mention of cultural studies, in spite of all manner of talk about denaturalization, social construction, intersectionality, performativity, inter-disciplinarity and queering popular culture (Sullivan 2003). What this manifesto seeks for queer theory is that it should become nothing less than a *discipline* in its own right, in spite of its ingrained suspicion of disciplines (Seidman 1996), and in spite of a mysteriously 'unknowable' self-image as a discourse 'in the process of ambiguous (un)becoming' (Sullivan 2003: 205, Morland and Willcox 2005: 5).

Two main strategies have been adopted to give cultural studies a more solid grounding, even at this late stage. The first of these is to emphasize the *practical* character of cultural studies, central to which is the feeling that the *methodological* side of things can be productively developed. The second is to try again to develop cultural studies as *social theory*. One way of tackling methodology is by inculcating empirical procedures and techniques. This is seen as necessary in order to compensate students for the sheer plurality and undecideability of available theoretical frameworks, and so encourage a new 'epistemological modesty' (Gray 2003: 190). Methodology might even be capable of providing a 'management template' for marshalling the burgeoning batches of cultural studies 'questions, considerations, assumptions and practices' (White and Schwoch 2006: 5). But, truth be told, this version of methodologism tends to succeed only to the degree that it *dilutes* the specificity of cultural studies because heavy borrowing from existing social science research pedagogy in such texts is very evident. For example, Alasuutari (1995), a professor of sociology, advises his cultural studies students to be thoughtfully eclectic about which methods to adopt, and to be clear about the route that takes you from original question to the selection of techniques, thence to investigative phases in the 'field' (whatever that happens to be), and onwards to the articulation of evidenced generalities and theoretical reflection. In all this, Alasuutari is really only reiterating what can also be found in any number of similarly useful manuals, the orthodoxy in all quarters now being that whilst research skills need to be dutifully learned, our choice of methods follows from the nature of our substantive concerns, which are various. In particular, no longer is there any duel to the death between qualitative and quantitative methods, partly because as Ann Oakley (2000) and others have argued, this distinction was always highly gendered. Oakley's message has consequences for feminism and other successor discourses too, however: that if the very distinction between qualitative and quantitative should *dissolve* rather than just *balance out*, then those in the successor discourses cannot hide behind their own 'special' method, or behind outdated offensives against 'positivism', but must expertly grasp all methodological tools in a social science research process that is often 'experimental' and compound. And it is also being accepted that whilst there is a definite ethics of research practice, and a pre-conditional empathy, there are many circumstances that require us to ensure a certain academic *distance* from our researched community, even if we might want to be deeply involved in 'mutual dialogue' with it.

The second way of understanding the importance of 'methodology' for cultural studies has less to do with matters of investigative technique, but rather constitutes a kind of ongoing 'argument' about research practice, or a 'path of reasoning' that is taken in the research process (Couldry 2000: 143, Gray 2003: 2, Johnson *et al.* 2004: 1). The guiding principle here is *reflexivity*, something that is still routinely contrasted with bad 'positivist' approaches that are thought to exist in sociology (Gray 2003: 16, During 2005: 30). In Chapter 9, I will be questioning at length the degree of faith that, in sociology as well as cultural studies, is being placed in reflexivity, so I will not pursue this matter here. But we can note that this second move in cultural studies methodology does represent an appeal to *meta-theoretical* norms of understanding rather than to the nuts and bolts of empirical excavation. This puts it within reach of *pragmatism* because such work tends to be pluralistic about the range of meta-theoretical perspectives in play, and about the spread of available substantive theories, selection amongst which is not likely to be terribly principled. This is why Richard Rorty's pragmatist post-modernism has become attractive to some cultural studies teachers of practice (Barker 2003: 27).

Wary, perhaps, of this kind of methodological and pragmaticist turn in cultural studies, McRobbie (2005) constructs the 'uses of cultural studies' rather differently, by showing how the 'difficult' ideas of authors like Hall, Gilroy, Bhabha and Butler offer insight into empirical and political phenomena such as Blairism, rap, postmodern film, and TV makeover programmes. This 'how to' strategy is not only interesting in itself, but seems closer to the original spirit of cultural studies enquiry, leaving aside McRobbie's reluctance to engage critically with her chosen figures (other than Bourdieu). Yet a range of thinkers less directly associated with a particular agenda in cultural studies might have been put to work in the same sort of way. This suggests that 'social and cultural theory' in general is becoming a shared resource for sociology and cultural studies alike, and indeed both discourses are well represented in current social theory Readers (Elliott 1999), and in advanced forums for research and debate, such as those bearing the *Theory, Culture & Society* imprint.

Conclusion

As if to warn against too rosy a view of the association between cultural studies and sociology, intense hostilities between the two can flare up again at the drop of a slur. In his advocacy of cultural studies as 'discourse analysis', for example, Jeremy Gilbert feels he has to identify himself as actively '*contra* sociology' on account of its supposed 'naïve realism', its treatment of culture and politics as 'mere surface effects of the social' (Gilbert 2000: 55). In reverse direction, Bourdieu and Wacquant's (1999: 47) denunciation of cultural studies as a mere creature of fashion and the media stands out, as does Turner and Rojek's polemic against 'decorative sociology', which is partly directed at the growing influence of cultural studies *within* sociology. Yet it is not at all clear that cultural studies people would disagree with what these authors construct as the central concerns of sociology: the dialectic of 'scarcity and solidarity', the process of 'action and interaction', and 'social analysis from the standpoint of human embodiment' (Turner and Rojek 2001: vii, 3). Indeed, recent cultural studies has been almost *obsessed* with this last dimension. Rojek (2003) followed up with a book-length discussion of Hall that consistently damned with faint praise, in return for which he received a furious riposte from Bill Schwarz (2005), who saw in Rojek's account a particularly crass variant of (in my terms) the 'sociological revenge' scenario. In response, Schwarz insisted that if sociology contributes much to the analysis of cultural formations in the way of systematic *theory* and investigative *method*, it habitually lacks the kind of historical *sensibility* without which the nature of Hall's trajectory and thinking – and that of cultural studies more generally – cannot be appreciated.

For all that, the scenario of reflexive pragmatism has allowed sociology and cultural studies to gravitate towards one another again. This can be seen in the place that issues of culture and the recognition of cultural studies find in the voluminous presentations of basic sociology (Fulcher and Scott 2004: 63–7, Macionis and Plummer 2005: 123–6), while cultural studies primers for their part are coming to resemble those of sociology in topic coverage and pedagogical temperament. In one such expression of cultural studies teaching today (Baldwin *et al.* 2004), the team of authors is drawn from several different disciplines, and the selection of the central issues (culture/structure, cultural practices, relativism) is cast in a broadly 'sociology of knowledge' mould. At more advanced levels, a kind of equilibrium between the pulls of structure and culture has been attained within some of the key cultural studies journals, and within sociology this is evident in current ways of thinking about central concepts such as 'class' (Devine *et al.* 2004). As a final example, the excellently straightforward volume *British Cultural Studies* (Morley and Robins 2001) is notable not only for the number of sociologists involved, but also for the absence of marked intellectual differences amongst its variety of specialist contributors. In concluding this analytical overview, then, I paraphrase an earlier summation by Janet Wolff (1999): the best of cultural studies work *is* sociological, but it can be other things too; and whilst people in cultural studies can and should pursue the concern with structures, institutions and categories of differentiation, these concerns are never optional for sociologists.

3
Explanation, Articulation, Imagination

I argued in Chapter 1 that if the idea of sociology requires 'tradition-alist' benchmarks for enquiry, these remain indispensable even under postpositivist lights. Then, in Chapter 2, I showed that if sociology and cultural studies are significantly different in some aspects of their intellectual styles and characteristic interests, there are many respects in which they share the same investigative and pedagogic terrain, and common resources in theory and methodology. Thus, if poststructuralism and post-Marxism undoubtedly influenced the framing of cultural studies in the last twenty years, there are plenty of statements in the periodic set-piece collections (Grossberg *et al.* 1992, Morley and Chen 1996, Ferguson and Golding 1997, Gilroy *et al.* 2000), which call for a determined 'recovery' of those materialist, experiential, institutional and structural dimensions of analysis. At the very least, we need to register a plurality of perspectives in cultural studies, some of which strike a definite sociological note, albeit pitched within an inter- or post-disciplinary conspectus (Morley 2000: 247–8).

In this chapter, I give analytical depth to the way in which I have summarized the interface between sociology and cultural studies to this point. If our two discourses represent *connected but different* forms of understanding, occupying the same sort of substantive ground, how exactly is this relationship to be envisaged? I tackle this question by adapting W. G. Runciman's (1983) account of sociological methodology, albeit glossed liberally for my own purposes. Using Runciman's categories, we might imagine sociology as primarily, but not exclusively, engaged in *explanatory* understanding, with the prevailing mode in cultural studies then being positioned as a combination of *descriptive* understanding and *evaluation*. Let us see how this works.

Four forms of social understanding

The first volume of Runciman's trilogy, *A Treatise on Social Theory* (1983), stands as one of the most systematic meta-theories of social investigation in recent times, yet it has barely been discussed in sociology, never mind cultural studies, where it appears to have made no mark whatsoever. Runciman is therefore an unlikely figure to bring to the elucidation of the logic of cultural studies, but I bring it into play for two reasons. First, Runciman achieves a level of conceptual 'crafting' in the service of substantive theorizing that is generally lacking both in sociology (Mouzelis 1991, 1995) and in cultural studies, where exercises in 'theory' tend to be summative and assertive rather than worked through in any stepwise manner. Second, Runciman's central problem – in what sense are the social sciences *explanatory*? – while central to sociology, has vital analogues in cultural studies too.

Runciman identifies three different moments in the constitution of social theory: reportage, explanation, and description. Each of these modes is said to operate according to its own governing criteria – respectively, accuracy, validity and authenticity – though collectively and in practice these are often closely interwoven with a fourth dimension of understanding, namely *evaluation*, which involves often explicit moral, political and personal judgements about whether the phenomenon under investigation is good or bad, progressive or reactionary, and so on. Reportage involves compiling bare-boned inventories of people and events. In principle at least, these are both verifiable by the 'recording angel', and acceptable to theorists of different explanatory inclinations. Since Runciman is well aware that even the barest reportage is likely to be neither purely factual nor actually demonstrable, his point is really to remind us that rival theorists often *do agree* on the empirical status of a wide range of occurrences. Much effort goes into clarifying just what is at issue in any theoretical dispute on the basis that certain other things (times, places, social phenomena under some low-level characterization) can be taken as agreed. Moreover, one central purpose in establishing reportage as a potentially consensual element is to insist that *description*, being post-explanatory, and often bound up with normative questions and intentions, is a much more complex and significant operation.

Descriptive understanding, as Runciman sketches it, conveys and reinterprets how social situations impact upon people's *experiences*. Descriptive theorizing relies upon particular reports and explanations, but its distinctive emphasis is neither to construct factual lists nor to engage in abstract relational analysis; it is to vividly reconstruct and encapsulate particular forms of life. Descriptive theorizing is not an undisciplined activity: it requires and presupposes determinate connections to evidence, reportage and explanation, and additionally strenuously needs to avoid the habitual pitfalls which characterize bad practice in this domain, such as oversimplification, ahistoricism and ethnocentricity (Runciman 1983: 244). But having said that, description clearly has greater license to move as it sees fit, evoking people's cultural experiences/resources, refiguring their predicaments and utilizing a range of expressive, conceptual, narrative and metaphorical tactics in the process.

Explanation, in Runciman's terms, is a narrower but more stringent enterprise. He hands down a ruling at an early stage in his account that explanation is not to be equated with looser notions such as 'making sense' of phenomena, 'exploring' them, 'elucidating' or 'gaining insight' into them and so on (1983: 20). These loose senses might well gesture towards the business of social understanding as a whole (which he defines as covering the descriptive and evaluative dimensions too), but they dilute the specific contribution of explanation. Explanation is essentially about establishing valid *causal relations*. Postpositivistically, Runciman accepts that social science cannot, and has no need to, produce universal covering laws, though it does *consume* general laws of many different sorts.

Instead, the procedure of social explanation is 'quasi-experimental', involving suggestive contrasts between alternative possibilities in an effort to identify the crucial antecedent(s) that bring about a social event. Nor is Runciman worried about causal relations including the kind of *functional* and *intentional* connections between social factors that orthodox empiricists used to exclude. And overall, it is acceptable if social theories are 'weak but adequate' rather than definitively well-grounded.

When it comes to 'evaluation', Runciman is dismissive of the 'purists of value-neutrality', but at the same time feels that normative commitments in the pursuit of social theory can be minimized if necessary. Evaluations, he says, inevitably enter into the picture, and we develop, variously, 'nostalgic', 'utopian' or 'exposure' veins of writing in justifying our explanatory and descriptive work. But still, each of these veins can be couched in an unacceptable 'pre-emptive' mode, or in an acceptable 'discretionary' fashion (1983: 335–7, 340).

From that distillation of his outlook, Runciman has articulated both an area of continuity between social theory and the natural sciences (chiefly around causal explanation), and yet a field of crucial differences too, notably in the realms of post-explanatory description and evaluation. Far from diluting the social scientific achievement, the modes of description and evaluation make social theory a rich and satisfying human endeavour. Explanation aspires to valid causal know-ledge; description re-presents the experience of social life in a given domain/period; and evaluation involves arguments as to whether a reported, explained and described state of affairs is a good thing or not. Evaluation in that sense stretches to cover the way in which ideological commitments and concerns interweave with our sense of the signific-ance of explanatory and descriptive accounts. The vitality of human *understanding*, for Runciman, lies not in any one of these elements of social theory as pitched against the logic of any other, but in the comple-mentarity between all four.

Yet differences of object, style and emphasis between the four analyt-ical sectors, and between the disciplines, do exist, so one plausible scen-ario is to place sociology mainly within the *explanatory* moment of social theory, with cultural studies framed principally within the moment of theory-informed *description and evaluation*. There are no hard-and-fast boundaries here, but intuitions to the effect that cultural studies is more urgent and engaged – some might say impressionistic – where sociology is more retrospective and formally analytical – some would say boring and scientistic – are satisfied too. Runciman himself is not the type to dwell much on cultural studies (McLennan 1995b: 103–4), and indeed he hardly dwells on the question of disciplinarity at all, but he clearly thinks of anthropology and history as being more involved in 'thick description' than sociology needs to be, and this Geertzian catchphrase is ever-popular as a proxy for cultural studies practice. We would expect Runciman himself to prefer to rank the sociological explainer above the cultural studies describer, but unfortunately for him, the relation-ship as stated does not allow this. Whilst explanation is a core pursuit, it is embedded within a fuller account of the many-sidedness of the socio-cultural realm; description, for its part, is definitively separated from mere reportage because it is a *theoretical* activity from the start, trading on various explanatory understandings.

Extrapolations

That re-characterization of the relation between sociology and cultural studies has a certain elegance and economy, and it leads to further inclusive theoretical moves. For example, it helps us finally to get past the formalistic tendency to treat 'the social' and 'the cultural' as distinct 'zones' or 'spheres' of the more general social totality (Bocock and

Thompson 1992, Crane 1994). It also gives greater license to the many sociologists who want to explore the symbolic field and to see their discipline in more 'passionate' terms, rather than force them to disown their (partial) identity as sociologists (Game 1991, Game and Metcalfe 1996).

The conceptual apparatus we have been utilizing also helps us to return afresh to the sociological 'classics'. The re-emergence of Simmel, for example, as a high-profile figure in the pantheon of sociology seems appropriate, for Simmel has been widely praised for developing the cultural dimension of sociology and for exemplifying sophisticated sociological 'impressionism' rather than abstract totalization. That characterization, though, is slightly misleading because it continues to pitch cultural understanding *against* systematic social understanding. In what is still one of the best discussions of sociology's house-rules, Simmel makes that lazy move difficult. Simmel certainly draws a distinction between the analysis of the 'major social formations' of society and the 'interspersed effects of countless minor syntheses', the former referring to those 'consistent structures such as the state and the family, the guild and the church, social classes and organizations based on common interests', whilst the latter comprises all those moods, meanings, routines and interchanges amongst people that touch on our sense of 'the colour and consistency of social life', its 'striking and yet so mysterious' quality (Simmel, in Wolff 1964: 9–10). This is the Simmel who has rightly been celebrated as inaugurating a 'sociology of the senses', something perceived as missing in the sociological mainstream but present in cultural studies (Barrett 2000: 17).

But to leave it there would be superficial. He is also proposing a further pair of conclusions. First, he implies that no analytical pursuit – and this would include cultural studies as well as sociology – can be expected to unlock *all* the secrets, all the 'mysteries' of lived experience. Simmel certainly has a more vitalistic sense of the flow of social life than, say, Weber or Durkheim (Simmel, in Wolff 1964: 12). But it does not follow from this that there is any fundamental antagonism between macro and micro, or between structural and cultural approaches. Simmel insists that we need an account of the major 'organs' *and* of the innumerable 'tissues' of the social body, and an account of how these dimensions mutually interact. In particular, he dispels any presumption that the description of the flux of cultural interchange is possible without *synthetic abstractions*, nor can any privilege be accorded on the basis of the greater *concrete reality* of its object. Rather, Simmel intimates, the differences between the two moments of understanding are differences of *distance* and *purpose*, and he is attempting to *characterize* those differences: he is not arguing that one is more legitimate, deep or real than the other (1964: 11–14). It is not too forced to suggest that Simmel is occupying, in his own way, the schema I have derived from Runciman. The moment of rich description, to reiterate, is necessary for a properly cultural sociology, but it *is* still a theoretical moment, carrying no more intrinsic weight or approved concreteness, than more distanced theoretical summaries, which are still indispensible in order to map out the principal characteristics of social structure in a given formation.

Our schema, furthermore, makes sense of some previous 'foundational' work in cultural studies too. Raymond Williams, with his concern first of all to develop the idea of the 'structure of feeling' of a social era, moved on latterly to reformulate the Marxist base-and-superstructure configuration so as to yield a better account of the relationship between culture and *ideology*. Essentially, this represents a shift in Williams's work from the descriptive to the explanatory moment of sociological cultural studies. These take different slants, of course, but they do logically complement one another. Related changes of emphasis, indeed coexisting forms of practice, along the same lines, can be read into the work of the Birmingham Centre. Hall (1980) outlined how the paradigm of culturalism within cultural studies buckled in the 1970s under the weight of a new structuralist leaning, and he argued that the preferred orientation lies somewhere between, in fact *beyond*, the combined strengths and excesses of the two.

Articulations

The discussion so far has sought to inject some freshness into habitual considerations of *canonicity*, but how does it impinge on more recent ways in which the theoretical purchase of cultural studies has been cast? Recalling our scenarios in Chapter 2, we are now able to sharpen it further. We saw there that in 'Birmingham' it was a key part of the repertoire to castigate 'sociological' accounts of working-class culture, education, community studies, race and ethnicity and so on. In each of these critiques, sociology was portrayed, and flayed, as being insufficiently dynamic, structural and materialist. The descriptivism inherent in empiricist sociology, whereby the realities of the world were held on the surface by reference principally to the current self-images of social agents, was thought by cultural studies critics to be both idealist and repressive. The implication was that cultural studies understanding could be more *explanatory*, achieving proper depth and perspective, so that transformative political practice would follow as a consequence.

With the shift to postmodern conjuncturalism, such ambitions to plumb the hidden depths of the social formation were questioned, and it has seemed to critics of this phase of cultural studies that nothing else *other than* the descriptive self-images of social agents was of any interest. As noted, this is not adequate as a characterization of what was going on post-Birmingham. A better purchase is gained if we consider what from that time to now stands as probably the most distinctive methodological theorization in cultural studies, 'the method of articulation'. The concept of articulation comes in different shades, none of which are fully convincing as a way of separating cultural studies from sociology (Wood 1998), but its role in taking cultural studies clear of any accusation of sheer descriptivism is decisive. In the postmodernist conjuncturalist version thematized by Grossberg, articulation questions the very notion of stable structures and different 'levels' of experience/analysis, since 'there is always a multiplicity of positions, not only available but occupied, and a multiplicity of ways in which different meanings, experiences, powers, interests, and identities can be articulated together' (Grossberg 1993: 31). This intimation of wholesale conceptual *open-endedness* is consolidated by assertions – fairly bland ones it has to be said – to the effect that 'a particular articulation can be both empowering and disempowering; people can win something and lose something'. Instead of conventional social-structural analysis, the emphasis falls firmly on evocative encapsulation. In focusing on popular culture, for example, postmodern cultural studies is framed primarily as a way to re-articulate the 'visceral responses' which define the popular, the 'sensibilities' which organize it, and the 'affective and libidinal' work that it accomplishes (Grossberg 1993: 51–2, 62–3).

Clearly, this version of 'articulation' looks like a bid to vacate and devalue the explanatory domain in order to elevate the descriptive mode. Yet, this cannot completely be so, since Grossberg continues to see postmodern cultural studies as governed not only by literary and psychoanalytic 'vectors', but also by orthodox sociological ones. Cultural studies, for example, must 'comprehend the specificity of the historical context of modernity and modernization within and against which contemporary cultural practices function'. And again, cultural studies 'is concerned with describing and intervening in the ways "texts" and "discourses" are produced within, inserted into, and operate in the everyday lives of human beings and social formations so as to reproduce, struggle against and perhaps transform the existing structures of power'. So it can only be in a relative, and not in any fundamental, sense that the new standpoint 'challenges the sociological pull of cultural studies'

(Grossberg 1993: 32–4, 58–60). The background reason for the tension in play here is that whilst this phase of theoretical cultural studies ostensibly rejects the 'philosophical' character of 'totalization', implicit within the entire educational-political *project* of cultural studies, there is a deep, inescapable logic of totalization (Osborne 2000: 16–17).

Balancing out Grossberg's Deleuzean enthusiasms with Hall's (1996b) original interview statements on articulation, Jennifer Daryl Slack couches the 'epistemological' dimension as 'a way of thinking the structures of what we know as a play of correspondences, non-correspondences and contradictions, as fragments in the constitution of what we take to be unities' (Slack 1996: 112). Playing on the double sense of articulation as both interconnecting and bespeaking, Slack argues that it is necessary to identify structural connections in the analysis of any concrete conjuncture in order to avoid mere happenstance observations and 'random' relations. Yet the conferral of structural status on certain relations is held to be the *product* of our organizing *discourse* (including its evaluative/political dimension), rather than the result of invariance in the object world itself (Slack 1996: 115, 199, Hall 1996b: 141). We are back, apparently, to the kind of neo-Kantianism that we saw the doyen of sociology Neil Smelser articulating in Chapter 2.

The problem with Slack's interpretation is that there is no justification for regarding some elements in the governing discourse as more 'structural' than others. In fact, this presentation of the method of articulation is curiously void of any kind of *content*, its status as an *explanatory* frame being dubious because ambivalent and unspecific about determination. However, regarded as a general heuristic and descriptive aid in mapping out the key dimensions of contexts, conjunctures and formations (Slack 1996: 125), it is altogether more acceptable. In fact, the language of 'mapping' has always been popular in cultural studies perhaps chiefly *because* of its ambivalent site between the registers of explanation and description. For example, the stated aim of the *British Cultural Studies* volume is 'to map the state of British culture now, seeking to identify its new configurations and to trace its new fault lines' (Morley and Robins 2001: 1). There is undoubtedly a structural and explanatory connotation in this depiction, but overall the goal is to figure out plausible figurations, not to provide definitive causal accounts.

The influential 'circuit of culture' figure which organized the Open University's 'Culture, Media and Identities' series of texts stands as a more applied theoretical 'mapping' of the terrain of cultural studies. Introducing the circuit, Paul Du Gay cites Hall's (1996b) interview, just as Slack did, as the source of the notion of articulation which generates the master diagram, presenting it as 'a theoretical model based on the articulation of a number of distinct processes whose interaction can and does lead to variable and contingent outcomes' (Du Gay 1997: 3). Du Gay adds that amongst the key 'moments' of the circuit – representation, identity, production, consumption and regulation – no priority to any one element can be given, partly because of the blatant inadequacies of more conventional sociological models, in which *production* seemed to be the first and last point of interest.

Two critical observations can be made about this application of 'the method of articulation' to the circuit of culture. First, the sense in which it is a 'theoretical model' is not completely obvious. We can certainly *orientate* our thoughts about the generation and uptake of cultural artefacts through this device, and so once again it could be seen as a valuable heuristic trigger. But it does not in itself propose any general positive ideas about the causal structures of cultural circulation, other than the observation that lots of different things come into the picture and that these are closely interrelated. Of course, these latter pluralistic sentiments appear weighty against the background story about how orthodox sociological accounts are *monistically* concerned with the moment of production alone. But – my second critical observation – this background story is not believable. Indeed, the nearest thing to sociological orthodoxy this century was probably Talcott Parsons's account of the way that the social system operated in terms of a circulating four-sector logic, and there is an intriguing parallel between this Parsonian image and the OU team's circuit of culture model. Parsons too was trying to develop an analytical descriptive *mapping* in terms of a consistent plurality of interdependent nodal points, with specific 'generalized media of exchange' circulating amongst them, but with no particular causal or analytical priority to be specified – unless it was the 'moment of culture' itself (Long 1997: 10).

So, in many ways, it is not *conventional sociology* that Hall and Du Gay are putting to the sword in their warnings against reductionism; what they are doing is taking their leave of the remnants of *Marxism*. But leaving to one side the question of whether Marxist accounts themselves have ever been quite as reductionist as the 'production and production alone' phrasing suggests (Hall 1977), there remains the problem that no determinate account of the workings of culture, that is to say no *explanation*, can be generated without some kind of reductionist intent. This is one of the very meanings of 'explanation' – the lessening of surface complexity through the use of a theoretical 'key' that brings to light selected, but central, generative processes. The circuit of culture model, however, does not seem to be designed to work in that way, rather it allows us, descriptively, to place various concrete phenomena and experiences in one of the four sectors, and that, in itself, helps us 'make sense' of things.

Demanding explanations

I have been arguing that Runciman's version of the distinctions between reportage, explanation, description and evaluation and the overlaps between them, is of interest in working out the relationship between sociology and cultural studies. And I have suggested that prominent cultural studies theorizations and mappings are less explanatory, in a formal sense, than descriptive. However, the debate is not to be left there because there are complications about the whole notion of 'explanation' that now have to be reckoned with. First, we should note that our main source, Runciman, is committed to giving a firm answer to a very traditional problem in the philosophy of social science: in what sense is sociology a *science*? His answer is that it is explanation specifically that makes sociology scientific, and that explanation, in turn, is a matter of providing causal answers to why-questions (Runciman 1983: 19–20). This classic concern impels him to accord analytical weight to explanation *as against* description and evaluation, and to associate explanation with causal accounts in a conventionally narrow sense.

At the same time, we have already noted that 'weak but adequate' explanations may have to suffice, and that these will include intentional and functional relations as well as (or as variants of) causal forces. Runciman also accepts that there may be so many antecedent conditions of a social outcome that *the* cause cannot decisively be singled out (1983: 183). Partly, he concedes, this is to do with the fact that social theorists often disagree with each other in terms of their 'presuppositions', 'models' and 'theories', though generally this seldom amounts to outright incommensurability (1983: 193). Moreover, whilst description, for its part, is set up as aiming for 'authenticity' in accounting for social experience, this is neither a straightforward reporting exercise, nor is there any prospect of isomorphic resemblance between account and phenomenon. Descriptive social theorists, just like explanatory theorists, require 'ideal types' to fulfil their task, and whilst these may be more specific in content than those of the explanatory theorist, each set of constructs is, in its own way, both 'creative' and 'fictional' (1983: 292). This is because, in spite of its connotations of situational accuracy, description works by way of reinterpretation and composite exemplification, rather than through average-typical representation. All descriptions are therefore partial, just as all explanations are provisional (1983: 242, 227).

Those finer details help further to situate the kind of 'mappings' in cultural studies already referred to, and to define the requisite level of abstraction of such widely adopted concepts as 'New Times', 'the Black Atlantic', and 'cultural hybridity'. These theoretical notions may not be strictly explanatory, in the sense of identifying any definitive set of relationships or causal properties; but nor are they 'merely' descriptive. A better way of conceptualizing them is in terms of those 'colligations' that philosophers of history identified as the way in which theoretically minded historians go about capturing the very core of sociohistorical epochs and moments (Walsh 1974). Instead of formalistic causal hypotheses, or veritable theories of history, colligations apply when we want to bring to light the *internal affinity* of various diverse and sometimes intangible phenomena. Colligations capture particular occurrences and beliefs neither as stand-alone items nor as parts of a completed system that we already understand fully, but as elements of *congeries* or *syndromes*. It follows that the *plausibility* of any colligation will be that bit more dependent upon the presenter's way of pressing upon us this tying-together of disparate contemporaneity than in scientific or systematic causal explanation. This, quite possibly, is what Schwarz was getting at when he chided Rojek for his inattention to the historical mode of apprehension that is sometimes prevalent – or at least ought to be present – in cultural studies.

In fact, the distinction between explanation and description distinction within philosophy of science today is far more fluid than it was when scientific deductivists battled it out with historical particularists in the philosophical discourse of the late 1950s. Three issues are worth highlighting here: the *range* of properly explanatory questions; the question of the *reductionist intent* of robust explanations; and the *pragmatic/rhetorical context* of explanation.

On the first matter, some theorists now emphasize that *what* and *how* questions are just as explanatorily important as *why* questions. Scientific explanations work, therefore, not only by specifying *causes*, but also by giving us a causal *story*. Moreover, we sometimes explain, not by causal specification at all, but 'by telling us of an entity what it is' (Kinoshita 1990: 304), that is, by giving an account of a phenomenon's *identity* or *constitution* (Ruben 1990: 219). Much is explained, for example, by the idea that water is H_2O, though no causal relation is specified in that characterization alone. Within the human sciences too, we often try to decide whether a certain concatenation of actions, intentions and outcomes is best designated as, say, a 'revolution' rather than (only) a 'riot', as capitalism rather than (only) industrialism, or as patriarchy rather than (only) personal sexist inclinations. In other words, we are trying to identify certain *dispositional* or *tendential features* that might give us a comprehensive grasp of the phenomena in question. Causality can thus be broadened out of its traditional remit to *include* those various relations of determination, or dependence, or structural correlation, or 'constitutionality' that characterize the things and processes in question (Kim 1993). The idea of explanation thus broadens out considerably, so that we explain something when we can show either 'what is responsible' for it, *or* 'what makes it as it is' (Ruben 1990: 233). Those who insist on interpreting explanatory responsibility in terms of theories of causality – such that, almost by definition, 'a theory is a description of a repertoire of causal mechanisms' – can still easily accept that what is to count as a 'cause' in the first place is somewhat variable, and above all something to be left to the practitioners of the inquiring discourse rather than being subject to some over-generalized philosophical specification (Miller 1987: 139).

What about the perennial question of reductionism? For Runciman, explanation is 'general in content, free in operation and simplifying in effect', whereas description is 'specific in content, restricting in operation and complicating in effect' (1983: 293). In this model, to switch to a formulation due to Bruno Latour, explanation involves the existence of two 'lists', and the idea is that we have to get the items that are on one list over to the other, paring them down in the process so that fewer remain on the one side than the other (Latour 1988: 157). Explanation, then, could be seen as always involving reduction, that is, the replacement of one set of terms used to describe a phenomenon by a supposedly more basic set (Kitcher 1988). 'Mere' description, it would follow, involves comparing two Latour lists, but without seeing either as being superior or as containing more basic terms. There would also be no motivation to cut down the number of items on either list. The centrality of reduction to explanation in that sense has long been assumed to be self-evident, but now it too is open to debate, as theorists of very different sorts pose again the fundamental question: why is explanatory 'power' desirable in the first place? Why do we *demand* explanations at all (Latour 1988: 159, Gasper 1990: 293)?

Reductive explanation, we need to appreciate, is not necessarily being rejected as such in these deconstructions. Latour, for example, thinks that it is the *distance between contexts,* and our feeling that we need to exercise *power over* one context from the distance of another, that characterizes explanation-seeking. But whilst this demand for power is often unhealthy, in his view, it also appears to be ineliminable. Moreover, that distance between the analytical and the object space *also* characterizes even the most 'ultra-reflexive' attempts at non-reductive re-description (Latour 1988: 169). Description may well involve trying to connect the several items on one list to those of another without reductive elimination, but any kind of analytical register requires that there is a theoretical distance between the domain of experience and the domain of understanding, and a presumption that the latter can legitimately subsume the former.

The third reason for closing the gap between explanation and description lies in the increasing acceptance that explaining is at least in part a pragmatic, *rhetorical* activity (Garfinkel 1981: 173, Achinstein 1983). In a handy slogan: explanations are not only *about* something, they are *for* someone (Edmondson 1984: 1). Traditionalists see affective and pragmatic persuasion as belonging to the realms of description and evaluation *rather than* to explanation, where the securing of conviction seems to be a purely rational affair. This seems implausible, though, especially when explanation works at least partly by way of 'suggestive contrasts' and 'striking parallels', and where 'weak' explanations, whilst typical in the human sciences, are routinely found to be 'thoroughly convincing' (Runciman 1983: 168–9, 183). Let me take this issue further by drawing on Ricca Edmondson's thinking on rhetoric in sociology.

Edmondson accepts that sociology does not explain or convince on the basis of law-like hypotheses or iron-clad causal statements. Rather, sociological explanation typically works by way of 'rhetorical induction', that is,

a guide to expectations in which an author goes from a limited number of observations to a statement about what can reasonably be anticipated in general. It is characteristically sociological not only in being subject to the limitations intrinsic to information about social situations, but also in its strengths. It has the strength of enabling the reader to interpret situations which are not exactly like those described; it does not involve the artificial modesty of pretending that the author can only talk about what he or she has directly observed; nor does it imply the excessive claim that the author can infer from the observations actually made to all possible cases of a comparable type. (Edmondson 1984: 106)

Rhetorical induction is thus a matter of symptomatic or *diagnostic* interpretation, and the source of conviction for a reader lies more in acceptance of the author's presentation of 'epitomes' – accentuated sketches of particular social roles and identities – than through (impossible) statistical fullness. For the reader to take it on trust that such epitomes and 'anticipations' of social states of affairs are fitted for their explanatory purpose, the 'communicative attitude' of the author is crucial. That is, the reader must be able to believe what the analyst says in the absence of definitive proof, which seldom if ever exists. Thus, the overall confidence, openness, coherence and eloquence of the discourse play a central role in securing 'successful' explanation. Even in the most monologic enunciations, therefore, there is still an underlying dialogue at work, a reaching-out, at the heart of explanatory understanding (1984: 107).

So whilst we may rightly continue to think, as Edmondson herself firmly does, that social science discourse is fundamentally about 'searching for opinions which are adequate to reality' (1984: 165), the way we respond to explanations in terms of descriptive power and the author's evaluative persona and cultural situation, makes 'adequacy to reality' a debatable and distant criterion in many cases.

Imaginings

In the discussion to this point, I have been suggesting that a close and productive parallel exists between Edmondson's thesis that *explanation* works through rhetorical induction and Runciman's claim that *descriptive* theorizing works through 'composite' representation. When brought together, these tools can be usefully applied across the genres of sociology and cultural studies to show not only the many respects in which they occupy the same ground of enquiry, but also as a method of appreciating, or questioning, great and exemplary works. For example, I have myself looked again at the continued communicative force of the *Communist Manifesto* with these guidelines in mind (McLennan 1999). But perhaps we are still giving *too much* credit to the work of explanation specifically, and above all to its *realist* underpinnings? If theories are indisputably 'products of intelligence' (Bevir 1998: 178), and if this includes emotional intelligence and the purposefulness that desire, motive and affect impart to all our beliefs about what is really going on out there, why not go much further? Why not proceed completely to submerge our understanding of explanation within an emphasis on creativity in social and cultural thinking, openly accepting its role as giving expression to ideology, need and situation?

Michele Barrett has argued along these lines in her book *Imagination in Theory*, and in her harshly critical review of sociology's abject failure to grip the imagination, or to insinuate sensibility, in her contribution to a *Without Guarantees*, a volume in honour of Stuart Hall. In the former, Barrett enthuses about poststructuralist ideas because they 'invite us to view theory as another form of writing', with the effect that 'the crisp boundary between creative, imaginative or fictional writing on the one hand . . . and knowledge, theory and analysis on the other . . . becomes less stable' (Barrett 1999: 2–3). This proposal, which we should observe falls *short* of abolishing the said boundary, could be taken as an endorsement of approaches like that of Edmondson. Indeed, there is nothing very unorthodox here at all: from Mary Hesse (1966) onwards, a great deal of work in mainstream philosophy of science has emphasized the crucial role performed by metaphor, analogy and counterfactuals in constituting scientific images of particular fields, and the image of science in general. That being so, it would be bizarre to think that social science for its part could *avoid* metaphorical, analogical and narratalogical vehicles for description and explanation, all carrying significant imaginative and ideological freight.

But that point still does not seem fully to grasp what Barrett is after. In her piece on Hall, she makes it clear that she finds sociology's concern for explanation *boring*; that any kind of talk of realism *after* poststructuralism is faintly ludicrous; that 'physicality, humanity, imagination, the other, fear, the limits of control' are all simply *missing* – 'in their own terms' – in the (by this time rather feeble) sociological imagination (Barrett 2000: 18–20). This is ultimately why sociology cannot be the proper or single home for someone like Hall, his own consistent allegiance over time to cultural studies rather than sociology speaking volumes. The point about Hall here is true enough, but the argument that sustains it is not right. If Hall is undoubtedly an 'imaginative, sensual' thinker (Barrett 2000: 19), then that is a point about *him*, not about cultural studies in general. There are as many tedious descriptions and wooden sensings in cultural studies – some of them pertaining to bodily physicality and the process of writing – as there are boring explanations of abstract social relations in sociology.

But what is the force of this 'boredom' anyway? In what sense is it fair or logical to ask of sociology that it embrace the understanding of 'fear', the 'limits of control' and so on *in their own terms*? Sociology explains in *sociological* terms, and it can do no other. Whatever it is that sociology (or cultural studies) does, it can do well or badly, but sociology cannot, any more than can the practice of psychoanalysis, the writing of fiction, engagement in politics or participation in sport possibly cover, 'adequately', the many aspects of life and experience that sometimes need to be appreciated in terms appropriate only to themselves. Perhaps the point is that, unlike these other quests to capture experience, sociology is intent on *gutting* these other areas of their specific meanings? But only an overly-romanticized attachment to the purity of experience, and only an understanding of all sociology as bad sociology, could sustain that complaint.

Barrett finds Runciman boring, or at least she sees him as the kind of theorist who makes sociology boring, declaring (Barrett 2000: 16) that she could not even get past the first page of his book *The Social Animal* because it contained the sentiment that postmodernism had come and gone, and 'good riddance' too. I take a slightly different view, finding stringently imaginative, in its own terms, Runciman's ability, throughout his *Treatise*, to conduct vast swathes of *counterfactual* thinking, all the while sustaining a rich grasp of the *actual* details and plights of groups and societies throughout human history. There is no accounting for tastes, perhaps. Yet if Barrett *had* got past that first page of Runciman, she would have reached another interesting distinction that he draws out, between *evoked*, *acquired* and *imposed* social behaviour. Runciman asks us (1998b: 9–10) to imagine attending a match at the Yankee stadium, and knowing enough about baseball and the crowd situation to understand, and sense, much of the total experience that is involved for both player and spectator. This understanding and sensing can be broken down a little, as long as we can see any point in theoretical analysis. Thus, 'evoked' behaviour refers to the 'direct response of players and spectators' to the episodes of the game's narrative as it transpires. Accounts that dwell on this dimension, it is implied, will be fully descriptive and evocative. 'Acquired' behaviour then refers to the 'idioms, styles and fashions that attach to this particular sport' – and no doubt much else on the scene that Runciman does not have time to itemize (because he is performing, we should observe, one of Edmondson's rhetorical inductions). This level of social phenomena can support a more *causal* account, but one that will still have to be descriptively conducted in terms of the specific ways in which particular traditions are passed on, improvised, and modifed. 'Imposed' behaviour, finally, refers to such relational background conditions as the fact that the sport has a certain place in the national culture and way of life, that the players are employees, that the spectators had to pay the going price for this cultural product, that they conduct themselves according to certain ritualized norms, and so on. These issues are more fully explanatory in a sociological sense, in that they refer to the roles and structures, and resources and rewards, without which, in its *societal* logic, the baseball game could not be understood.

What I want to press in thinking about the interconnection between these different levels of understanding is, first, the inadequacy of anticipating some kind of dual to the death between the different moments of understanding, and, second, the intellectual irrelevance of any question of 'boredom'. To be sure, much is (necessarily) left out of the explanatory strategy when taken on its own, and it might well have been useful for Runciman to have an Erving Goffman to help him out on the descriptive front. Or a Don DeLillo. Runciman's historical and theoretical writings contain many telling references to novels, but De Lillo's *Underworld* is not amongst them. This is a pity because that novel of 1997 opens with an evocative fifty-page 'prologue' in which is re-imagined the legendary 1951 baseball final between New York Giants and the Brooklyn Dodgers, a contest settled by Glasgow-born Bobby Thomson's dramatic closing home run for the Giants – the 'shot heard round the world'. This extraordinary segment laces together vibrantly immediate detail with social observation and cultural encapsulation. The scene is set when a Harlem youngster risks life and limb by jumping the fence and settling down amongst racists to watch the game, and it ends by him catching and keeping the winning ball as it soars into the crowd. Unbeknown to all the players in the situation, including Sinatra and cronies, and Edgar Hoover, who have all been woven into the frame, this game was unfolding at exactly the same time that another shot was going off around the world – the explosion of its first atom bomb by the Soviet Union. It is the *ball*, rather than any character or historic event, that features as De Lillo's central focus in the novel. The contingently changing trajectory of that ball, as it passes through different hands, acts as the very prism through which all the structural and cultural contradictions of America in the second half of the twentieth century are refracted – the personal and the political, the deep and the superficial, the destined and the happenstance.

For some readers, De Lillo is all too much: too much the distant observer, too much the contriving overlayer, too much in control of – in words that are slipped into the novel very early on – 'the sly contrivances of the game, the patterns that are undivinable'. For others, this entwining of the living and the dying in cultural experience is fascinating, at once highly intellectual and profoundly disturbing. De Lillo's writing is sociological in a strange way, and even rationalistic up to a point: 'I write to find out how much I know. The act of writing for me is a concentrated form of thought' (interview in *The Independent*, 19 August 1991, pp. 18–19). But the novelistic aim cannot, of course, *be* to convey knowledge in thought; it is more to do with De Lillo showing through his creations that he 'understand[s] the hidden triggers of experience, the little delves and swerves that make a state of being'. Torn from the pages of *Underworld*, this thought rather alarmingly resembles some inflationary exercise in cultural theory, so let us leave the last (and more appropriately pedestrian) word to Runciman: 'the novel, fictional though it is, can perfectly well perform the function of sociology. Novels *are* sociology to the extent that their authors make them so' (1983: 21). We might add that novels are never *just* sociological, and if they do contain good sociology, this will not be a matter solely of their imaginative accomplishment.

Conclusion

Beyond the realms of polemic, there have been few expansive discussions of the theoretical or methodological issues that underlie intimations of either antagonism or complementarity between sociology and cultural studies. In this chapter, I took this task forward by going beyond the 'usual suspects' in both sociology and cultural studies, utilizing some under-discussed writers on the logic of explanation and description (Runciman, Simmel, Latour, Edmondson). In working through the key issues, the essential *continuity* of sociology and cultural studies has been proposed, whilst at the same time finding space for recognition of the different heritages and styles in the component discourses. For all the complexities, there is mileage in the assumption that sociology is more committed to explanatory understanding, with fuller-throated evaluative description of social life coming more from the cultural studies end of the spectrum. But this is a relative judgement only, and it only makes sense within a broader overall scenario of 'sociological cultural studies'. With some methodological ground opened up, I turn now to more ideologically charged theoretical matters.

4
Eurocentrism: The 'Rise of the West' Revisited

Having outlined some key elements in the case for sociological cultural studies, I now want to address an issue that appears to jeopardize the project on something like ideological grounds: sociology's *Eurocentrism*. With cultural studies today very much associated with *postcolonialist* normative and theoretical standpoints, sociology's Eurocentrism could hardly be overlooked or just set aside. Indeed, by comparison with related disciplines such as anthropology, sociology has appeared to be more hesitant about embracing postcoloniality, and more reluctant to change in the face of it. Partly, this is due to scepticism in the mainstream about the wholesale shift to *postmodernist* assumptions and conditions, of which postcolonialism is frequently taken to be a component or consequence. In that context, standardly accused of being a 'modernist regime of truth', sociology's resistance to postmodernism has seemed more than in other cases a matter of core, almost necessary, defensiveness. But the challenge of postcolonialism is more interesting and complicated than this, because some commentators want to say that postmodernism is *itself* a Eurocentric formation, and indeed a fellow-traveller of the sociological imagination, because specific aspects of the 'advanced' West, postmodern-style, are still tacitly associated with what is happening to 'society' in the most general way.

For strong postcolonial theorists, two tasks seem pressing in confronting the sociological imaginary. First, the typically Western tendency to speak of its own specificities in the name of Society needs to be exposed in the substantive *contents* of sociological discourse – the types of social relations it deals with, the historical and geographical contexts it excludes, and the forms of social life that interest it most. In all these respects, Western, metropolitan, white, and middle-class formations tend to be privileged over those that do not match this cultural template. Second, sociological theory constitutively exhibits another Western cultural specificity, namely *epistemological universalism*, in its persistent hankering after solid scientific foundations. When faced with the postcolonial challenge, then, sociology's discomfort can be taken as a sign of what Hall (1996a: 242) calls a 'powerful unconscious invest-ment' in the value system that is under scrutiny, such that postcolo-nial thought represents a 'signifier of danger' for sociology, rather than something it can easily embrace.

Without wishing to withhold from sociologists the therapeutic uses of discomfort, I want to open up this question of sociology's Eurocentrism for further debate, not least because it is often thought to be beyond all debate. We can begin by noting the complications that immediately arise if we want to say both that sociology's modernism is typically Euro-centric, and that postmodernism is too. This is problematical because the strongest type of postcolonial criticism of sociology does tend to be generated by a postmodernist cast of thought; so that where postco-lonial thought does *not* appear to be strongly postmodernist, it can be seen to share with sociology the pursuit of universal principles of invest-igation and critique, in which case the original depiction of sociology as defective and Eurocentric in at least that respect falls.

The second thing to stress initially is that there are considerable differ-ences across the varieties of postcolonial theory, so quite what the strength of the criticism of Eurocentrism is and what needs to be articu-lated as a postcolonial alternative to it are matters of ongoing discussion. On the one hand, there is the form of poststructuralist or discursive postcolonialism associated with writers such as Bhabha (1994) and Young (1991), a current that came to be strenuously opposed by those committed to an older leftist anti-colonialism, such as Ahmad (1992, 1997). Slightly different again is the ever-developing 'world systems theory' perspective represented by Immanuel Wallerstein (1997), which increasingly pursues issues of postcolonial theory and practice. Now, whilst something of a battle for the soul of postcolonial theory and politics took place amongst these currents earlier on, the lines are less clearly drawn today. Anti-colonialism *per se* hardly does justice to the kind of critical perspective developed by Ahmad, for example, whilst Wallerstein's writings on this topic (Wallerstein 1996), especially the statements issued during his time as president of the International Soci-ological Association (Wallerstein 1999a), overlap with poststructuralist campaigns to unsettle the kind of modernist, Westernist epistemology that is held to define the entire sociological tradition.

Meanwhile, one of the central writers in the poststructuralist wing of postcolonialism, Robert Young, has made signal efforts in his recent work (2001, 2003) to take a more historical, materialist, and activist approach to the discourse. Thus, postcolonialism is framed by Young (2003: 3–7) as still utterly challenging of the continuing equation that is made between 'white culture' and 'civilization'. But the challenge now comes less by way of abstruse discursive critique and more as a matter of 'political and philosophical activism'. The thrust of postcolonialism in that mood is above all to contest the economic and political disparities between the societies of North and those of the South. Postcolonialism, consequently, is not to be conceived as a singular 'theory', but rather as a 'series of juxtaposed perspectives' and 'contestatory dialogues between Western and non-Western cultures'. And if, still being suspicious of the 'protocols of objective knowledge', postcolonialism tends to be 'largely based in cultural studies', it can still borrow from 'a wide range of disciplines', including sociology. Now kitted out with its own series of beginner's guides, postcolonialism is thus accordingly presented to student audiences as a 'manifold subject matter' sustaining 'myriad reading strategies' (McLeod 2000: 3).

Sociology, in any case, has responded positively, if fitfully, to anti-Eurocentric interventions. Since the mid-1990s, the presentation of the discipline at introductory level has shifted, slowly but surely, towards issues of postmodernism and postcolonialism generally, and towards a more inclusive sociological *canon*. Steven Seidman, for example, has consistently introduced sociology as a formation whose concepts and projects have underwritten Western practices of 'exclusion, marginalization and devaluation', thus being complicit in 'promoting colonialism as a benevolent gesture of social progress' (Seidman 1994: 129). And Charles Lemert, in his carefully titled 1993 collection *Social Theory: The Multicultural and Classic Readings*, denounced even Marx and Weber as having an affirmative view of the destiny of 'Euroculture'. Lemert also greatly accelerated the process, still developing, by which an author like W. E. B. Du Bois, previously unappreciated (by Eurocentrics), could be acknowledged as a great sociologist of not only African–American life, but *tout court*. These commentators do see themselves as apostates within sociology, or at least heterodox, but concessions to the virtues of classical sociology are also made (as they were by Du Bois), with Seidman accepting that the European canon can itself 'be used to combat... Eurocentrism' (Seidman 1994: 275), and Lemert emphasizing that Marx and Weber were 'great white men' precisely because they did *not* 'buy the official story of the modern world uncritically'

(Lemert 1993: 9, 13). This kind of toggling between a totalistic ideological view of the Eurocentric intellect, and a more complex, contextualized, and appreciative account continues to operate, for instance in assessments of the critical realist philosophy that some think underlies radical sociologies like that of Marx. Thus, in one realist collection, a chapter that sees realism itself, and all who reside in it, as Eurocentric to the point of legitimating 'modernist technofascism' (Kanth 2004: 173–4) sits right alongside another depicting Marxian realism as the very condition of comprehension of Eurocentrism (Hostettler 2004).

In short, postcolonialism is converging on that mood of 'reflexive pragmatism' or at least 'contested heterogeneity' that I said in the last chapter was characteristic of cultural studies in general at the present time. But even if – especially if – the connotations of the charge of Eurocentrism are implicit rather than explicit, it is important to try to get closer to the analytical core of the matter, which means re-examining the 1990s literature. To that end, I divide my discussion into two separate chapters, dealing first with the strand that takes Eurocentric sociology mainly as a form of *ideology* in a clear pejorative sense. And I examine this paradigm in relation to a recent round of historical sociological writings around a classic image: the 'rise of the West' itself. In the following chapter, an interpretation and critique of postcolonial theory in the poststructuralist mode will be offered.

Specifying 'Eurocentrism'

It is surprisingly hard to find consistent and compelling definitions of Eurocentrism. If Eurocentrism is frequently specified as being a major obstacle to emancipatory social science, it is also a 'hydra-headed monster', not amenable to over-generalized definition (Wallerstein 1997: 94), easier to grasp in its 'manifestations' than in its essential properties (Amin 1989: 106). James Blaut, however, furnishes one essential encapsulation prior to his extensive historiographical trawl through its almost innumerable symptoms. For Blaut, Eurocentrism's suspect mentality is rooted in the belief that the West has some unique historical advantage, 'some special quality of race or culture or environment or mind or spirit, which gives this community a permanent superiority over all other communities, at all times in history and down to the present' (Blaut 1993: 1).

Is this generalization adequate as a precise guide to Eurocentric ideology? It is hard to imagine what historical account could *not* be interpreted as highlighting 'some special quality' of Western development, and yet at the same time precious few historians or social scientists today would hold that the Western 'community' had a *permanent* superiority over other 'communities'. Taking things forward, Samir Amin identifies two main 'axioms' of Eurocentrism. One is the assumption that historical development is 'internalist' in character, and the other is that the trajectory of Western capitalism can be generalized to the entire planet (Amin 1989: 109). What is not explicitly brought out by Amin, but clearly holds in his presentation of the issue, is that the 'specialness' of the West in Eurocentric perspective, both in historical terms and in our current imaginings about human futures, is more than a question of 'factual' assertion, so to speak. For Eurocentrism to apply, in Amin's account, we not only must believe that Europe witnessed the constitution of the modern capitalist world, but also need to claim 'mythologically' that it could not have been born elsewhere (Amin 1989: 105). Relatedly, Eurocentrism cannot merely be an expression of the kind of 'ethnocentrism' we find in almost every society; it must be an explicitly held, specifically modern *theory* (1989: vii). Finally, in Eurocentrism proper, it is not a question of thinking that as a matter of fact the whole globe has become more capitalistic; rather, it must be 'impossible to contemplate any other future for the world' than its progressive Europeanization (1989: 107).

Wallerstein goes further still, listing five main criteria for Eurocentrism. In the dimension of 'historiography', it is the assumption that whatever triggered the Western lead into industrialism can retrospectively be seen as a 'good thing' because capitalist modernity is a good thing. In terms of 'universalism', the paradigmatic villain of the piece is the claim or assumption that the emergence of European-type society was not only a good thing, but also inevitable, irreversible and applicable, in principle, everywhere. Under the aspect of 'civilization', the benchmark ideology is that which presents and defends European culture as uniquely civilized. When it comes to 'Orientalism', Wallerstein replicates the charge of Edward Said and others to the effect that in its politics and culture alike, the West has categorized and stigmatized the non-West as either a stagnant or an exotic 'other', disallowing any independent momentum or complexity in those ultimately subordinate cultures. Finally, under the heading of 'progress', the Eurocentric fallacy lies in believing that progress is already an achieved reality, and indeed an inevitability, involving the application of some variant of the functionalist 'modernization' scenario to the developing world.

Amin's and Wallerstein's specifications of Eurocentrism thus aim to provide a more graduated menu of qualities than Blaut's single-statement summary. However, they have not managed to avoid the latter's dilemma. Couched strongly in the vein of ideology-critique, it is the more strident and culturally imperialist versions of Eurocentrism which are targeted, and rightly so perhaps. But by the same token, it is hard to see how any classical bourgeois theorist of modernity, or intelligent historical sociologist, or indeed any everyday empirical historian, could be fitted up as identikit Eurocentrics if the full list of elements specified were to be taken strictly and cumulatively. Will just one dimension do to convict someone of Eurocentrism, or does it have to be all five? What if the assertions of European specialness in the work of social scientists refer chiefly to what *happened to happen*, or to what seems simply to be the overwhelming nature of the current global order, rather than constituting anything more obviously 'mythological'? Is that then Eurocentric or not? In other words, if Wallerstein's and Amin's axioms of Eurocentrism are to be taken literally, then ironically, as in the case of Blaut's umbrella characterization, they have the perverse effect of *undermining*, not confirming, the thesis shared by these authors that Eurocentrism remains hegemonic in scholarship today.

Leaving these reservations aside, it seems possible to extract four workable criteria for Eurocentrism that might be 'tested' on three pairs of theorists in historical sociology, all of whom revisit to a greater or lesser extent the pivotal question of the 'rise of the West'. First, Eurocentric theories or histories emphasize the leading civilizational role of the West in modern times by reference to some special and primary features of its socio-economic life, whether material or cultural. Second, the specialness of the West is figured as something essentially *internal* to European development, an autochthonous emergent property, and therefore not something borrowed from outside and simply grafted on. A subsequent causal asymmetry occurs here, though, in that what has proven special to modern development in the West is later spread by diffusion to the 'Rest'. Third, the development of the West is held to constitute a universal step forward for humanity as a whole. This sentiment can take shape in more or less moralistic ways. It can mean that the West has been the first to go through the broad sequence of civilizational advancement that *each and every* nation/society inevitably must experience. Or it can mean that humanity *as a whole* goes through that sequence of steps, so that the West's pioneering role enables other societies to accelerate through the sequence, or to skip stages altogether (thus perhaps leaving the West itself behind in due course). Or it can amount to the triumphalist assertion that European civilization as we know it represents substantial and irreversible progress for all peoples.

The fourth aspect of Eurocentrism is meta-theoretical, referring to the aspiration towards an objectivist, unitary theory of historical development as a whole. Critics hold this to be Eurocentric because a feature of specifically Western thought is being generalized as a universal goal and advance. Writers such as Amin and Wallerstein are hesitant about ranking faith in scientific reason as a criterion of Eurocentrism, since they themselves rely on some notion of universal cognitive progress in both accounting for, and overcoming, the dire effects of Eurocentric ideology. Blaut is the most straightforwardly traditionalist in this matter, enjoining us to demystify Eurocentrism simply by invoking the definitive historical 'facts' of the matter (Blaut 1993: 2, 9). Amin, for his part, calls for a 'genuine' universalism in theory and practice, one that is liberated from the limitations of Eurocentric ideology (Amin 1989: 116). Wallerstein is more ambivalent. On the one hand, he calls for a 'reunited . . . structure of knowledge' such that the 'true' and the 'good' may no longer be considered separate categories, thereby proposing a confluence of the normative and the factual realms which directly contravenes a core tenet of modern scientific meta-theory (1997: 106). On the other hand, he clearly thinks that the pursuit of science is a necessary human compulsion, evident in all societies, and he is fully committed to the idea that rational social progress is possible.

Historical sociology: Hall and Gellner

The historical sociologists John A. Hall and Ernest Gellner boldly address the need not only for an historical sociology, but for a 'backcloth vision of history' (Gellner 1988a: 12), a project defined by opposition to the kind of revisionist, relativist movement which posits the radical equality of all cultures and histories, and which therefore denies the West any special role at all (Hall 1986: 9, Gellner 1992: 55–6). Concerned to maintain a sense of 'what it is about us that is truly different and novel' as a direct alternative to worldviews such as that of the Ayatolla Khomenei (Hall 1986: 3, 8), Hall develops the proposition that the West did indeed lead the progressive march of humankind, in terms of releasing a whole new quantum of productive power and social energy. The special mechanisms responsible for this epochal upgrade involved a precarious balance struck in early modern Europe first between the dynamic, pluralizing effects of market society on the one hand, and the stabilizing, this-worldly spiritual cohesiveness of the Christian churches on the other; and secondly between the restless exercise of civil and political liberties on the one hand, and the unusually constructive social brokering role of the incipient nation states on the other, whose happy size (not too big, not too small) and commercial military rivalries contributed further special effects to Occidental dynamism.

By contrast, Hall argues, that kind of catalytic combination was firmly *precluded* in the configurations of society typical of the Eastern civilizations. Hindu social order, for example, was in effect *anti-society* in its rigid imposition of social segregation, with consequent 'blocking' effect on the development of an autonomous civil society (Hall 1986: 80). The Chinese path, for its part, was locked into a cyclical struggle between the mandarin cadres of the 'capstone state' and the powerful but constantly checked rural landlords, with corresponding variation in the amount and form of tax/rent generated, such that little surplus was freed up for coordinated momentum at the level of society as a whole. In the case of Islam, a universalist religion of mightily cohesive quality combined with the traditionalist practices, transience and interests of pastoral nomadism to choke off any independent political culture. Ruling elites cultivated no sense of the role of the state in providing infrastructural support for economic life.

Where Hall tends to emphasize the *political* prerequisites for the rise of the West, Gellner returns to the question of its distinctive *mentality* and culture, which he frames more in terms of secular rationality than the Protestant ethic. For Gellner, the hallmark of modern Western society, and the source of its world-historical dominance, lies in its distinctive 'objective, unified, referential style of cognition' (Gellner 1988a: 197). Convinced that this cognitive style 'has totally transformed the human social condition' such that 'the way back is blocked' (Gellner 1988a: 204, 1992: 60), he paints a broad-brush picture of world history, comprising three profoundly different evolutionary stages: hunter–gatherer society, Agraria, and Industria. Regarding the emergence of industrial-objectivist society as the work of 'one society, and only one' (that is, the West), Gellner sees the worldwide dominance of its mode of cognition as thoroughly embedded, and its universal effectiveness as an 'indubitable datum' (1988a: 199, 202–3).

These powerful scenarios would seem to match exactly the kinds of evaluative contrasts and causal stories that in the eyes of postcolonial critics perpetuates 'the Eurocentric myth of world history' whereby capitalism, progress and the West are 'synonymous' (Gills 1995: 157). Special causal features of modern Occidental civilization are singled out, their existence is treated as 'internal' to the West and defined by contrast to their notable absence in the Orient. Certainly, being nowadays far more sensitive to the achievements of non-European cultures, and placing the West itself within a very long-term historical perspective, this kind of sociological panorama is nothing like as 'Eurapologetic' as the imperialist/racist rationalizations of previous generations. Nevertheless, it is plausible to argue that Eurocentric 'diffusionism' is still in place here (Blaut 1993: 29–32), and that if the 'West for itself' has gone, the 'West in itself' remains a powerful discursive force (Latouche 1996: 3).

However, if we refer back to our specification of Eurocentrism, even in the case of the more judgemental historical sociologists, some important complications become apparent. Not only is the nature of the rise of the West open to widely different interpretations (political culture and societal dynamism in Hall, intellectual styles for Gellner, technical superiority for others), but the 'specialness' of the causal processes involved is far from settled. Hall says that it was the 'presence of political liberties' which 'ensured the creation of organic polities', which in turn 'became translated into liberal systems of rule', which uniquely fostered the dynamic market economy (Hall 1986: 158). But the exact causal sequence here is difficult to determine, and elsewhere Hall seems to put over-riding emphasis on the role of 'military competition' within the context of 'long-lasting states' (Hall 1988: 38).

Gellner for his part is more interested in characterizing the qualitative generic differences between Industria and Agraria than with bothering too much about how the one grew out of the other. Taking his distance from the historical details, he reckons (Gellner 1988a: 158) that there are at least fifteen 'candidate' variables involved in the production of the Western 'miracle'. Both Hall and Gellner, moreover, are agreed that the whole phenomenon of the rise of the West is to be seen as miraculous just because it is *un*exceptional in explanatory terms, being more a matter of happenstance than teleology. So when an anti-Eurocentric detective such as Blaut tracks down many more than those fifteen cited triggers for the West's rise, and discounts each and every one by showing either their non-specialness within the European configuration or their notable existence in parallel non-Western contexts, his chief targets would probably not disagree.

The specialness of the West, then, is not, amongst our historical sociologists, thought to reside in any primary 'internal' factor, nor indeed is the rise of the West held to be in any way inevitable or predetermined (Hall 1986: 5). This is why, surprising as this will sound, Gellner declares that one of the more recent rounds of debate on these issues is decidedly *not* about constructing a 'Europocentric vision of history', pointing out that to be engaged in deciding why and how some eventuality is *possible* is not the same as asserting that it was *necessary* (Gellner 1988b: 1, 3).

Moreover, Western civilization is not held to be 'universal' in the sense that the West prefigures and represents the historical destiny of each and all nations. *That* form of Eurocentric assumption 'has now been abandoned' (Gellner 1988b: 3). The specialness of the West, indeed, becomes simply a 'factual' matter in many ways, and, up to a point, it is hard to contemplate many anti-Eurocentrics disagreeing. Their chief complaint is that the agreed sequences and happenings of modern history have been subject to 'inappropriate extrapolations', notably the estimation of Western dominance as basically a 'positive achievement' (Wallerstein 1997: 101, 103).

But even on this score, it is not as if writers such as Hall and Gellner are unaware of their biases, so the formula whereby Eurocentrism consists in blithely generalizing European values on the assumption that they are the eternal values for all humanity needs significant amendment. Indeed, it is because they know that their evaluations are to a considerable extent optional or surplus to the historical record that these writers name their genre as *philosophical history*, rather than the kind of 'boring modern sociology' which we must presume is thought to catalogue the bare happenings only (Hall 1986: 3). The notion of 'reflexive Eurocentrism' as applied to Gellner may again come as a surprise to those impressed or infuriated by his Olympian style, as in his summary judgement that where *cultural* relativism slides into *cognitive* relativism, it 'simply and totally misdescribes our collective situation' (Gellner 1992: 55). But the valid elements of cultural relativism are not disavowed. Thus, Gellner acknowledges that it is only from the point of view of a citizen of Industria that Agrarian society appears to be 'unacceptably stifling' (Gellner 1988a: 23). And he is quite willing to characterize his own worldview as 'rationalist fundamentalism', accepting thereby that commitment to this perspective involves a leap of faith: it cannot be proven by reference to what the world in itself necessarily is. Indeed, the tendency of all fundamentalisms, including his own, is to 'absolutize' its own status, such that it 'leaves its shadow on the world'. Rather than simply *reflect* external reality, in other words, the rationalist fundamentalist framework 'engenders an orderly, symmetrical Nature', a figured world that we may have no independent grounds to verify (Gellner 1992: 81).

That clarifies things considerably, but critics might still insist that for all the magnanimous concession to cultural relativity, Gellner still shows a bellicose attachment to the supposedly 'factual' view that the Western cognitive style can increasingly be expected to 'be generalized to the entire planet' (Amin), and to the idea that it is now in an evolutionary sense 'irreversible' (Wallerstein). Without doubt, Gellner is saying something like that, persuaded not only that the way back is 'blocked', but being virtually unable to see any coherent pathway beyond the present of late Industria. Under that pressure, the bold lines of *Plough, Sword and Book*, in its treatment of 'future possibilities', fade into broken dots and uncharacteristic rambling. But again, there may not be such a huge difference between, on the one hand, accepting, as many anti-Eurocentrics do, that there is an unprecedented and ever-growing cultural homogeneity, application of science, and capitalism around the globe; and, on the other hand, believing that this state of affairs is pretty near irreversible. Not even such a scourge of the 'megamachine' of Westernization as Serge Latouche can bring himself either to positively *desire* the decline of the globalizing West or to accept 'cultural solipsism' as a realistic alternative (Latouche 1996: 118–19).

Methodological Eurocentrism: Mann and Runciman

If the meaning and force of the charge of Eurocentrism are compromised even in the case of the more opinionated of the contemporary historical sociologists, the case is weakened further when we turn to theorists such as Michael Mann and W. G. Runciman. The charge is that it is Eurocentric to try to pass off particular cultural and ideological preferences, even at the 'methodological' level, as sanctioned by the authority of 'history' or 'social science' themselves. And the further assumption is that although couched in the language of sophisticated scholarship, modern sociological investigations remain bound to a teleological 'God's eye view' of the social world, one that favours specifically Western categories and images of effective causality. Runciman in particular would seem at first consideration to be fair game for this kind of criticism, seeing as he is outspoken in his defence of sociological evolutionism as the appropriate methodology of social theory – and there is continuing unease in many quarters about even a merely connotative connection between this and earlier racist traditions of Eurocentric thought. Moreover, Runciman accepts that a certain mode of sociobiology has a role to play, something about which many in sociology and cultural studies alike remain highly suspicious. As it happens, Runciman is emphatic that the role for sociobiology is by no means to replace, or even find a place *within*, sociology as such, just as he meticulously demonstrates why sociological evolutionism is *not* the social evolutionism of old (Runciman 1989a, 1998a).

In fact, as developed in treatise form, Runciman's perspective turns out to be rigorously *anti*-teleological. There is undoubtedly, he affirms, a dynamic of competitive selection and adaptive success at the heart of social as well as natural evolution, but neither the precise content of the social practices which are selected, nor the identity of the *systacts* – the typical group interests and social roles within a given society – which carry those adaptive practices, can be specified in advance or given an evaluative coloration. Nor are those practices, or those systacts that represent evolutionary development at any time, likely to *continue* in that position for very long, in macro-historical terms (Runciman 1989a: 37–48). It follows that whilst we can try to build up a static 'Linnaean' typology of societal structures within the different generic stages of human history, and whilst we can certainly (at least in principle) identify the 'Darwinian' leading edge formations and practices at key dynamic-evolutionary moments, this programme entails nothing whatsoever about whether any human society, past or present, is ultimately 'progressive'. All opinions on such progressiveness or its lack, even if sociologically informed, are entirely distinct from the form and content of sociological explanation as such (Runciman 1983: 15–26).

Taking these guidelines to the case in hand, the West's rise to dominance, and within that Britain's emergence as the leading industrial power, was largely a 'random' process, 'a unique coincidence of jointly necessary factors' (Runciman 1989a: 340). Such necessity is not given in advance by the moral preferences of History itself, but is, strictly as a matter of the preconditions of success in the given circumstances, retrospectively analysed. The transition from feudalism to capitalism needs to be seen in that way too: it happened in Europe and not elsewhere 'for good sociological reason' and as a matter of 'unarguable social fact' (1989a: 367–8); but, still, this does not mean that it was preordained in a transhistorical sense. There *may* be inevitable outcomes within particular settings: Runciman cites the case of the French revolution, which he thinks was quite superfluous to the evolutionary change it reflected, which was happening anyway (1989a: 367). But again, this entails only relatively 'local' adaptive advantage, not unilinear programming. There is also no necessary internal mechanism whereby all societies must embark on an ever-forward evolutionary track. Runciman suggests that but for external contingencies, feudal Poland, for example, might well have sustained itself indefinitely (1989a: 374).

Runciman's argumentation is undoubtedly forceful, but it may still leave critical readers feeling that he is trying to have his cake and eat it too: that it is really not possible to have a convincing evolutionary theory which leaves everything to chance. In that case, we could turn to Mann instead. This is because Mann, unlike Runciman, eschews *all* notions of evolution and necessity in history, and is keen to look at the development and sources of social power without the aid of such modernist, presentist (Westernist?) concepts such as the state, nation, class and private property (Mann 1986: vii). Indeed, Mann would do away with the idea of 'society' itself, regarded as a coherent totality of institutions or levels between which a process of diffusion takes place, just as he dismisses the kind of rigid endogenous/exogenous typology of causal factors that follows from seeing society as a single unit of comparison (Mann 1986: 1–2, 35). This explicitly counters the charge against Mann and others made by Blaut in particular. Equally dubious, he feels, are conventional contrasts between sacred and secular societies, the modern and the traditional, and status and contract (1986: 31). These manifesto statements contrast with some of Runciman's conceptual priorities, and they move sociology sharply away from the sort of 'large collective terms', 'abstract generalities' and 'fixed entities' that some critics see as indirectly but emphatically *orientalist* leanings in sociology's classificatory mind (Said 1978: 154, Wolf 1982: 7–8). Seeing the socio-historical process as the multi-causal, contingent development of overlapping networks of power, Mann decisively disallows any assertion of special causality, progressive meaning, or ultimate primacy in socio-historical theory.

In the case of the West, its leading role was the result of a 'gigantic series of coincidences' (Mann 1988: 16), a multiple causal intersection, one aspect of which indeed included a specifically *colonial* power-transformation (Mann 1993: 18). That there took place in Europe a massive economic development is not to be gainsaid, but the aetiology of even this material phenomenon involves a potentially infinite regress which eventually blurs the East/West divide altogether. For example, to explain the industrial revolution, we need to appreciate the nature of the previous agrarian revolution, and for that in turn there are the still earlier innovations in trade and navigation, and to trace those we find ourselves back on the trail of the yet older (much underestimated) trading pathways which criss-crossed their way in and out of different cultural and political settings, both East and West (Mann 1988: 7). In the end, Mann attributes Western development to a number of contingent features in combination: a marginal ecological advantage, convenient transport options, technological innovation, a 'multiple' and 'acephalous' political structure, and a certain 'rational restlessness' in psychological make-up (Mann 1988: 7–15). For all the hesitations about the status of these causal agencies and their inevitability/progressiveness, it is a familiar list of contingent Western advantages, reproduced within a seriously decentred theoretical overview.

The outcome of this reading seems to be that any charge of outright Eurocentrism would be mistaken. However, it is perhaps more in the *rhetoric* of the governing terms of a sociological perspective, rather than in the detail of its causal stories, that its cultural and ideological leanings become most apparent. For example, even – especially – when pitched as a matter of description, a positive value attaches to the notion of the 'miraculous' rise of the West and the 'breakthrough' into Industria, even though one purpose of these labels is to render them radically contingent rather than predetermined. Similarly, at the level of generic differentiation between forms of society, Hall, for example, continuingly refers to the 'release' or 'blockage' of social creativity, dynamism and energy. Not only does this kind of 'social physics' evince a distinctly Western quasi-scientific frame of reference, it automatically has the effect of commending some historical trajectories (the West) whilst devaluing others (the Rest).

That kind of evaluative discourse would be discounted by Runciman and Mann, but their own master concepts still reflect a distinctly Western mode of apprehension. Mann, as noted in Chapter 1, wants to evict all teleological and 'presentist' impulses, and to that end tries to focus on power by reference not to group intentions or social functions, but to *organizational capacities*. Groups and institutions prevail, he argues, by way of organizational outflanking, and we must try to understand this process not by ascribing 'ends' to people or societies, but by paying attention to whatever needs-meeting organizations are effective in achieving their goals (Mann 1986: 5, 7). Refreshing though this perspective is, its theoretical overlay is a modernist one: that of means-ends rationality and a calculus of success couched in a neutral or technicist discourse of organizational, logistical appraisal. The whole idea of power conceived as a congeries of overlapping networks fed by multiple causal pathways amongst which no ultimate primacy can be assigned is a coding stemming from institutional communications discourse within the advanced societies.

There is, finally, a significant commonality of conceptual priority amongst the theorists selected for examination, in that *power* is held by all four to be the primary force in human history, and power in turn is jointly believed to comprise just three definitive, but also definitively *autonomous*, sources or dimensions – the economic, the ideological and the political. It might be argued that this very separation of spheres, along with the separation of facts and values in the assessment of their inter-relationship, is precisely what sociological theorists, from Weber through to Gellner and Habermas have picked out as the central, novel feature of Western modernity itself. Yet here we see these sophisticated historical sociologists rather un-reflexively 'applying' that cultural grid to history as a whole, from the earliest times forward. Whilst it is difficult to distance oneself from these modernist touchstones, it might be worth considering whether, some centuries from now, power and power alone, divided into just three mutually non-reducible dimensions, will seem so obviously the right way of conceptualizing multilinear social development across the ages.

Multidimensional comparisons: Eisenstadt and Arnason

Reading the focus on power as fundamentally Eurocentric is worth considering, but it is somewhat tenuous. In any case, other contemporary historical sociologists have been trying to qualify the analytical primacy of power in the comparative analysis of civilizations, by giving at least equal weight to other moving forces. Historian William McNeill, in retrospective acknowledgment that his seminal (1963) study of the rise of the West contained Eurocentric residues, called for a 'multidimensional discourse' in this field. He adds that this is something of a 'daunting task' because such an analytic should continue to strive to be 'clear and elegant' about the 'shapes of world history' (McNeill 1995: 319). The further development of multidimensionality, without sacrificing shape, has been the aim of sociologists such as S. N. Eisenstadt, extended in a slightly different direction by Johann Arnason. Their special effort, arguably, has been to highlight the *cultural* dimension of socio-historical change.

Eisenstadt has long been engaged in a 'far-reaching reformulation of the vision of modernization' that dominated American sociology, especially in the mid-twentieth century (Eisenstadt 1987a: 6). The elements of this reformulation, tabled in Eisenstadt's general manifestos for sociological theory as well as in his more specific investigations, are in many ways familiar: that our thinking about social structures must be thoroughly historicized; that the permanent potential for conflict in society, and not only integration, must be acknowledged; that there is no evolutionary tendency towards global convergence in terms of advanced industrial society; that any categorical distinction between traditional and modern societies must be relativized and held as a contingent research question, rather than a theoretical given;

that human populations are usually strung across a multiplicity of social systems and collectives; and that 'different integrative mechanisms' across a whole range of levels of culture and power are highly autonomous, complex and fragile (Eisenstadt 1973: 98–9, 1985: 10–17). When applied to the story of the West, these general stipulations have the effect of breaking any necessary connection between Westernization and modernization, and of rendering the latter a thoroughly diverse process, open to significantly different forms of adaptation and resistance wherever Western influences encounter more traditional formations. Eisenstadt theorizes the resulting institutionalized patterns as 'civilizational complexes' rather than static or closed 'societies' as such.

The civilizational approach of Eisenstadt emphasizes not only a diversity of vectors of social stability and change, but also within the cultural arena itself, the normal existence of a plurality of 'cultural visions' – premises about authority, justice and cosmic meaning – is underscored. Moreover, these are carried by different sorts of social elites, and different coalitions of elites (1987a: 7–9). This conceptual apparatus clearly renders explanations of the various degrees and effects of modernization across different civilizational complexes extremely specific and contingent, and the interesting outcomes can be observed in Eisenstadt's many works dealing with what he designates as historical bureaucratic empires, axial civilizations, and modern revolutionary episodes, and with more recent Eastern interactions with Western currents. The forms of social order observed in each category are emphasized as unique to them, and are often articulated by Eisenstadt in terms of their distinctive cultural orientations. Thus, the trajectories of certain pre- or proto-modern societies are framed as disruptions and challenges posed by the emergence of tensions between different sorts of secular and spiritual authority, tensions that are resolved partially by the construction of 'transcendent' cultural models (Eisenstadt 1986). The distinctiveness of the modern West itself is held to be its unique and dynamic *pluralism*, both in terms of group life and organizational competition and perhaps pre-eminently in its *symbolic* pluralism (1987a: 47).

The universalization of certain features of Western modernity, for Eisenstadt, is thus not at all a matter of simple diffusion or imposition, but rather a highly variable and partial uptake of the impulse to cultural innovation generated by modernity's ability to express a range of contested social images and agencies. This might be sufficient for postcolonialists to regard with suspicion his claims to have broken with the modernization paradigm (Wallerstein's fifth token of Eurocentrism). Eisenstadt freely acknowledges that he continues to find parts

of the Parsonian apparatus valuable, endorsing the centrality to sociology of 'the problem of social order' and its attendant 'mechanisms of
integration and control' (1985: 8, 19). He insists that the institutionalization of systemic properties, normative or otherwise, is a matter of
'continuous process of construction' (1985: 18), but he still concludes
that different civilizational complexes do settle down into comprehensible patterns of order, vision and counter-current, a pattern in which,
theoretically speaking, the 'allocation of basic resources' and stabilization of power relations follow from cultural premises/orientations rather
than the other way round (1987a: 9).

In his critical overview of Eurocentrism, Wallerstein identified a
kind of 'anti-Eurocentric' brand, and this might be just the type
that Eisenstadt's overall discourse exemplifies. The point is that, even
when scholars try to break the connection between Westernization
and modernization, and identify the variety and reversibility of quasi-
modernizing tendencies in a *number* of civilizations, the modernist
package of processes and attributes is basically regarded as a 'positive
achievement' (Wallerstein 1997: 104). Particularly offensive, for Wallerstein, is the tendency, even amongst knowledgeable and critical scholars,
to accept that the characteristic differentiation of social and cultural
spheres in Western modernity, such as the separation of scientific
cultural norms from political life more generally, is remorseless and legitimate. In a general sense, Eisenstadt fits this categorization in that he
is attitudinally upbeat about the 'pluralistic and multi-centred' process
that the West has visited upon the world (Eisenstadt 1987b: 8). But
does this constitute Eurocentrism or not? Much depends upon whether
one regards the tone of scholarly disinterestedness – so characteristic
of Eisenstadt – as itself ideologically disingenuous. Rather than taking
up that complex matter, Wallerstein just opines that the formally 'anti-
Eurocentric' position outlined represents 'a very feeble way of opposing
Eurocentrism' (1997: 103).

Arnason, for his part, has acclaimed Eisenstadt's contribution to
discussions of modernity and its diverse encounters with other civilizations, but notes critically that Eisenstadt still tends to write of
modernity as an integral civilizational type, over-reliant on the 'tension-
transcendence' coding of cultural order and change (Arnason 1997:
66–7, 374). Accordingly, Arnason draws on theorists such as Elias,
Touraine and Castoriadis to provide a lens on his concrete interests
that is thoroughly cleansed of Eurocentric smears, and every deposit of
functionalism too. All the key aspects of the revised view of the rise
of the West are thus emphatically rehearsed (1997: 5–7), leading to a

radically open-ended comparative schema, and to the suggestion that accounts of the distinctiveness of social formations must be treated in hermeneutic fashion as 'narrative reconstructions'. Where any interest in integration seems legitimate, moreover, this must be open-endedly accompanied by a concern to establish differentiations (1997: 353). The 'impact' of modernity is to be rephrased in terms of highly variable 'intercivilizational encounters', and in fact the very nature of modernity in the West requires considerable further pluralization too, in terms of a constitutive 'field of tension' between conflicting forces and impulses or 'incompatible projects' (1997: 374, 354). Giving empirical substance to the growing number of voices who are now calling for differences within modernity – and *counter-modernities* – to be fully recognized, Arnason develops accounts of the Soviet Union (1993) and Japan (1997) in terms of distinctive cultural *dualities* and para-modern *constellations*.

Accusations of Eurocentrism against this kind of historical sociology would seem to be quite hopeless – except along one possible line of thought. Like Eisenstadt, Arnason tends to slip between, on the one hand, a multi-factorial concern to acknowledge the autonomy of culture, amongst other causal and constitutive processes, and, on the other hand, a certain type of *culturalism* – in Arnason's case, a Castoriadian conception of social subjectivity. The latter, when pressed, would stymie any genuine computation of a range of causal processes and explanatory factors, because the 'magma of imaginary significations' that is regarded as inherent in modern plural subjectivity is also nothing less than 'the most distinctive component of social-historical being' itself (Arnason 1997: 57). This is a familiar thought in contemporary social theory, having the effect of enthroning fluid and indeterminate subjectivity at the core of our very idea of society in general. But arguably, there is yet again an illegitimate historical and cultural universalization going on here, whereby what seems ontologically central to complex social subjectivity in Western postmodernity is assumed to hold for other cultural and historical formations. Moreover, from the kind of Left-critical standpoint discussed earlier, this kind of privileging of the social imaginary is doubly Eurocentric because it also inevitably involves playing down the role of power and wealth in the consolidation of Western civilizational advantage.

Conclusion: Ethnocentrism and ideology

My argument in this chapter has been neither to vindicate particular theorists, nor to finally trip them up, when it comes to the charge of

Eurocentrism in contemporary works of historical sociology. Rather, the point has been to examine the genre in some detail with this charge in mind, and to insist as a result that the issue is complex and problematical. This is in large part due to the fact that debates of this kind raise questions about *consciousness* and *ideology* that in many ways remain quite unresolved in social theory. For example, I referred earlier to a comment by Amin to the effect that for Eurocentrism proper to apply, it must not be a matter of banal *ethnocentrism*. But if some terms in the general discourse of historical sociologists can undoubtedly be said to reveal aspects of Eurocentrism, whilst not yet amounting to Eurocentrism proper, is this to be taken as an expression of the depth of cultural imperialism, or as one kind of escape route from it? Wallerstein recognizes this difficulty when he offers two significantly different characterizations of Eurocentrism.

One of these is as a variant on the idea of Eurocentrism as ethnocentrism, Wallerstein presenting it as an all-embracing epochal *weltanschauung*, nothing less than the 'constitutive geoculture' of the modern world, and in consequence a culture whose values – humanism, secularism, modernism – altogether 'permeate social science' (Wallerstein 1997: 93). With that definition in play, however, it would be well nigh impossible for social scientists or anyone else to escape its influence, or even to grasp in any clear way what is 'bad' about being subject to it. No person, author, or academic tradition could be simply *condemned* for exhibiting Eurocentrism in this sense, and, indeed, the critics of Eurocentrism themselves are bound to be contaminated in various ways. Being too general, then, Wallerstein moves away from the *weltanschauung* conception towards the five criteria that specify Eurocentrism as a robust dominant ideology. But as I have argued, it is (increasingly) hard to identify exponents or dupes of this pernicious mindset. In the end, then, the question of Eurocentrism as applied to sociological discourse, whilst not having been dispelled as such, has certainly come unstuck. Its further uptake as an issue, moreover, is unlikely to be productive without more sustained thinking about the status of 'ideology' as a concept that both facilitates social explanation and encourages moralistic judgement.

5
Eurocentrism: Postcolonial Theory

Through the 1980s and 1990s, numerous 'special issues' on postcolonial theory and politics were published in the journals; but not in the sociology journals, where only a very few individual articles on these themes appeared (Mouzelis 1997, Parker 1997). Meanwhile, popular textbooks on the sociological classics (Hughes *et al.* 1995, Craib 1997) barely touched on the questions that Seidman and Lemert were raising about Eurocentrism in the founding fathers. And until the late 1990s, otherwise up-to-speed reviews of modern sociological theory (Maynard 1989, Craib 1992, May 1996, Ritzer 1996, Layder 1997) were devoid of mention of the postcolonial issues that seemed so pressing elsewhere. Throughout this period, cultural studies once again raced ahead of sociology as the discourse of contemporary existence, by fully taking on board those theorists of postcolonialism that were conducting explicit 'disruptions' of Western modernity and its disciplinary discourses.

In this chapter, I develop a critical engagement with postcolonial theory in that 'disruptive' genre. As pointed out before, this series of positions has been modulated in various ways since the statements that I will examine were written. But it is striking that even now few properly critical engagements with the main postcolonialist authors and concepts can be found. In formulating one kind of argument in response, chiefly in relation to the figuring of sociological understanding in postcolonial theory, my intention is not to deny that sociology *is*, in some important sense, an ordering and classifying enterprise, born into the world to scientifically and politically master the social structures and social problems of modern urban life in the West. But when this point is generalized to the effect that any kind of concern with classification is Western, modernist and oppressive, we are in the realms of sheer obscurantism. And if sociological theorists have not managed to embrace postcolonialism because of its close association in some minds with *postmodernism*, which many sociologists are cautious about, then that may just mean that there is a bit more yet to hammer out.

In some ways, the characterization of postcolonialism as not only part, but the very essence, of postmodernity itself is an attractive proposition. Thus Bauman says that the typically postmodern traits of pluralism, ambivalence and decentredness are condensations of 'the erosion of the global structure of domination upon which the self-confidence of the West and its spokesmen has been built' (Bauman 1992: 96). Against this stands the point, made by several postcolonial authors, that postmodernism is but the latest form of self-privileged Eurocentric theory, obsessed with the dilemmas of epistemologically challenged metropolitans (Williams and Chrisman 1993: 13, Ashcroft *et al.* 1995: 2, During 1995, Ahmad 1997: 365, Rattansi 1997: 494). Both these views have something going for them: postcolonialism is not *equivalent* to postmodernism, but nor are these syndromes fundamentally *antithetical* to one another.

Partly as a result of unresolved debates of this kind, the field of postcolonial studies has been reported, for about a decade, as having reached something of an impasse (Slemon 1994: 29, Young 1995: 163, Moore-Gilbert 1997: 186). One aspect of the standstill concerns postcolonial theory's prevailing textualism, its tendency to evade the constraints of structural investigation into the divisions of labour of our times (Hall 1996a: 257). It is in that context that cultural studies people reach to recover the sociological part of their make-up, alarmed by 'the repudiation of foundations and objective validity' that literary deconstructionism is thought to entail (San Juan 1998: 8). What is needed, some think, is the revival of Marxist notions of totality and universality within the contemporary global analysis of culture (Lazarus 1999: 29). Similar notes, more guardedly struck, can be found throughout Gayatri Chakravorty Spivak's *Critique of Postcolonial Reason* (1999), the verbose convolutions of which seem otherwise to confirm rather than relieve the troubles within postcolonial thought.

With those guidelines in mind, I want to reconstruct and appraise the way that sociology's ostensible Eurocentrism is brought to light in the work of Hall, Bhabha, and Young, the three principal interpreters of the postcolonial problematic. Sociology, we should note straight away, is seldom referred to explicitly or at any length in these statements, but overall the logic is damning: sociology, unlike postcolonial theory, is assumed to be constitutively Eurocentric because of the structural(ist) and rational(ist) lenses through which its knowledge is characteristically focused. The whole idea of a postcolonial sociology, in that case, would appear to be a contradiction in terms.

Postcolonial theory: Off limits

Stuart Hall has suggested that although the field of postcolonialism is far from homogeneous, there is a common feeling amongst those at work within it that something both substantial and novel is going on (Hall 1996a: 245). However, Hall's ecumenical gesture soon takes on a more stringent character, for he goes on to designate the *differentia specifica* of postcolonialism as an engagement in the process of 'thinking at the limit'. Postcolonialism could, of course, be defined in more orthodox ways: as a Third World or anti-imperialist political movement, or as a stage in the historical struggle/process. But whilst Hall is sympathetic to those who sustain these activist and historicist senses, they have not caught the cutting edge of the phenomenon. The first, for example, encourages a self-definition which merely inverts, and therefore reaffirms, the dominance of the category of First World, whilst the second, even though it announces the potential for genuinely *new* social and cultural formations, still represents a variation on a familiar stageist conception of history. But for Hall, these 'reversals' of dominant political discourses do not quite reflect what is excitingly different about postcolonialism, namely the prospect of a complete change of *frame of reference* for theory and politics, at the highest level of abstraction. Instead of envisaging the 'posts' – postcolonialism, postmodernism and so on – as simply introducing new elements along familiar conceptual chains of meaning, we should see them instead as profoundly interrogating or undermining the norms of 'centrist', European-forged thinking.

In particular, radical postcolonialism should be envisaged as interrupting the 'false and disabling distinction' between colonialism as a system of *rule* on the one hand, and as a system of knowledge or *representation* on the other (Hall 1996a: 254). That enables an interesting and rigorous extension of the scope of the postcolonial phenomenon, from the demise of the geo-political empires, to the hybridization of cultural life within the metropolitan centres themselves, to creative disaffiliation from the dominant, almost unspoken mainstream structures of cultural thought (Hall 1996a: 246–8). This latter target of postcolonial criticism is what others arrestingly call 'the invisible Empire' (Sayyid 1997: 129) and 'the Empire within' (Young 1991: 175). 'Thinking at the limit', then, in postcolonial style involves not only, perhaps not even, offering a *different* version of politics and social thought, but rather a bypassing or 'bracketing off' of conventional representational, linear and necessitarian modes of understanding. The point of critique is not to produce another, better representational account of 'our' problematic history, but to incite a proliferation of histories.

Occasionally, sociology gets noted in the postcolonial literature as a useful resource for counteracting the *literariness* of much current work (Mongia 1996: 2, Moore-Gilbert 1997: 8, 186). Under the strong form of postcolonial critique, however, it is doubtful whether any such legitimacy could be conferred on sociology as a form of understanding and explanation. In major part a representational discourse, staking claims for descriptive accuracy and universal cognitive gain, sociology might be thought definitively to exhibit the kind of 'scientific and aesthetic disciplining of nature through classificatory schemas' which embodies the 'imperialist ordering of the globe under a panoptical regime' (Shohat and Stam 1994a: 100). Sociology, in this formulation, could only be part of the *problem* for postcolonialism, not part of the solution. Ultimately, Hall for his part hedges the issue as to whether the ideas of postcolonialism as defined are to be entirely endorsed, or whether they are to be seen mainly as creatively unnerving. But the radical path is clearly attractive, if only because of the frequent swings of opinion noticeable amongst less adventurous postcolonialists often producing unsatisfactory conceptual entanglements. Some try to argue, for example, that whilst the anti-universalist, postmodernist sort of postcolonialism is wholly suspect, the goal is still to achieve 'an identity uncontaminated by universalist or Eurocentric concepts and images' (During 1995: 125). Others believe uncompromisingly that Western colonialist thinking and 'ethnocentric essentialism' remain firmly lodged within the 'bad epistemic habit' of academic theory, history and film (Shohat and Stam 1994: 10), though, remarkably, this case for the persistence of colonialist history is supported by reference to only one article, by Paul Johnson, the right-wing historian turned polemical journalist. Even such firm critics, however, baulk at the threshold of outright discursive postcolonialism, for fear of the depoliticization that might follow with an abandonment of all forms of Left universalism. Such combinations, then, seem highly contradictory, awkwardly caught on either side of the 'limit' rather than moving boldly off limits. Couze Venn, for example, still thinks it possible to uphold an account of the specificity of modernity as being 'bound up with the history of colonialism and capitalism' whilst at the same time roundly rejecting arguments deriving from 'the claims of structural relations' (Venn 2000: 2). What, then, does the poststructuralist-postcolonial critique involve, exactly, and what are its ultimate implications for the discourse of sociology?

Translating Bhabha

The work of Homi Bhabha, neglected by sociologists, is omni-present in debates within and about postcolonialist theory. One problem in assessing his contribution to the themes of this book is the opaque quality of his keynote collection of essays, *The Location of Culture* (1994), which consequently requires a relatively free translation in order to connect to problems of sociology and disciplinarity. As it happens, the discursive politics of *cultural translation* and the problematic status of intellectual transparency in discourses such as sociology are pivotal to the way in which Bhabha casts his version of postcolonial theory. His starting point is to accept, along with other postcolonialists, the pervasive and oppressive history of Western colonialist politics and culture. However, Bhabha refuses to picture the subjective and imaginary relations between colonizer and colonized as a simple, undialectical one in which the rule and mindset of one either wholly reconstructs that of the other in its own image, or by contrast unleashes a 'pure' form of resistance and oppositional consciousness. Rather, there is constant intellectual, political and psychic negotiation *between* the colonizing and the colonized subject positions, so that variable hybrid moods, conditions and products emerge over time. Today, that initial hybridity has been intensified by the greater presence of migrant peoples within the West itself, and marginal groups therefore engage in new processes of cultural hybridization, as colonizer and colonized identities repeatedly clash and mix, thus shaping unstable – and always different – postcolonial interpretations.

For Bhabha, neither in the past nor in the present can social/psychic being be regarded as exemplifying the kind of subjective certitude which is governed by binary categories such as colonizer/colonized, white/black, West/East, home/foreign, inside/outside, self/other and so on. Cultural and imaginative life constantly traffics ambivalently *between* these poles, and transgressively *across* those borders, with no particular practice or understanding forever fixed in a given location. All the time, cultural translations of ideas, images and practices from one register and mode of being to the next are taking place. Even the dominant colonizing consciousness, which aspires to emit self-images of mastery and to construct regimes of hierarchical certainty, does so only in the enabling rhetorical presence of the 'Other' – that which is figured not only as colonized, weak and silenced, but also as feared, forbidden and threatening. And so it is, we can surmise, with dominant Euro-centric *theories*. In the Western academic tradition, schemes of cognitive penetration are construed as gloriously independent, translucent and consensual, but their sense and power is made possible, we should see, only by means of a prior murky process of negotiation with, and separation from, other suppressed or forbidden currents.

These strands of thought are evidently connected to postmodernist thought, and also to earlier styles of phenomenological philosophizing. It is worth repeating then that for Bhabha the definitive 'unhomeliness' of the unsettled modern consciousness is *not* a matter of 'Man's' onto-logical alienation (1994: 9), any more than the 'master–slave' dialectic that plays such a large part in European thought is an arbitrary exempli-fication of the workings of power as such (Young 1991: 5). Instead, these topoi are to be regarded as extrapolations from the specific psychic ambi-valence generated by and through *colonialism*. Bhabha is thus comfort-able with postmodernism, but only insofar as there is a 're-naming of the postmodern from the position of the postcolonial' (Bhabha 1994: 175). The impact of this formulation can be seen in two important segments of discussion in Bhabha. The first is his notion of the 'time-lag' as some-thing that disrupts the representational coding of Western social theory (1994: 171, 238). As I read it, the idea is this: even if it is increasingly accepted that the social history of modernity has been a specifically colo-nial history, 'postcolonial' sentiments cannot then just be re-inserted into accounts of 'the rise of the West' or the 'making of nations' or 'the class struggle' and so forth. Nor can we readily re-periodize and re-name the object of enquiry to fit our revised inclinations. This *post*colonial interruption, unalterably, has come *after* the substantive and epistemo-logical framings of pre-postcolonial understanding, and it points *beyond* the shared cultural reference points that have given life to the received histories until now. Past and present time, then, is now *out of joint*, there is a *lag* which cannot be made up, and a corresponding visceral and cognitive *lack* in the very mode of historical apprehension of histor-icity for which there is no adequate substitute or relief. That is why Bhabha says, construing Fanon in support, that the struggle against colo-nial oppression not only changes the direction of Western history, 'but challenges its historicist idea of time as a progressive, ordered whole' (1994: 41). And again, 'The cultural inheritance of slavery or colonialism is brought before modernity not to resolve its historic differences into a new totality' (1994: 241).

A second way in which postcolonialism makes a difference to post-modernism lies in Bhabha's casting of the familiar point that Western thought is oppressive in its universalizing aspirations, its habitual search for a *totality*, for a rational summary of the *common* structures which govern all social thought and action. In postcolonial light, this need to speak on behalf of human society as a whole is a desire and demand typically located within the horizon of Western *cultural majorities*. From the point of view of cultural *minorities*, such total-ization is thought to have no intrinsic merit and fulfils no social need of theirs. Why, then, should minority or hybrid subjectivities, growing in cultural presence today, have any deep-rooted cultural or cognitive interest in sustaining this kind of universalist intellectual theme? The aim is thus to 'rearticulate the sum of knowledge from the perspective of the signifying position of the minority that resists total-ization', and not only from the angle of more general postmodernist scepticism (1994: 162).

The dislocation of sociology

These reflections of Bhabha's have decisively negative effects for three sorts of sociological consciousness. One is the kind of 'oppos-itional' postcoloniality that advocates liberation from colonial and other oppression, sees the distorted forms of Eurocentrism as Western capitalist ideology, and wishes to radicalize the progressive parts of Eurocentric universalism. There is manifestly a sociology at work in these social and intellectual alternatives to the dominant system, whereby a basic international relation of exploitation between classes gener-ates socio-economic interests, which in turn overdetermine many of the specificities of cultural life and consciousness. This perspective also assumes a thoroughgoing top–down process of social control, whereby the cultural 'translation' process that is going on in neo-colonialist *insti-tutions* is far from significantly 'negotiated' or truly 'hybridized'. But for Bhabha this kind of 'sociology of underdevelopment' continues to reveal a searching desire to locate a pure politics of Otherness, or even 'nativism', involving the kind of 'unitary representation of a political agency or fixed hierarchy of values and effects' that are now thought to be misguided (1994: 28, 173). Critics of Bhabha (Ahmad 1997) find it by turns deliciously and infuriatingly ironic that Bhabha should see the consequent embrace of 'aporia, ambivalence and indeterminacy' (1994: 173) as postcolonially *radical*, when for them it is the clear sign of a *retreat* from radical politics into liberal angst.

But this will not quite stick because Bhabha is equally concerned to problematize any form of sociological liberal pluralism. The latter involves the assumption that in the cognitive space of sociology and in the political culture of liberal democracy, cultural difference can be both *recognized* and *represented*. As political life in the Western nations becomes more complex, the liberal argument goes, the empirical map of its constituent ethno-cultural groups will need to be carefully drawn up so as to ensure that the various interests gain a voice and that the cultural institutions reflect that. But for Bhabha this is a recognition of cultural *diversity* that fully remains within the conventional totalizing, knowing frame of Western rationality. It is not an appreciation of serious cultural *difference* (1994: 35–6). The latter, he argues, is a matter of living with the 'insurmountable ambivalence' that accompanies the question of 'knowing' of other cultures within a framework that cannot truly shift very far (1994: 154–7). It follows that there is no single representative space to be found within pluralist political culture in which all the multicultural subject positions can be 'equally' voiced, because that idea of a *single*, if conflictual, space is precisely the hallmark of just one cultural tradition – that of Western liberalism itself. Against the sway of the kind of multiculturalism or pluralism which conceives of cultural and political discourse as 'mirroring' the multicultural complexity which exists in the society, Bhabha thinks that whilst each specific cultural voice 'adds to' the dense fabric of cultural and political exchange, there is no (diverse) totality that 'adds up' (1994: 163).

The logic of this argument is not hard to grasp, and it applies to many instances of 'incoherent' totalization. Students, for example, are often told that the concept of social structure that preoccupies all sociologists can be broken down into a series of divisions, identities and perspectives – not only class, race, and gender classically, but also age, sexuality, dis/ability and so on. However, none of these posited agencies and perspectives 'add up' exactly because each, in order to make its distinctive impact and sense, is compelled to declare a priority of vision and politics that inevitably *weakens* the strength of the other 'factors'. The thought of a multi-factorial whole in which all those elements have 'equal' representation is thus something of a fraud.

And in any case, who is the reader/student/expert that is *positioned* in these pluralist modes of address? Ellen Rooney (1989) has analysed the workings of pluralistic literary criticism in terms of its assumed culture of 'reasonableness'. According to Rooney, in the latter, differences of being and interpretation can be recognized and perhaps even celebrated, but any truly awkward discrepancies are over-ridden by the very terms of the discourse of common understanding. The expectation is that we are going to agree to agree, or agree to differ, but always in reasonable enough ways, even if we then go on to articulate and press our separate passionate commitments, some of which will be thoroughly incommensurable with others. But if we are used to being 'seduced' by this academic-liberal spirit of reasonableness, Rooney concludes – and Bhabha says something similar (1994: 175) – we need to see that it amounts to a form of cultural *violence*.

Once again using Runciman for illustrative purposes, we can envisage a sociological equivalent of that presumption of liberal pluralist reasonableness in his argument that whilst, undoubtedly, intensely contrary value-laden assessments exist in social theory, such conflict occurs in the 'descriptive' and 'evaluative' sectors of understanding rather than in the zones of 'reportage' and 'explanation'. In the ideal type of these crucial dimensions of thought, situations and causal accounts must be such as to command the considered assent of all 'theorists of rival schools' (Runciman 1983: 195–6). As we saw in Chapter 3, Runciman has little time for the postpositivist mantra that theoretical disagreements, being the products of particular socio-cultural commitments, go 'all the way down'. His belief is rather that the 'facts' of reportage and the 'soundness' of well-founded depictions and arguments outstrip the ideological and socio-cultural background of both reader and advocate.

We must presume that the same rules govern how we appraise Runciman's scheme of explanation and understanding itself. That is to say, when evaluating its conceptual merits, he would wish us to remain quite unaffected by the fact that he is a senior aged man, a practising capitalist and a social democratic ameliorist. We should also, presumably, be wholly unmoved by his own candid admission that the *Treatise on Social Theory* could have been produced within no other cultural frame than that of the 'Western European intellectual tradition' (Runciman 1983: 52, 1989b: 15). But the Rooney–Bhabha point in this context would be that Runciman's appeal to us to engage in pure intellectual evaluation *outside* cultural consideration is one that only makes sense within the cultural horizon of *just* such a person, and just such a social type. The seduction of sociological reason, with its appeal to a certain kind of rational hygiene within the borders of reportage and explanation, could also then be seen as exercising a kind of cultural violence to those who desire to, or have no option but to, remain outside those borders. Operating under postcolonial values, then, the point might be made that it is no longer the assertion of *substantively* 'Westernist' propositions about culture and politics that today constitutes the most pervasive expression of Eurocentrism. Rather it is this tenacious insistence on the possibility of ideal rational consensus, at a time of intensely rational challenge to liberal reasonableness itself (Sayyid 1997: 128).

The third critique of sociology implicit within Bhabha's writings follows from the last, in that a very different *style of theorizing* is regarded as timely and necessary. Instead of the 'traditional sociological align-ment' between self and society, whereby the interests and positions of individuals are comprehensible in terms of a 'background of social and historical facts' (Bhabha 1994: 42), the life of the self must be re-figured in terms of image, fantasy and disjunction. Instead of the 'paradigm of social action' that dominates sociology, we must seek 'a more affective and iterative' register (1994: 193). Instead of the 'senten-tious and exegetical mode' in which writers such as Runciman both distinguish and entrap themselves, we need to 'catch' the forms of spatio-temporal being which lie 'outside the sentence', moving from a paradigm of 'knowledge *that*' to one in which the modes of justification and explanation are inextricably mixed up (Bhabha 1994: 181–3, 127, Spivak 1996: 32–3). Instead of seeing culture as an object of social enquiry, even one which is subject to radically different interpreta-tions, we need to reject the idea of a representational frame in which these different accounts are convened at a 'safe' distance from the 'phenomena' themselves. Indeed, we need to develop a symbolic vision which treats the cultural not as an epistemological object *at all*, but rather as an 'enunciatory site' in which meanings are creative, not mimetic, in character (1994: 36, 177–8). Now, if, accordingly, the 'place of the theoretical' cannot be as a 'metanarrative claiming a more total form of generality', and if we need to see theory instead as itself an act of cultural *performance*, one which necessarily 'deforms' as it apprehends, then it seems as though the reconceptualizing of theory that Bhabha is engaged in must be a movement *beyond theory* (1994: 30, 179, 242). This style of theory thus promotes the 'development of unmeaning' as a way of progressing 'beyond modernity and its sociology'(1994: 239,255).

The ambivalence within

Bhabha's work has provoked a number of critical reactions, the most informal of which has been a frustration with its obscurity and pretentiousness. No doubt some sociologists will share this impression, concerned to quickly disqualify 'discursive' postcolonialism as either over-inflated or hopelessly opaque. Certainly, Bhabha's arguments are couched in a form that makes them hard to confirm or refute, and sometimes they are indeed strikingly overblown, as in the High Street new-ageism of phrases like 'the Third Space', or when pronouncing portentously that the path of enlightenment lies in 'neither the one nor the Other but something else besides' (Bhabha 1994: 28, 39). Other authors in postcolonial theory also find something seductive in grandiose tautology, as when Bobby Sayyid, for example, explains to us that 'what is extraordinary about Islam is that, although it can be used to articulate so many divergent positions, it maintains its specificity – it remains "Islam"' (Sayyid 1997: 44).

The 'difficulty' and portentousness of Bhabha's style, however, are not insurmountable, as I hope my interpretative summaries have indicated, and there is an intellectual consistency in his position that demands attention. He is not 'doing theory' in the normal sense, and it is important for him to make 'us' feel uncomfortable with rationalist and representationalist forms of argument. Not all writers need to seek to convey their truths in the conventional way, and Bhabha firmly believes that a more performative stylistics within cultural theory is necessary and beneficial. Moreover, the complaint that he is minimizing his critical audience, or failing to convince us by virtue of his cryptic aura alone, involve exactly the sort of assumptions about the 'availability' of a culturally transparent, fair-minded and consensualist reader that he is unhappy with, and for interesting reasons.

Other common criticisms of Bhabha's work target its pseudo-radicalism, the line being that such a mannered and finely-honed perspective could only be developed by a *de-classe*, re-centred and ex-marginal social stratum, embedding itself within the metropolitan *avant guard*, and leading us down a profoundly apolitical cul-de-sac. This is the view of those universalistic postcolonialists who wish to recover and extend the materialist explanatory bearings of anti-imperialist politics. This line is also, as indicated before, a strongly *sociologistic* critique, in its account of the world in which such a view becomes influential, and as a way of explaining bourgeois ideological frameworks in general. Adjusting those themes to this chapter results in significant paradoxes emerging for Bhabha's contribution. On the one hand, he might want to refute (as many sociologists would) the *reductionism* involved in the leftist portrayal of 'his' stratum. After all, there are many non-Western intellectuals at work in Western institutions, and many of them are convinced universalists, not deconstructionists. More broadly phrased, the sociological characterization of the intellectual subculture might well be informative in its way, but the intellectual potency of the positions generated within that formation is another matter altogether.

But the problem with this riposte is that at some level it still demands the kind of assent to sociological and rationalist norms that Bhabha appeared to place permanently under erasure. As we also saw at the very beginning of my exposition, Bhabha *requires*, and can in no way obliterate, a background sociological account of the ways in which contemporary hybridity, as an emergent cultural movement, has come to take on such urgent and disturbing significance within and 'beyond' the intellectual discourses of the West. Just as postcolonial assaults on the notion of historical truth and representation tend to reveal, beneath the headline sensations, a minimal commitment to 'mundane' realism and 'conventional historiographical consideration' (Schwarz 1996: 21, 26), so postcolonialism relies upon a baseline sociology of cultural movements. If new energies and forms of social interaction are happening, these emerging formations must be carefully, mundanely, tracked. And when they are carefully tracked and opened up for further debate, assertions about either the *prevalence* or ruptural *significance* of hybrid consciousness might have to be seriously qualified (Werbner and Modood 1997). It would be simply foolish for postcolonialists to insinuate that such tracking and revising was illegitimate due to its reliance on discredited 'representationalism'. When Bhabha speculates, for example, that 'the truest eye might now belong to the migrant's double vision' (1994: 5), this is another assertion that presupposes, and does not bypass, substantial sociological understanding, and a basic minimum of representationalism. Taken as a stand-alone rhetorical flourish, critics like Friedman (1997: 81) might observe that this sort of statement could only come from postcolonials 'who can afford a cosmopolitan identity'.

Similar factors come into play in any assessment of the anti-universalism involved in radical postcoloniality. As we saw, *explanatory* universalism is considered severely limiting, and other subterranean affective sources are felt to be busy at work underneath narrowly cognitivist understandings of whatever sort. The watchword is that rather than looking for the truth *within* sociological totalizations, we should be considering the truth *about* them. For Bhabha as for others, the suggestion is that it is in the ambitions of colonial *desire* and the workings of psychic ambivalence that the most revealing reference point is to be discovered, or indeed 'enunciated'. Some specify these forces of 'other-desiring' in Lacanian–Derridean terms, such that Western 'logocentrism' is thought to express a repressive 'disavowal' of loss, lack and split in the subject, falsely arresting a primal instability of the self (Venn 1996, Sayyid 1997: 42). But the problem here – reflected in the very unreservedness of the assertions – is that these reference points act as new *foundationalist* gestures, signalling a deeper and more inclusive truth, and a different but still compulsive *explanatory* solution. The surface of Western cognitivism is penetrated, and deeper mechanisms are then discovered to be doing the real work.

The ethics of intellectual exchange gets interesting and sensitive at this juncture. In one sense, the discourse works to present postcolonial theorists as occupying a superior moral and subjective state: *they* can see, but the blinded representationalist cannot, that when postcolonial questions are asked, the 'demons are released' and the play of colonial desire across power and knowledge is revealed when 'thinking at the limit' is on the agenda. Yet at the same time, the new explanatory hinterland is potentially embracing of *all* subject positions, for how could postcolonial subjectivity be simply exempted from the terms of critical assessment without essentialism being reintroduced? When we do see counter-cultural claims being made of radical alterity, as in theorizations of Afrocentrism for example, the results can easily be picked apart, both politically and conceptually (Howe 1998). It can, then, legitimately be asked of the postcolonial theorist's subjectivity *itself*: what is the play of power and knowledge, the desiring and demonizing, that is going on *here*? Some might argue that such a *tu quoque* manoeuvre is improper because postcolonial theory cannot be practised, or even understood, by people who do not share in the subjectivity of exile or diaspora (Moore-Gilbert *et al.* 1997: 5). That indeed is a challenging thought, and one worth elaborating in existential and political terms; but such elaboration has *not* been forthcoming in the discursive postcolonial project because its residual element of explanatory as well as political universalism will not permit such exclusiveness.

These complications need to be underlined in bold. If *explanatory* universalism persists within the postcolonial project, then, contrary to the rhetoric of wholesale intellectual disruption, some of the background norms of liberal and Left discourse – the striving for common understanding, the ideal of an inclusive totality, some kind of minimal representationalism – cannot, after all, be dispensed with. The same applies to the question of *political* universalism: in spite of nominally anti-humanist rhetoric, the background assumption of all postcolonialism must surely be that if there is a problem with Eurocentrism, this is because of the latter's contribution to racism and exploitation, and it is *these* that are the things that need to be eradicated. The adoption of a postcolonial framework, it follows, cannot be anything other than an aspiration to political and moral progress, and as such it must take its share of the burden of universalism (Bhatt 1997: Ch. 1).

Bhabha's work, and postcolonial theory generally, highlight the importance of states of ambivalence and hybridity, but by this stage in our assessment we must wonder whether persistent ambivalence *in the theory itself* is ultimately something to commend it. Take the idea that, in Appiah's terms, postcolonialism is about the 'manufacture of *alterity*' (Moore-Gilbert 1997: 6, emphasis added). This implies a root-and-branch alternative vision, an ontology and politics that are incommensurable with the political and intellectual mainstream, the kind of altogether fresh pathway that is intimated by Bhabha's references to the Third Space and to the production of a 'counter-modernity' (1994: 241). Yet in other renderings, alterity cannot possibly be a matter of total contrast. Counter-modernity, it seems, is a matter of living 'otherwise' than modernity but not *outside it* as such (1994: 18). And if we do encounter 'insurmountable ambivalence' at every turn, then we would be wise not to put our trust in *any* declaration of cultural certainty. In this regard, Bhabha has strongly questioned the aspiration to political and cultural Otherhood in the postcolonial understanding, and is clearly in favour of some kind of cosmopolitan multiculturalism.

Chetan Bhatt has probed this dilemma further, showing that in spite of its rhetorical anti-Eurocentrism and anti-rationalism, the terms and categories of Bhabha's discourse parallel those of long-standing currents within European philosophy. For example, the pitching of the One against the Other, in order to come out with something new and Different Again, stands as the briefest tracing of the Hegelian dialectic. And if, for lack and fear of rational certitude, we feel it necessary to gesture towards the sublime, the ineffable that lies *beyond* the fixity of knowledge, then that might serve as a thumbnail sketch of the Kantian system itself (Bhatt 1997: 13–14).

The Young Hegel

The single-minded effort of another postcolonial theorist, Robert Young, to demolish the entire Marxist and modernist tradition in social theory comes to grief by way of a related philosophical parallel. Young has more recently effectively withdrawn from the full conviction of his earlier onslaught, but the reasons for this have yet to be fully spelled out by Young himself. In *White Mythologies*, Young suggested that Marxism's 'collusive Eurocentrism' stems from its Hegelian foundations, in that Hegel's imperialist dialectic involves a coercive metaphysical 'appropriation of the other' on the part of the knowing subject (Young 1991: 3, 83). Hegel, as rendered by Young, constantly sought to 'escape' rather than fully 'recognize' the intractability of the stubborn *tensions* which exist between the constitutive poles of the knowledge relation: subject/object, general/particular, self/other. Foucault, by stark contrast to Hegel and all his neo-Marxist progeny, *did* recognize such intractability, and is therefore deemed by Young to be superior as a philosophical resource for postcolonialism.

But this argument is doubly misguided (quite apart from any exegetical dispute about the extent to which Marxism *is* really Hegelian). First, Young's presentation of Hegel is highly idiosyncratic. The whole point of Hegel's effort, in explicit counterpoint to the intractable 'antinomies' into which Kantian thought was locked, was to lodge within the very *identity* of each antinomial pole of consciousness its tense but indispensable relation with the other, opposite pole. Hegel's Reason, in unshrinkingly *recognizing* rather than seeking to *escape* the tensions entailed by identity-in-difference, is thus able to claim a new level of understanding (Berthold-Bond 1989). Arguably too, Hegel felt that the limitations of static presentations of the antinomies of knowledge and experience were due to the adoption of a narrowly *epistemological* framework. But the second unimpressive aspect of Young's argument now becomes clear, because Young has marked the theoretical advantage of *Foucault* in precisely *Hegelian* terms. Indeed, Young places the assessment of Foucault himself within a sequence of theorists running from Althusser to Bhabha, each of which is judged by Young according to the extent to which each exhibits this quasi-Hegelian realization (and therefore partial transcendence) of contradiction-intractability.

Hall (1996a: 249) notes that Derrida, the crucial reference point that grounds Young's critique of other theorists, is actually absent from Young's discussion. But if that is an ironic instantiation of the deconstructionist catchphrase that the centre is always present through its absence, it is also the characteristic expression of the movement of the Hegelian Absolute Idea. More generally, we need to draw attention to the several key moments in which the sudden appearance of 'orthodox' social theorizing decisively puncture Young's coruscating anti-modernism. For example, Young (rightly) demands to know of Bhabha himself: how exactly does Bhabha's intervention fit into the wider 'text' of colonialism? (a *totalizing* question); who exactly are the colonized and colonizers anyway? (a *sociological, realist* question); and exactly what kind of political resistance does pan-subjective ambivalence incite? (a conventional Leftist question of *historicist* timbre) (Young 1991: 151–2).

The point of my argument here is twofold. First, that a lot of pseudo-philosophical concept-mongering goes into the semblance of radical alterity in the postcolonialist theorists' self-imaging, and, second, that there is no reason why whatever is important about postcoloni-alism cannot be embraced by a sociological version of cultural studies. Though pitched as profoundly novel, the quasi-metaphysical reflec-tions on being, consciousness and agency in the work of the post-colonialist theorists are either already familiar within conventional (Western) sociological and philosophical thought, or their novelty and difficulty requires considerable collective further endeavour. One of these difficult issues is about how to conceptualize *time*, something that is being increasingly addressed across a whole range of disciplines and 'spaces'.

Another complex matter is the role that *binary categories* play in the process of understanding. In one sense, we cannot begin to think about social life without contrastive categories first being installed – distinc-tions between subjective and objective, structure and agency, culture and material life, sacred and profane and so on. But then a further bifurc-ation typically occurs, with these distinctions being read either as strict oppositional dualisms or as mutually constitutive 'dualities'. And the deadlock between dualism and duality then typically generates further moves towards synthesis or towards dissolving the very terms of the opposition. This is the modality of all manner of 'third ways', including Bhabha's own 'Third Space' locution, however distinctive or esoteric it is dressed up to be. However, in due course it is often then discovered that the terms of the original opposition *reappear*, duly reconfigured, in the synthetic or surpassing discourse, just as theorists who once thought of themselves as synthesizers and supersessionists are assumed by the next generation as having always been fully committed to one or other pole of attraction (Holmwood 1996). 'Structure and agency' is the most familiar of these tropes in sociology, but a moment's reflection reveals countless more.

Intrinsically interesting from any meta-theoretical point of view, these issues around the structural or dialectical logic of thinking and debate have been castigated by some postmodernists and post-colonialists as a matter of the typical binaristic structure of *Western rationalism*. The implication is usually that non-Western forms of thought, and anti-modernist ways of theorizing are not marked by such central encompassing dualities. Without requiring a sort of Cook's

Tour of theories and cultures to show the sheer empirical implausibility of this critique, perhaps all we need to do is point out that it is wholly reliant itself on the construction of a rigid meta-level binary, namely the very contrast between binary and non-binary thinking. Promising to relieve us of this particular dead end of the modernist 'dialectic of enlightenment', postcolonialist thought is fully part of it.

Conclusion

I have supported the claim that the form and the content of postcolonial theory are indeed troubling for modernist discourses like sociology, and suggested that this unsettling effect should be met with interest and self-scrutiny rather than sheer defensiveness. At the same time, I have insisted that sociology has resources with which to reformulate these concerns, and that some of the general conceptual strategies at work within postcolonialism cannot be sustained without generating internal instabilities of its own. In making this assessment, what emerges with particular force is that the whole question of the purpose and structure of *theory* and *analytical categories* in the critical human sciences, for all their rehearsals over the generations, remain extremely demanding. It is often hinted that, for example, by highlighting performativity and liminality rather than structural positioning and rationalist assessment, postcolonial cultural studies offers a wider canvas and a more inclusive sense of the richness of social experience than staid old sociology. But in many ways, this is just the latest form of the eternal complaint that the grey paint of theory fails to do justice to the green fields of life. Its superficiality lies in thinking that it is possible for *any* distinctive analytical discourse – and in spite of its energistic terminology, postcolonialism *is* an analytical discourse – fully to capture the raw edge of life as it is actually felt and lived. Constitutively, all theories and categories reduce experience to their own conceptual priorities, and rigorously exclude rival theories and categories that counteract them. Postcolonialism is no different in that regard, and indeed poststructuralist postcolonialists might be expected to be warier than most of the implicit naive realism which lies behind the gripe that sociology misses out on much of what is 'really' interesting. The contradictoriness of the accusation that sociology is no longer (if it ever was) 'adequate' to the nature of the social is that it sets up an almost unattainable image of what should constitute 'adequate' theory, such that its proponents are always likely to be disappointed beyond the initial attraction to apparently radical alternatives. Notwithstanding notable differences of emphasis, tradition and political resonance between sociology and postcolonial cultural studies, there is then, after all, an extensive area to be explored between them, one in which initial uneasiness brings in its train greater interest and depth.

6
Critical Multiculturalism

Long recognized as an important ethos in educational philosophy and policy, multiculturalism did not finally emerge as a central idea in *social theory* until the 1990s. In the wider public sphere, only by that time had it become clear that multiculturalism posed fundamental issues about the institutional and moral fabric of liberal-democratic nation states. Within academia, the cultural turn that had taken place around that time validated the 'culturalism' half of the label, whilst a prevailing intellectual pluralism affirmed the 'multi' part. One of the major attractions in multiculturalism is its positive, normative quality: it gives us something to be *for* and not just something to be *against*. It compares favourably in that regard with negatively phrased causes such as 'anti-Eurocentrism', which looks over-intellectualized, and 'anti-racism', which has come to be regarded as *insufficiently culturalist*. An added bonus is that multiculturalism seems to be eminently progressive, whilst lacking any taint of political impossibilism.

Within cultural studies, multiculturalism has met with a slightly mixed reception. Some take it without ado to be a 'core value' (During 2005: 160), and largely equivalent to postcolonialism itself (Shohat and Stam 2003). Other postcolonialists are cagier, but accept that multiculturalism constitutes a 'transruption', capable of 'unsettling' liberal Western hegemony (Hesse 2000). At the other end of the spectrum, multiculturalism's prominence within cultural studies has been lambasted for decisively blocking any proper comprehension of racism and other global structures (San Juan 2002). Partly because of this mixed response, it is not easy to project any simple clash of paradigms between sociology and cultural studies on the matter. Both disciplines have much to say about multicultural societies and their component ethnicities and subcultures, such that *descriptively* at any rate multiculturalism stands as a productive point of mutual orientation, a definite area of 'intellectual trade between sociology and cultural studies' (Turner 2002: 223). The only real sticking points are about how fully *coherent* multiculturalism is as theory and practice – what it is that makes it an 'ism' – and the way in which it might be deployed within social science as a *critical* perspective.

It is these sticking points that I want to open up to scrutiny in this chapter, with a view to disturbing the consensus that exists around critical multiculturalism. I begin with remarks on the basic idea of multi-culturalism, moving on to the way that *monoculturalism* gets established as its discursive counterpart. I then take issue with the variants of multi-culturalism that critical texts in the 1990s sought to articulate. This focus is justified in the same way as other discussions of 1990s liter-ature in this book: if poststructuralist interpretations of identity and social relations have waned in the intervening period, it is not because those who are attracted to them have worked out how to replace or extend them. I go on to review proposals, before closing, that 'radical democratic pluralism' is the theorized political perspective that gives multiculturalism traction, by addressing some unsuspected issues that are only now emerging with full force. One of these concerns the way in which a *Marxist* version of critical multiculturalism might be sustained. The other relates to the growing challenge to the *secularism* that charac-terizes Western political life and thought, a secularism that still marks projects like sociology and cultural studies.

The basic conundrum

In spite of many attempts to define multiculturalism, its essential logic remains troublesome. In probably the clearest discussion, Bhikhu Parekh restricts the primary or 'strong' meaning of multiculturalism to recogni-tion of the existence and importance of 'communal' cultures, those that represent a deeply embedded way of life. Insofar as multiculturalism refers to different lifestyles, habits, and politico-cultural diversity across a wide range of social groups, this meaning, though not illegitimate, must be regarded as *secondary* or 'weak'. For Parekh, these often hybrid cultural spaces and identities, however interesting, 'do not represent an altern-ative culture', they do not really depart from the society's 'dominant system of meaning and values' (Parekh 2000: 3).

This foundational distinction immediately raises difficulties. What does it mean to represent an 'alternative' culture, and how are we to decide what does or does not depart from a society's 'dominant system of meaning'? Just empirically, many observers think that the deeply communal or ethnicized cultures to which Parekh gives conceptual and moral priority are eroding, whilst the second multiculturalist syndrome is growing. If it is then insisted that many people are moving *back* to their traditional cultures and values, and reclaiming their ethnicized or deep communal identities, this can be regarded as a matter of *informed choice* within a shared setting of global politics and capitalist techno-culture. As such, it does not represent the kind of inherited, as it were unthinking or natural, quality of allegiance that alone would prompt us to distinguish deep cultures from various subcultural options. In any case, many instances of the latter are not simply 'choices', but themselves possess (varying) degrees of sociological depth and compulsion. There are sources of identity – class, work, sexuality – that are not necessarily cultural *tout court*, nor always trumped by cultural identities of an ethnicized kind. And some of these (queer cultures for example) might be thought *more* threatening to the dominant system of meanings and values than some of the ethnicized ones.

Sensing difficulties of this kind in Parekh's weighted preference, Tariq Modood (2005: 18–19) argues that multiculturalism 'recognizes the legitimacy of both developments'. This parity of recognition is held to be in tune with the influential view of the UK as a 'community of communities', as proposed in *The Future of Multi-ethnic Britain* (CMEB 2000). Unfortunately, this formulation compounds rather than unlocks the basic conundrum, which has three aspects. The first is that the 'community of communities' rhetoric implies that all the people of the nation do fall squarely into one kind of community or another, and this is perhaps questionable. Of course, we hear every day about the existence of not only the ethnic community and the deaf community and the gay community, but also the police community, the shopping community, the student community, and the train-spotting community. But this only plays up the difficulty in the idea of what a relevant community is, and leads us to question the presumption that *being* members of some community is the principal way that everyone should think of themselves.

Second, the understandings of the process of (contemporary) social life that lie behind the two senses of community, between which Modood proposes parity, are close to irreconcilable. As Hall (1988) first pointed up, the emphasis on the growing number, and increasingly fragmented or hybrid forms, of 'new ethnicities' – such that 'ethnicity' begins to seem the wrong word to use in this context – runs directly *against* the 'strong' multiculturalist concern for profound singularity. Instead of regarding culture as *inherited*, it is read as *constructed*; where cultural *incommensurability* once held, we now have extensive cultural *porosity*; where culture used to be inhabited by settled and *saturated* selves, now *nomadic and fragmented* subjects roam all over the place.

Third, the difficulty evident in stabilizing the sense of community translates directly to the meta-level of multiculturalism, because it is not clear what we are then to make of the idea of a *community* of communities. What identity is characteristic of *this* community, the meta-community? If we favour the strong, deep notion of culture, then we might think, and hope, that multiculturalism itself would develop into the kind of deep culture that would bind its members together through commitment to its values and participation in its extensive social practices. The paradox here, however, is that to take on that degree of multicultural commitment, to see ourselves as belonging to the higher-order community of communities in any deep sense, means discounting and superseding the depth of commitment and belonging that we might show for any particular *first-order* community. If, conversely, we really do belong to a deep first-order community, there is no reason to accept the higher-order value of multiculturalism, which after all is duty bound to treat as equally legitimate other first-order values and communities that might be anathema to us. Of course, we might *pragmatically* accept the higher-order compromise, just to preserve and protect our own first-order culture as much as we can, but in that case to say that we have a *community* of communities and a deep *value* of multiculturalism is somewhat disingenuous.

Running instead with the second, 'weaker' understanding of cultural selfhood and identity, it quickly becomes clear that we might not be very concerned at all about puffing up multiculturalism into a strong value and deep culture, because this involves a further 'essentialization' of the notions of culture and community that are already overstated in relation to the first-order socio-cultural structure. So whether we take the stronger or weaker interpretation of multiculturalism's own value, and the community of communities it seeks to construct, a coherent and satisfactory concept or ethic appears to be unobtainable. Now it could be that we need to specify multiculturalism in *other* terms in order to attain the right sort of coherence, such that what is felt to be good about multiculturalism is that it assists or extends more general principles – egalitarianism, or individual cultural creativity and freedom, or even, dare to say, socialism. But this is odd because the promise of multiculturalism was that it was to be a *new kind* of social philosophy, not something to be subsumed under existing values – indeed those were the things that multiculturalism was meant to challenge and 'unsettle'.

Mono . . .

Critical multiculturalists have sometimes sought to ease those potential inconsistencies by stressing that multiculturalism is not something we have to *believe* in, rather it is a pluralistic label for a given 'multicultural condition' (Goldberg 1994: 2) – 'it simply is' (Kincheloe and Steinberg 1997: 2). But no sooner is the possibility of a purely descriptive multiculturalism raised than work in that vein gets pressed once again into service 'in the name and for the sake of the multicultural' (Goldberg 1994: 27). What pushes us in this affirmative direction is the construction of a definitive binary contrast in which *mono*culturalism stands as the undesirable opposite of *multi*culturalism. According to Goldberg (1994: 4, 11), monoculturalism refers to an 'ethnoracial Eurovision' which stood as 'the more or less unchallenged ideological common sense of the first half of this century', leaving the voices of marginalized cultures 'unable to speak'. If these 'barbarians uttered unrecognizable sounds . . . eventually, these sounds came to be named multiculturalism'. In this view, then, we are back with the identification of multiculturalism as 'an assault on Eurocentrism', where the latter represents the 'discursive residue of colonialism' (Shohat and Stam 1994b: 296).

In the last chapter, I accepted much of the overall drive of anti-Eurocentric thinking, but also raised some problems about it. Both the strengths and the overstatements can be seen in this context too. For example, even if the marginalized voices came to be *named* multiculturalism, multiculturalism is not necessarily what those voices came to *speak*. And if Eurocentric discourses were in their way monocultural, then it is not as though what they were replacing or crushing was any *less* monocultural. Perhaps the problem with Eurocentric discourse was not so much its monoculturalism, but the fact that it served to rationalize oppression and exploitation on a global scale. But that kind of separation of elements is not to the liking of anti-Eurocentric multiculturalists. There is something, they think, in the very mindset of Eurocentrism that requires special exposure and condemnation. One candidate for its uniquely bad feature, for example, is the *supremacist* belief that the West is destiny (Shohat and Stam 1994b: 296), another is the basically *elitist* sense that both 'non-whites and the poor are inferior' (Kincheloe and Steinberg 1997: 3).

Perhaps most of all, the critique of monoculturalism suggests that the latter's most basic problem is to do with its denial of intellectual *pluralism*, in both an epistemological sense and more generally. With the epistemological angle in mind, Eurocentric modernism is held to involve a 'scientific epistemology and one-correct-answer ideology' that passes itself off as the only language 'for capturing truth' (Kincheloe and Steinberg 1997: 35). Such an ambition seemingly commits a fundamental 'epistemological error' (McLaren 1994: 50). In more general terms, Western universalist values – science, rationality, freedom, enterprise, equality, progress – are arrogantly believed to be valid for all people in all cultures (Goldberg 1994: 4–5).

As in our earlier discussion of Eurocentrism, we need to note that these portrayals of ideological contamination can be taken in a very broad way (equating to *ethnocentrism*) or more narrowly (deliberate inculcation of a *dominant ideology*). The problem with the first is that *all* cultures are ethnocentric, so there can be little wonder that people express the values of their culture. Indeed, strong multiculturalists might be expected to be particularly attracted to this view, seeing as they portray cultural saturation, affirmatively, as going 'all the way down'. The second take on Eurocentric ideology calls for the sort of detailed approach to key questions that is hard to find in critical multiculturalist discourse. What is the exact timbre of Western destinarianism? What are the variations on the scale of Eurocentric monoculture? How extensively were such views held? What was the balance between monocultural attitudes and matters of material gain in the dynamic of colonialism?

In the 'epistemological' dimension of critique, few multicultural arguments get beyond the stark equation cited above: Western culture equals science equals a 'one-correct-answer' ideology. Apart from underestimating the considerable degree of pluralism about knowledge *within* the Western scientific tradition, the implication is that multiculturalists can readily step right *outside* that tradition, so that they themselves are *not* looking for 'one correct answer'. But this is patently not so because what they want to do above all is reveal the hidden cultural truth about Western objectivism, the *truth about Truth*, so to speak – for example that it exhibits 'the phallocentric logic of white supremacist ideology' (McLaren 1994: 55). A damaging irony in such arguments is that investment in *rigid binary categorizations* is frequently highlighted as a necessary part of that phallocentric logic, something, presumably, that we are then meant to forget entirely when taking up the definitive 'multi *versus* mono' construct.

The feminist philosopher Sandra Harding has given one of the most developed arguments to the effect that the very idea of *science* is quintessentially Eurocentric and monocultural. The belief of Europeans, according to Harding, was that their particular civilization is 'fundamentally self-generated' (1994: 346), and on that basis, a number of other things emerge: that science habitually denies its non-European influences; that science cannot transcend culture; that all the benefits of science go to Western elites; and that, contrary to the dogma that scientific truths have a privileged free-standing logical status, they are in fact 'caused by social relations' (1994: 353). This is a more credible version of the charge of epistemological monoculturalism, in the main arguing for a sociology of knowledge that would show how scientific progress takes place in socio-economic contexts that profoundly mark both the sequence of discovery and the character of the intellectual product. In this way, Harding notes how metallurgical and astronomical developments were directly spurred on by the surge in mining and navigation in the early modern (colonialist) economy.

Harding seems to willingly commit what mainstream philosophers call the 'genetic fallacy': the (in their view) mistaken claim that we can explain the *validity* of science in terms of its original motivation and context. For example, in a move that rehearses an old theme in Soviet Communist philosophy, Harding proposes that modern science's obsession with revealing the *law-like* structure of the natural world reflects its intimate association with bourgeois *legal* culture (1994: 355). As an afterthought, Harding backtracks slightly, adding that 'of course, no one would deny that there are aspects of the modern sciences, their cultures and practices that can and should be used to benefit all peoples living in every society' (1994: 359). The addendum is crucial, however, because it involves *opting out of* the genetic fallacy, and it rules out any strictly relativist reading of the work of the sociology of knowledge. This is because those 'aspects' of the sciences that are agreed to be valid in a cross-societal, that is *universal*, sense can only be those cognitively robust aspects that have survived the long haul of testing, theorizing and debating in the scientific culture.

Bhikhu Parekh (2000: Chs 1 and 2) gives a more general reading of the mono/multi contrast in his overview of European political thought over the centuries. Those considered relatively *monistic* include the Greeks, the Christians, Locke and Mill, with relatively *pluralistic* exemplars being Vico, Herder and Montesquieu. Parekh's preference for the latter strand is based on the now familiar refrain that the former group try to specify binding universal values, whereas the latter do not. And the problem with *that* is that universalism is heavily coloured by specific-ally Western prejudices, such that cultures that do not conform to the prevalent benchmarks of reason, science and liberalism are then neces-sarily regarded as inferior.

But we need to note that this debate between pluralist and monistic thinkers is taking place *within* the Western tradition, something that immediately runs against the complaint that Western thought, *as such*, is monistic. Also, most of the views considered are universalistic. Some, to be sure, may be more universalistic than others, but even the least temperamentally monistic thinker, Vico, was attempting to provide a generally valid reading of the nature of all history and culture. Finally, Parekh's preference is accepted as being *relative* rather than absolute, because he is aware that ultra-historicist, pluralist and organicist views of cultural specificity (Herder's for example) can also be taken as justifying cultural supremacism. Montesquieu, another giant who is placed on the pluralistic side, accepted cultural relativity, but grounded this objectively or 'naturalistically' in terms of the combination of physical and cultural causal forces that had cross-cultural determinative status. And so it goes: today endless debates are to be had about whether Marx's scientism cancels out his anti-imperialism, or whether Kant's rationalism nulli-fies his eloquent early plea for cosmopolitan peace, or whether Hume's comments on the inferiority of black people give the lie to his incom-parably anti-rationalist philosophical outlook. When Parekh comes up to the present time, he finds residues of monoculturalism in Kymlicka's proposal that multiculturalism can only be viable if it is restricted to *national* peoples, and if it takes a *liberal* form within those national cultures. Even Rawls, whom Parekh prefers, is thought strong on moral pluralism, but short on 'thick' cultural pluralism. But we are back to square one here, because as noted earlier, Parekh's persistent critical theme – that 'cultures are not superstructures' (2000: 122) – can only definitively favour multi over mono, and relativism over universalism, if deep, saturating, cultures themselves are taken to constitute the *infra-structure* of society and history. And that claim is entirely contestable.

Multi . . .

In condemnations of monocultural closure, the obvious suggestion is that multicultural discourse is by comparison open and plural-istic, signalling its 'antihegemonic thrusts rather than its univocity and singularity' (Goldberg 1994: 3). Accordingly, a large number of possible interpretations of the multicultural label itself can be entertained: pre-modern, conservative, assimilationist, liberal, left-liberal, managed, corporate, managed, pluralist, nativist, left-essentialist, postmodern, post-structuralist, resistance, insurgent, reflexive, and of course critical. In effect, though, only four broad options are in play, and they are given relatively short shift.

'Conservative' multiculturalism (McLaren 1994: 50, Kincheloe and Steinberg 1997: 3–5) turns out to be a misnomer, needing to be unmasked as the very bastion of monoculturalism itself. This is because conservative multiculturalists are advocates of integrationism or assimilationism, understandings in which critical multiculturalists find no substance whatsoever. Where intellectual conservatives do declare themselves as wishing to embrace something of multiculturalism, they are summarily dismissed as duplicitous. Thus, Arthur Schlesinger's arguments about the disintegrative dangers of radical cultural multiplicity, and his defence of *citizen* identities – plausible concerns that are by no means restricted to a conservative political framework – are translated without hesitation as racist aspirations to 'homogeneity' (Goldberg 1994: 20, May 1999b: 15–17). Not only is this reading dogmatic in itself, it allows critical multiculturalists to overlook the likelihood that there is something *inherently* 'conservative' about *every* form of multiculturalism.

Liberal multiculturalism, the second variant, comes in three shades. Where cultural identities are effectively denied in favour of an individualist ontology and ethics, liberalism is clearly anti-multicultural, having no place for group belonging (Goldberg 1994: 25). Where liberalism seeks to build bridges between isolated individuals, the claim is that this is merely to put faith in universalist 'cliches' such as 'one race, the human race' (Kincheloe and Steinberg 1997: 10). Liberal *pluralism* is said to be a different kettle of fish again, being an expression of a long-standing 'corporatist' thread within modernist culture and politics. However, whilst accepting that corporate pluralism represents a genuine concession to multiculturalism, critical multiculturalists regard it as deeply flawed. Above all, it requires acceptance of the myth of the 'neutral' political state. But in a society of structural inequality, fair and equal treatment is impossible; indeed the liberal pluralist state will initially recognize and constitute only those cultural groups who will play by and benefit from the existing rules of the political and cultural game.

A strong note of class analysis and political economy was necessary to conduct that critique of 'inadequate' liberal multiculturalism. Critical multiculturalists, however, are generally ambivalent about the sort of Marxist perspective that yields such leverage. According to this

line, Marxism itself is Eurocentric, with the Western industrial prolet-
ariat acting as culturally specific proxy for the future of all humankind. Relatedly, Marxism's constitutive priorities require a devaluation of
cultural identity-formation in favour of class position and class interests,
this being reflected broadly in anti-racist stances. And being methodologically 'rationalist' in character, Marxism's aspiration to a science
of society and history contains distasteful 'foundationalist' dregs. Thus,
any kind of Left 'universalism' must be categorized as *anti*-multicultural
in spirit, not a genuine variant of multiculturalism (May 1999b: 11).

It turns out, then, that critical multiculturalism is not itself terribly
pluralistic after all, with respect to other possible variants of multiculturalism. These all appear either as fundamentally flawed, or not as
conceptions of (true) multiculturalism at all. On what basis, then, can
critical multiculturalism claim to be the thoroughgoing and surpassing
perspective?

Hetero...

The most persistent effort to establish a distinctive conceptual repertoire
for critical multiculturalism has taken a poststructuralist direction. True,
this orientation was never the only theme in the critical multiculturalist
camp, and increasingly it has been toned down. But the merit of the
poststructuralist move is to see that in order to give greater unity and
freshness to the busy and disjointed field of multiculturalisms, and in
order to be able to critique other Leftist versions which retain all the 'sins
of modernist theorizing' (McLennan 1996), a different sort of theoretical
and political ethos had to be forged.

For McLaren (1994: 53–62), 'critical multiculturalism starts from the
perspective of a resistance, poststructural approach to meaning', namely
the idea that signs are 'not fixed' but are rather 'multiaccentual' and
'polyvocal'. It follows that 'all representations are the result of social
struggles over signifiers and their signified' and that, conversely, 'society
needs to be seen as an irreducible indeterminacy'. Such propositions are
thought to constitute a new 'cultural imaginary', with the aid of which
we can go 'one step further' than left-liberal multiculturalism. Goldberg
concurs by adding that only a 'pragmatic anti-foundationalism' can
support the 'commitments' of 'the multicultural project', which are
'insurgent, polyvocal and heteroglossal' (Goldberg 1994: 20).

For illustrative purposes, let us pursue Goldberg's version of this
foundation for nominally anti-foundational critical multiculturalism.
Goldberg perceives the central problem to be the existence of a kind

of metaphysical horror in the West of impurity and heterogeneity. It is not only that conservatives and Left universalists in their different ways see commonality as *politically* important; rather, there is a cultural and visceral *obsession* with stability and orderliness. Visions and projects of cultural homogeneity serve to allay the unruly prospect of ceaseless mobility and mixedness (Young 1995). That is why Goldberg states that the homogeneity/heterogeneity couplet is more central than identity/difference to the critical multicultural cause (1994: 20). A true multiculturalism, it follows, must celebrate 'the transformative energy of impurity', and must scandalize pseudo-natural normativity with the troubling force of 'abnormal transgression' (1994: 25–6).

The sheer momentum of this line of thought is infectious. Unfortunately, it is also 'bullshit', in Harry Frankfurt's (2005) terms. That is to say, its authors present the paean to heterogeneity with such panoramic flourish, and with such a sense of indulgence in freedom from constraint, that they hardly seem concerned to establish its truth or validity. Now, undoubtedly, cultural analysis can be stretched to include matters of sensibility and even the kind of experience that appears to go 'beyond words'. Anthropologists have on that basis often enquired into diverse cultural framings of 'purity and danger' and the like. But when critical multiculturalists assert, without much in the way of descriptive and explanatory argument at all, that their mission is to explore 'new structures of experience', to 'remap desire', and to develop a cultural imaginary that will stand as 'a bold infringement on normalcy' (McLaren 1994: 67), some obvious counter thoughts come to mind.

First, no theoretical elaboration of the basis for heterogeneity would be likely to be able to dispense with all notions of 'normalcy'. Perhaps its basis might lie in Heidegger, perhaps in a variant of psychoanalytic theory, but almost certainly the specification of anti-normal being will involve further species of universalism and 'homogeneity'. Second, *all* cultures have their own ways of solidifying experience, their horrors in the face of the impure and profane, and their own ordering mentalities. To attribute the thirst for orderly understanding to modern Western societies alone seems ignorant and reductive.

Third, heterogeneity is a brute 'fact', we are told (Goldberg 1994: 25), suggesting that homogeneity possesses no equivalent facticity. Yet, stability and similarity are just the *necessary* other side of the coin of mobility and difference, and there is nothing intrinsically 'superior' about either modality. The root proposition in many of these statements, namely that homogeneity is somehow more 'oppressive', is obscurantist and glib. Perhaps there is something about Being itself that gives heterogeneity a privileged status? – but what kind of cosmic essentialism is this? Perhaps we should feel obliged to desire a ceaselessly mobile and disrupted social order? – but what could that possibly mean, unless we are to set the chimes of freedom ringing by driving on the other side of the road from everyone else, or by infecting our unwitting lovers with AIDS. And anyway, 'heterogeneity always includes within the possibility of its moment the forces that might render its moment impossible' (Golderg 1994: 27). Whatever this means, it represents a concession that heterogeneity too can take an exclusive and coercive form, a concession that altogether spoils the case.

Radical democratic...

Since no *direct* move can be made from post-structuralist tenets about meaning and selfhood to political multiculturalism, intermediary strategies must be posited that might enable the transition. One strategy is to invoke postmodernism on the grounds that postmodernism is above all about the workings of *power*, and 'how power is played out amongst groups' (Grant and Sachs 1995: 91–2). Since this applies to any conception of political theory whatever, a supplement is required that postmodernism is especially 'emancipatory and rational'. But this sense of a 'postmodern solution' to multiculturalism is, to say the least, counter-intuitive. If postmodernism is anything substantial or different from radical modernism itself, it must put into question *all* rational metanarratives of emancipation, including the hopes that critical multiculturalists place in 'equity and social justice' (Grant and Sachs 1995: 101).

A second approach is to acknowledge the difficult and variegated character of postmodernism, and to configure one possible strand of it. Thus Kanpol and McLaren (1995: 3) distinguish between 'ludic', 'travelogue' and 'resistance' postmodernism, believing only the latter to be suitable for critical multicultural purposes. Against this, we need to remember that feminists and Leftists have found it persistently difficult to wring any specific *content* out of the Foucauldian incantation of 'resistance'. This is not surprising, since Foucault distanced himself from Marxist and other 'oppositionalist' conceptions of power and ideology in treating resistance as a ubiquitous modality present in *all* social relations. There is thus no reason to think that Foucault would be any more favourable to a multiculturalist regime of truth than to any other form of governmental moralism.

A third strategy designed to bring poststructuralism to politics has been to draw upon version of radical democratic theory. These writers, after all, remain on the Left, express distinct poststructuralist leanings, and have been speculating for a long time about the pluralist character of democratic subjectivity and change. For Laclau and Mouffe, as for the critical multiculturalists, the notion of 'society' is understood as profoundly destabilized and 'unsuturable', just as subjectivity is uncertain, shifting and multiple. At the same time, undeniable social constraints establish key 'nodes' of stability, and political discourses of all sorts constitutively project a potential collective 'we' of action and solidaristic identification. If politics always involves a range of necessarily *imaginary* projects that can never fully be achieved, there may yet be new ways of convening all those social movements and voices against oppressive forces under a general radical, pluralist, dialogic, oppositional, democratic agenda, and this is what the term 'critical multiculturalism' signals (Kanpol and McLaren 1995: 12).

The radical democratic outlook does embrace the politics of difference, but it is harder to see why it should be called critical multiculturalism rather than just radical democracy. Indeed, the approach of Laclau and Mouffe is already beset with two main tensions before multiculturalism is added to the brew. The first is the retention of a structuralist and Marxist horizon in the identification of the key social 'nodes' around which democratic imaginaries contend. This residual sense of underlying constraint works against the more poststructural elements in Laclau and Mouffe, in terms of which social structure is a discursive hindrance to the idea of a politics of radical difference (Laclau 1990, McLennan 1991). That tension hampers critical multiculturalists also, because even more than Laclau and Mouffe, they want to leaven their post-structuralist probings with an orthodox dose of anti-capitalist political economy, in light of which they berate the liberal complacency of other multiculturalist currents (Goldberg 1994: 15, Kanpol and McLaren 1995: 3, McLaren 1997a: x).

The friction between the democratic and the *pluralist* side of radical democratic theory cannot be underestimated either. Democracy stabilizes political subjectivity in terms of national or global popular consciousness, whereas the ingrained pluralism of the Laclau and Mouffe sort takes on a kind of ontological status, summoning up radical plurality across the board – plurality of the social, plurality of subjectivity, plurality of political imaginaries. It is not only Marxist re-totalizations of the social, and of politics, that begin to come unstuck here, but any rendering of multiculturalism itself as essentially democratic. Advocates of the latter go along with the quasi-ontological line of thought for a time, repeating slogans like 'there is no single referent such as democracy', that politics lies 'beyond identity' and that 'cultural space is continually renegotiated' (Kanpol and McLaren 1995: 9–11). But such catchphrases give no particular priority to *group* identification, and the groups might be based on any number of ascriptions or affiliations. Overall, the continuous invocation of 'oppression' in critical multiculturalism, and related calls for 'counter-hegemonic' action, look incongruous when filtered through the discursive, contestable and pluralized modalities that are highlighted by Laclau and Mouffe, not least since these authors end up questioning the very concept of 'hegemony' itself.

Such considerations do not deter critical multiculturalists from inciting 'insurgency' and even 'utopia' (McLaren 1994: 66). But overall, a milder reforming zeal is tangible. Multiculturalism's main role might be to help formulate 'new projects of possibility' and encourage the 'creation of engaged and critical citizens' (Giroux 1994: 341, 1995: 116). Within critical educationist multiculturalism, a key expression of the radical democratic agenda is the idea of *border consciousness*, which in turn leads to *border pedagogy*. Here, the thought is that whites and non-whites together are to 'critique their "selves" and ideological configurations' (Kanpol 1995: 181); to become 'uncertain about the politics of one's own location' (Giroux 1995: 121); and to cultivate 'intersubjective spaces of cultural translation' (McLaren 1994: 65). One deficit in these writers is their failure to see that border spaces are, simply, parasitic upon *borders*, and another is their inability to accept that the kind of uncertainty and caught-consciousness that they regard as palpably radical has long been paraded as a core quality of the liberal mind.

What about the exposure of cultural *whiteness*? One problem here is that if *cultural identities* are generally to be accorded elevated status, and if this is to be couched under Taylor's famous (1994) rubric of the 'politics of recognition', then whites too are entitled to their forms of cultural authenticity and representation, not least in polities where they represent the majority. This would be particularly the case if we still hold that majoritarianism remains central to democracy. Of course, outright racism and violence is to be prohibited, but multiculturalists have no right to *legislate* against *ethnocentrism*, otherwise the whole notion of a self-determining 'people' is placed in jeopardy.

The proper route to multicultural democratic ethics, in that case, might better be driven through education. But this is also tricky ground. Critical multiculturalists seek to educate whites into 'unlearning' their practices of privilege and violence (Giroux 1994: 327), and they want them to confess their part in routinized 'white terror' (McLaren 1994). But this level of psychodynamic guilt-tripping is both ethically dubious and likely to be politically counterproductive, not least because it is generally white Professors of Education who seem to offer themselves as the very role model of how to unlearn privilege.

Unsettled liberalism, unsettled critique

After the heyday of poststructuralism, critical multiculturalist writings became notably more rounded, with an emphasis on political economy reasserting itself, and a dash of Bourdieu adding sociological subtlety (May 1999b). Three problems remain, however, that together suggest that we have reached the end of the road for critical multiculturalism rather than its maturation. First, there is the issue of intellectual momentum. After all, many of the flaws with poststructuralism as it moulded itself to the politics of difference were plainly perceptible at the time of enunciation. Goldberg's signature collection, for example, contained a devastating caution from Gates (1994) against radical moralism, and well-crafted reflections by Caws (1994) about the dangers of outright *culturalism* within multiculturalism. To now simply reclaim these elements, as if they were something new in the paradigm rather than what undermines it, involves a paradoxical loss of distinctiveness.

The second problem retraces an earlier antinomy: that it is very difficult to find the desired third way between the dispersalism that is carried in the emphasis on transgressive hybridities, and the over-essentialist depiction of deep cultures. It can now be claimed, of course, that hybridity theorists have both underestimated 'rooted' identities, and that they have over-pluralized the social totality. And it can be noted too that ethnic and national identities on their side really ought to become subject to 'non-essentialist, critically reflective' analysis, so that multiculturalism will not be seen as bound up only with ethnicity and nation (May 1999b: 24, 33). But now we are left a little unsure again: is this a critique of hybridity or an affirmation of it, a statement of multiculturalism, or its supersession?

In a similar line of thought, Hall (2000: 231–2) argues that we must regard as appropriate and tangible the 'multicultural drift' of all currents of contemporary thought, which has led to a situation whereby the 'double demand for equality and difference appears to outrun our existing political vocabularies'. To that extent, multiculturalism, or at least the 'multicultural question', stands inescapably as the horizon of our time. Even so, any stable or literal interpretation of multiculturalism as a coherent theory or positive value is problematic because not only has *race* been effectively problematized in recent times, but so has *ethnicity*. Once again, therefore, the whole notion of 'culture', as well as democracy itself, is eminently contestable and heterogeneous. Never one to trust purely philosophical solutions, Hall does not attempt to give this notion of heterogeneity any metaphysical underpinning, and he accepts what critical multiculturalists used to deny, namely that the culture and politics of late modernity require due recognition of *both* particularity *and* universality. If that appears to give a synthetic and positive rendering of the present mood, others read it in a more thoroughly reflexive, almost excruciatingly ambivalent way, in view of the sheer number and complexity of multicultural subjectivities and politics that it covers (Rattansi 1999).

Does the rediscovery of political economy and Marxism relieve that ambivalence? In the hope that it does, erstwhile poststructuralist radicals like Peter McLaren have turned their hand to lambasting all the 'posts' for their relativism and denial of totalization; for their exaggeration of indeterminacy and difference; for their abandonment of categories of exploitation and false consciousness; for their presentation of hybridity, and *mestizaje* consciousness as always intrinsically progressive subjectivities. In a remarkably *volte face*, we are now urged instead to take up quasi-modernist and indeed sociologistic framings, such as 'what is the relation among schooling, the production of ideology, and the formation of subjectivity within larger cultural logics of post-industrial capitalism' (McLaren 1999a: 174). Emphasizing the persistence of the 'materialist and non-discursive dimension of social life' (1997a: 193), and postmodernism's complicity in accepting the most important 'difference' of all, that 'between rich and poor' (1997b: 185), McLaren forswears any allegiance to multiculturalism *as such*, in favour of 'the reconstruction of the deep structures of political economy, culture and power' in general (1997b: 287).

All this amounts to a belated acceptance that multiculturalism's *defect*, not its *strength*, lies in its rejection of universalism, something that others worked out earlier on (Hollinger 1995; Kahn 1995; Joppke and Lukes 1999). Probably the most pertinent form that universalism might take in these gnarled debates is that of a revived radical *humanism*. But those who have rediscovered conventional Marxism are slightly exposed in that regard. On the one hand, McLaren pays homage to Bauman's notion of the post-postmodernist 'completion of humanity', and to Freire's injunction that only love of 'the world', of 'people', and of 'humankind' can finally sustain revolutionary pedagogy (McLaren 1997b: 284, 2000: 171). Yet at the same time, humanism is posed chiefly as a 'mediation' for class-based struggles and outcomes, and as supplying an altogether 'thinner' ethic than revolutionary materialism (McLaren 2001). Something has to give here, and one way of moving forward might be to view Marxist concepts and values as interpreting and extending humanist understanding, but not exhausting or surpassing it. In that sense the greater *breadth* – not thinness – of radical humanism emerges as its principal virtue rather than a weakness. Class analysis *per se* would then have to be regarded as incapable of fully encompassing all issues of human motivation and sociological situation.

Multiculturalism *versus* secular humanism?

After the fundamental problematization of humanism by Althusser, Foucault and Derrida, its revival in social theory could hardly have been expected to be dramatic. Humanism's re-emergence after poststructuralism, however, whilst unspectacular, has been steady (Soper 1986, Barrett 1991, Weeks 1993, Johnson 1994, McLennan 1996, Assiter 2003), to the point where once again it is taking centre stage, not least in arguments about multiculturalism. For Paul Gilroy, a leading cultural studies voice in this context, the kind of 'pragmatic, planetary humanism' that we require cannot be of a sort that is, so to speak, *pre*-multicultural. Like Hall, Gilroy takes the view that even if multiculturalism is an 'overloaded' idea, leading to all manner of interpretations and claims that will never rest easy with one another, yet still it is 'pivotal', necessitating continual open-ended engagement, especially in relation to 'thinking about cosmopolitan democracy' (Gilroy 2000: 243). What multiculturalism has helped achieve is to put older forms of universalism out of commission, along with the primacy of national identity, and any singular compression of the many modernities. Above all, it has helped us to see the catastrophic influence on Western culture (and thus the world), of what Gilroy calls 'raciology', in which the very category of *race* is installed as the governing imaginary for understanding all human and social relations, from the idea of the 'human race' itself through all its hierarchized, racialized sub-species.

But if the imperative now is to go 'beyond race' and thus beyond any 'anthropological' notion of humanity, indelibly marked as that is by raciological discourse, multiculturalism itself cannot be the last word either. This is because, for Gilroy, in its ethnicized forms, multiculturalism also carries the trace of raciology, in that multiculturalism's social identities are conferred by neo-essentialist assumptions about ethnic belonging and cultural rootedness. As an antidote, attention needs to be re-focused on the 'undervalued power of this crushingly obvious, almost banal human sameness', in terms of which a *post*-multiculturalist approach to the politics of a common future might be possible. If that power can be harnessed, not as 'a rather old-fashioned plea for disabusing ourselves of the destructive delusions of racism', but rather as an appreciation of our vulnerable and creative human predicaments, then the conjoint grip on our social imaginings of raciology and false universalism will be broken (Gilroy 2000: 28–30).

An elliptical writer, it is perhaps questionable whether Gilroy manages to tease cohesion out of the juxtaposition of 'planetary' humanism as an ambitious general prospect, and its qualification as 'pragmatic', and debatable too, whether the 'planetary' reference-point, either conceptually or empirically, can yet bear the weight that is being placed upon it. Even as things stand, though, Gilroy's interventions have advanced the possibility that the important things about multiculturalism can be retained whilst allowing us to develop more adequate theoretical and political platforms for cultural studies and sociology.

But at this point an unexpected, yet fundamental, twist in the tale reveals itself, because while there is an obvious link between radical *humanism* and radical *secularism*, radical secularism has been singled out as one of the largest obstacles to the further realization of multiculturalism (Parekh 2000: Ch. 10, Modood 2005: Ch. 7). This imagined connection between humanism and secularism is real enough. Many religious people are decent humanists, and all the main religions come in versions that can be interpreted as soft on humanism. But neither of these things holds, necessarily or uniformly, and anyway the great bulk of religious people regard their humanism as *derivative* rather than primary, since human dignity and equality do not come as stand-alone facts about the human condition, but only by way of *God's will*. For radical humanists, though, 'there are no supernatural or super-human beings to tell us how to live' (Norman 2004: 15), and so humanism is radically 'secular' just in so far as it requires a thoroughly *naturalistic* understanding of the state of the world, and a decidedly *this-worldly* vision of any egalitarian future. Quite obviously, humanists also argue that a secular polity is distinctly preferable to one governed by religious identities and theocratic aspirations.

Multiculturalists raise critical points that they think will be decisive against secularism, but some of these can quickly be agreed upon or discounted: that the origins of 'the secular' lie in the *Christian* tradition, that the organization and operation of modern secular states are never wholly *separate* from either their established religions or their otherwise 'biased' cultural formations, and that it is perfectly *legitimate* for religious people publicly to voice their *religious* reasons for adopting whatever *political* position they happen to hold. All that secular humanists require to do here is *deny* three things: that *all* meanings and uses of secularism are tainted by the term's origins (the 'genetic fallacy' would be committed otherwise), that the steady sacralization of political discussion and social identity are *progressive* developments, and that there should be institutional *equalization* of religious participation in politics and education rather than a reduction of *all* forms of special treatment for particular faiths. A further multicultural rejoinder then suggests itself: is not humanism itself a faith, just like the other faiths it seems intent on diminishing? But this argument is a contrivance. There are few grounds for any total *faith* in 'humanity' as such, if the lessons of history are anything to go by, and meanwhile what motivates the rejection of religious views of our human situation is simply the overwhelming balance of evidence and argument, not some primeval urge to replace one sort of religious belief by another – curiously non-religious – sort.

Parekh and Modood are particularly keen to drive a wedge between 'moderate' secularism, of which they approve, and 'radical' secularism, which is said to be rather extreme and 'ideological' (Modood 2005: 142). This characterization then permits the further connotative association between 'fundamentalisms' of different types, secularist on the one hand and Islamicist (for example) on the other. But this is a spurious equation, one that recalls opportunist tactics by liberal thinkers in the 1950s to delegitimize any challenge to their authority by simply tainting it with the 'ideological' label. Insofar as secular humanism is 'ideological', this just signals that secularists take their naturalism and humanism *seriously*, meaning that they would oppose non-secular opinions and actions that removed or questioned reasons for political engagement *other than* those of religious faith. And clearly, for secular humanists, democratic debate in the public sphere of democratic civil society is *an end in itself*: its virtue and worth are sanctioned by no external authority, nor serve any higher purpose. This is just what the ideas of secularism and humanism *mean*, and such meanings are only 'ideological' or 'extreme', in the sense that these are substantive and quite properly challenging ideas.

Nothing in those ideas, however, prevents radical humanists being 'pragmatic' and sensitive when it comes to religious people exercising their democratic right to put forward their own beliefs. Moreover, secular humanists are entirely capable of working hard to negotiate solutions between apparently opposed cultural values: indeed, it is hard to see how 'moderate' secularists could be in any *better* position to find workable solutions to cultural clashes than 'radical' secularists. We should note here that, contrary to the initial multiculturalist suggestion, moderate secularism is no less *ideological* than radical secularism, at least if it is to contain anything worth arguing about. For example, inculcating a deep public ethos of neutrality and tolerance between different identities, cultures, and values is no easy matter, and it involves the commitment to override intense conflict and special pleading when the terms of the multicultural polity itself comes under pressure.

Any robust form of multiculturalism, we should also perceive, is universalist in principle: whatever benefits multiculturalism is thought to bring are good things for *us*, for us *all*, qua human beings and global democrats, rather than as members of particular groups. Parekh, in particular, is awkwardly caught at times between the construal of humanistic reference points as part of the *trick* that Western monoculture has played on alternative cultures for its own ends, and an acceptance of those values as the very coinage of inter-cultural assessment. He does not quite face up to the fact that if multiculturalism is to engender a valuable and worthy deep culture – *its own* sense of 'community, solidarity, common loyalties, and a broad moral and political consensus' (Parekh 2000: 171) – then this could only happen at the *expense* of certain aspects of its component faiths and subcultures.

When Parekh defends the merits of religious worldviews, interestingly this is done in terms of the *generic* social and human benefits they can bring, that is to say, goods are *independently* valuable and not just as sanctioned by the sacred – a sense of civic and moral duty, the anti-egotism that goes with seeing the world as a large and mysterious realm, and the richness of religions as contributory to emancipatory social movements (Parekh 2000: 327–9). He soon concedes, rather damagingly, that religious creeds and powers can also just as easily *repress* as encourage each of these social goods. This is why, as Parekh fully accepts (2000: 332), multicultural religious *education* is what is needed in schools, not the teachings of the faiths as such. Again, what needs to be grasped here is that this is a *strictly* secularist position, even if it is conveyed with much apparent moderation.

Conclusion

By engaging in these important political and ethical debates, it might be thought that we have strayed a long way from questions of sociology and cultural studies. Nothing could be more mistaken. I have been trying throughout to defend the idea of sociology as an intellectual vantage point that can play a part in achieving progressive social and political change. In also arguing for a closer association between sociology and cultural studies, it is their shared heritage in holistic, explanatory and critical social understanding that I am underlining, even if considerable differences remain between them. This conception of the disciplines is grounded in radical humanist values, and its logic can hardly be other than secular in a broad sense. This necessarily brings the conjoint discourse of sociological cultural studies into conflict with versions of multiculturalism whose pivots are post-structuralist conceptions of subjectivity or post-secularist conceptions of political life.

7
Sociological Culturalism

If multiculturalism cannot provide a coherent intellectual or normative basis for sociological cultural studies, perhaps a culturalist approach to sociology that includes at least a significant element of multiculturalism can be developed? Over the past fifteen years or so, the 'new American cultural sociology' (Smith 1998) has emerged as a significant and confident intervention of this kind, designed to re-orientate sociology and cultural studies alike in quite fundamental ways. The sociological theorist Jeffrey Alexander stands at the centre of this development, and it is his works, especially those published in the current decade, that I want to examine in this chapter. The impressive scale and coherence of Alexander's project are indicated by the fact that it operates on four inter-connected levels of abstraction. The first of these provides a reading of postpositivism as the necessary philosophical backdrop for all social enquiry at the present time, and the second, couched within this frame, is his configuration of the project of cultural sociology. The third aspect is the embodiment of the theoretical platform in a series of substantive analyses, while the fourth features Alexander's thinking about the cultural politics of contemporary civil society, including multiculturalism.

Having indicated, in Chapter 1, what I think is skewed about Alexander's way of posing the first set of issues, I concentrate here on the other three dimensions. The theme I establish is that Alexander's long-term pursuit of theoretical 'multidimensionality' in social and cultural understanding is persistently dogged by an ultimately one-sided preference for *idealist* formulations and valuations. This tension characterized his earlier ventures in theoretical reconstruction (McLennan 1998), but in the new cultural sociology the awkward juxtaposition of idealist impulses with counteracting tendencies intensifies further. This not only brings into question his claims for general-level multidimensional synthesis, it also limits the critical purchase of his specific brand of cultural theory and progressive politics. My point, in short, is to block a path to sociological cultural studies that is based around the kind of residually *culturalist* way of comprehending the social that Alexander's project exemplifies.

For cultural sociology

In his centrepiece volume of 2003, *The Meanings of Social Life*, Alexander sharply differentiates the new cultural sociology from alternative 'sociology of culture' approaches. A definitive 'fault line', he argues, exists between these two competing understandings of cultural structures. Examples of the dis-preferred genre are Bourdieuian analysis, Birmingham cultural studies, and the Foucauldian 'governmentality' thematic. For Alexander, the primary task of cultural analysis is to interpret collective meanings by 'tracing the moral textures and delicate emotional pathways by which individuals and groups come to be influenced by them'. This is partly because 'it is such subjective and internal feelings that so often seem to rule the world'. These are particularly powerful today, because 'in our postmodern world, factual statements and fictional narratives are densely interwoven... Fantasy and reality are so hopelessly intertwined that we can separate them only in a post hoc way' (Alexander 2003: 5).

In this construction of debate, the 'single most important quality' of cultural sociology is the strong thesis that 'culture is autonomous'. In sociology of culture approaches, by contrast, culture is treated as a 'feeble and ambivalent variable' within a reified 'model' (2003: 6–7, 13). Of course, sociologists of culture and Birmingham cultural studies people may not *intend* to be inattentive to cultural specificity. But they do not accept that this specificity resides, precisely, in the *sui generis* quality of cultural intensities. Rather, they persist in the assumption that culture is to be understood as a matter of the 'reproduction of social relations' and its vehicles: 'self-interested ideologies, group processes, and networks' (2003: 13, 16).

Now we might be inclined to think that Alexander is railing against a straw person here. As I showed in Chapter 2, cultural studies has long since scattered in several post-Birmingham directions, both theoretically and politically, while sociology, for its part, has come to accept much of the force of the 'cultural turn'. Indeed, if there is a culprit needing to be exposed, it might be Alexander himself in a previous,

'neo-functionalist' incarnation (Alexander 1998a), given his persistence then with the Parsonian division between the social, cultural and
personality 'systems'. On the other hand, since that version of sociology of culture did not grant theoretical privilege to the *social* system
over the other two, it was hardly the kind of reductionist programme
that Alexander sees as the basic deficit of neo-Marxist or materialist
perspectives on culture. The question then becomes, how can those
still sympathetic to the latter modes of analysis respond to his new
challenge?

One response involves recapitulating debates about the 'relative
autonomy' of ideology and culture. In earlier exchanges with Althus-
serians and Gramscians, Paul Hirst (1979) made the Alexander-like assertion that the concept of relative autonomy was incoherent: autonomy
simply *means* the absence of extraneous determination. Ideologies must
therefore be engaged with as self-standing discursive forms, appraised
in terms of political rationality rather than those of epistemological
correction. Hirst's point was effective, but excessively formalistic. Just
because a dictionary tells us that autonomy means independence,
this hardly justifies social scientists regarding philosophical positions,
political platforms and cultural practices as cognitively and ideologically *separate from* the class positions, social locations and group
characteristics of their advocates and audiences. In any case, as John
Thompson subsequently (1990: 85–96) noted, the relative autonomy
debate tended to result in stalemate rather than resolution. On one side,
the assertion of autonomy is denounced as idealism, on the other, the
assertion of relativity is condemned as reductionism. Even so, 'impasse'
is a better way of condensing this perennial issue than settling for
'autonomism', because the idea that cultural appreciation must be altogether detached from considerations on the 'reproduction of social relations' remains less convincing than the assumption of their (complex)
connectedness.

Second, the reference in Alexander's argument to contemporary
society is ineffective. One part of the problem concerns his view that
because feelings – 'massive ones' (2003: 3) – appear to 'rule the world',
we need to give those feelings the powerful independent status they are
obviously due. But this conclusion does not follow from the premise:
it is precisely *because* massive feelings appear to rule the world that
critical social observers must try to gain some interpretative distance
from them, putting that 'obvious' symbolic power into wider socio-
historical perspective. The other note of contemporary urgency involved
Alexander drawing attention to the dense interweaving of fantasy and

reality in postmodern times. But here too there is a non-sequitur: complex interweaving is not the same thing as wholesale identity or utter inseparability, so distinctions can legitimately be made, even if judgement comes – necessarily – 'post hoc'. In any case, if fantasy and reality *are* to be regarded as 'utterly inseparable', then there would be good reason to think that what holds now holds for past societies too.

The third counter to Alexander's tendential idealism at the general level is to note how strongly, outside the headlines, he qualifies the main drift of his thinking on culture. Alexander states, for example, that 'wider social contexts are not by any means necessarily ignored'; rather they are 'every bit as important' as in sociology of culture approaches (2003: 26). But Alexander is shooting himself in the foot here: if the material context of meaning-making were *every bit* as important for him, then his foundational ranking simply falls apart. More specific considerations show Alexander to be quite cautious about the merits of 'autonomous' methods of cultural analysis. In particular, the Geertzian notion of 'thick description', lauded one minute as that 'moment where the social text is reconstructed in its pure form' (2003: 16), comes into question soon after. Thick description, on reflection, 'seems rather elusive', because we are often left with a situation in which 'the local explains the local', producing a merely 'novelistic recapitulation of details', in which the task of 'explanation' is abandoned (2003: 22).

Alexander enters another important rider: in Geertzian reportage, the 'precise mechanisms through which webs of meaning influence action are rarely specified with any clarity' (2003: 22). And the corrective is 'to anchor causality in proximate actors and agencies, specifying in detail just how culture interferes with and directs what really happens' (2003: 14). These references to 'causality' and 'what really happens' are entirely salutary, but they inevitably reflect some kind of realist and externalist frame of reference, not an internalist or 'textualist' one. The upshot is that Alexander faces a major dilemma: either he has to back down from his strident advocacy of Diltheyan cultural hermeneutics, and accept, in Weberian vein, a more pragmatic approach to the use of a range of investigative resources and ideal types, or he faces the charge of outright contradictoriness.

Substantive applications: Watergate and computers

If Dilthey is Alexander's inspiration for asserting the methodological primacy of culture, the intermediate schema that helps put sociological flesh on the bones of general hermeneutics is of Durkheimian derivation: 'culture should be conceived as a system of symbolic codes which specify the good and the evil' (Alexander and Smith 1993: 196). Equated without further ado with the related, but possibly different, sacred/profane and pure/polluted dualisms, Alexander's writing on the good/evil polarity is partly theoretical and partly applied. In the former mode (Alexander 2003: Ch. 4), the proposition is that when dealing with powerful, apparently 'natural' phenomena like evil, we need a strong dose of social constructionism to see what is going on. In particular, we need to examine the codings and iterations of what stands for 'goodness' and its necessary symbolic counterpart, 'evility'. Alexander writes,

> The line dividing the sacred from the profane must be drawn and re-drawn time and time again . . . through such phenomena as scandals, moral panics, public punishments, and wars, societies provide occasions to re-experience and recrystallize the enemies of the good (Alexander 2003: 115).

Although he returns to such points many times, the status of the discussion is rather elementary, lacking a distinctive purchase. After all, without some kind of basic social constructionist moment, in which 'natural' phenomena are repositioned as, to varying degrees, discursive and social products, social science does not get off the ground.

Things get more interesting when the preferred tropes are put to use. In one keynote module, Alexander (2003: Ch. 6) offers a sustained account of the character of the Watergate episode of 1972–74. He emphasizes the qualitative leap made in the general American consciousness of this 'event' from the time when the facts of the Watergate break-in surfaced to the phase of widespread agreement that the very values and practices of the 'centre' of American political culture had been profoundly contaminated, requiring the drastic reassertion and reconstitution of fundamental standards. For Alexander, the facts of the matter, broadly speaking, altered little across these two wholly different evaluative phases. Initially, there was a perception that Watergate-like machinations were 'just politics', examples of how the pursuit of the reasonable goals of official politics could sometimes go wrong. Some local rectification and punishment, of course, might well be the answer at this level. But as the heightened cycle of 'revelation' took hold, a Parsonian process of 'generalization' occurred, in which the normally separate normative-organizational strata of policies, goals, norms and societal values became thoroughly fused, explosively reconfiguring the Watergate events as 'fundamental violations' of the social and moral fabric. In this process of generalization, the relevant judgemental public is greatly extended beyond the circles of the political class to encompass the populace as a whole, achieved through 'the deepest ritualization of political life' (2003: 156–7).

This sea-change in the public mood and the conditions for ritualization were secured partly through a series of elite and 'counter-centre' mobilizations, labelling exercises, and alterations in the visibility of different kinds of institutional settings and controls. That much was predictable, no doubt, from conventional instrumental sociological tenets. But successful institutional resolutions in this kind of affair are far from guaranteed. For the social and political divisions inherited from the 1960s that carried through into the Nixon administration to express a full-throated cross-party consensus and a supreme concern for re-establishing high-minded 'Americanism', it is the quality and realization of collective moral sentiment and effervescence that must be fully appreciated. The Senate hearings of the summer of 1972, especially, were crucial in transforming the entire significance of the scandal. Once the battle over whether these hearings should be televised at all had been won, the nation's soul was laid bare in a perfectly 'liminal' experience, the courtroom constituting a world unto itself, partaking of the transcendental. 'Luminescent values' were in play and the sanctification and demonization of persons reached truly 'mythical' levels (2003: 162–6). Their very names, like 'Watergate' itself, took on intrinsically pure or polluted connotations.

Further instalments of liminality and sacralization were needed, though, to sustain this heightened register. Only with his dismissal of special prosecutor Archibald Cox, and with the 'transcript convulsion' that followed the release of the tapes of his thuggish private mediation of the cover-up operation, was Nixon himself placed decisively on the polluted/evil side of the moral drama. Then, the impeachment proceedings themselves: a most 'solemn and formalized' ritual, in which everything was polarized according to its coincidence with, or deviation from, the virtual unimpeachable image of the nation and its core values, now polluted beyond any sort of pragmatic, strategic or humanistic apology for the miscreant deeds and perpetrators. For Alexander, no merely 'functional' explanation can be adequate to this rampage of effervescence, and whilst, inevitably, post-Watergate politics had to revert to 'post-symbolic' atmospherics, the profound impact of the experience was to be felt in a series of institutional reforms and 'little Watergates' – up to and including the Iran–Contra scandal of the Reagan years, and of course, subsequently, Clinton's own 'Monicagate'.

This somewhat free rendering of Alexander's reconstruction of Watergate should indicate its drive and detail. It represents the best exemplar of the new cultural sociology at work, and raises an interesting issue about how to even go about assessing its value. Unlike exercises in 'pure theory', suggestive capsules of cultural sociology like this cannot be turned into propositional statements and decisively confirmed or refuted. As I suggested in Chapter 3, no one would think of doing this with Simmel's account of the experience of the Metropolis, for example. Rather, descriptive-theoretical reconstruction, unlike explanatory reasoning, is 'taken on board' and found more or less illuminating. There is, no doubt, plenty to take issue with in Alexander's account, for example his characterization of the polarization of American society in the 1960s and 1970s, and his excessive investment in the rather limited opinion poll data that he thinks give hard-edged support to his sense of the scale and swiftness of change in the societal consciousness (2003: 156). Certainly, too, Alexander's notion that the 'facts' of Watergate changed little throughout the episode needs to be pursued further. Kuhn-like, Alexander describes a veritable 'gestalt switch', such that the emphasis is all on the change in public *perception*. But whether in science or in social apprehension, sober gains in knowledge and assessment do reconstruct the relevant 'facticity' too, without the status of the facts thereby becoming simply an *attribution* of the (altered) apprehending mind-set. In that sense, subsequent to the hearings and debates, it would have been mistaken, not optional, to convey the initial Watergate 'events' in terms of a mere 'break in'.

Such reservations can be left to one side, however, because Alexander's Watergate exploration does reveal the interest and traction of the new cultural sociology. This is possibly because the case in point is 'exceptional', and the Durkheimian sacred/profane schema, arguably, comes fully into its own in such profound moments of cultural crisis. The new American sociologists might dispute this, holding that it is equally applicable to more *mundane* things and events. Here is where my second illustration of Alexander's investigative practice is relevant, for his account of the cultural significance of *information technology* (2003: Ch. 7) seems intended to demonstrate just such effectivity. However, this module strikes me as much less successful.

Within the conventional sociology-of-culture mindset, Alexander maintains, computer technology constitutes a quintessential expression of instrumental rationality, inviting its analytical placement within a disenchanted world of systemic and material forces. Marx, Weber and Habermas can all be seen to invest in this thematic. But, far from driving

meaning and values out of the social and cultural systems, new technology is coded in much contemporary experience as magical, awesome
and sacred. For example, there is a new priesthood of computer nerds
and literary cyber-gurus; cult Internet sites and new media superstars;
computer-centred compulsiveness and creativity; new aesthetic sensibilities and fluid constructions of virtual selfhood. Actually, I am extra-
polating a little here: Alexander does not furnish us with a huge number
of such unequivocal reference points. Clearly, though, there is a good
deal here that rings true. And we can see the purchase of his emphasis
on the *cathartic* work done by the new symbolism: relentless high-tech
innovation is simultaneously fantastically powerful and beneficial, and
yet also monstrous and destructive.

Still, the primarily semiotic register that frames this analysis carries
some penalties. For one thing, the account remains by turns impressionistic and doxic rather than rich in either an empirical or a textual-
critical sense. Relatedly, the constant reference to the sacred/profane
binary is excessively Manichean, and becomes simply wearying. To
counteract this singularity and formalism, we might point to the results
of an extensive UK research programme examining the rhetoric and
reality of 'virtual society' (Woolgar 2002). The broad findings of this
programme are that the 'cyberbole' around the new magical world of
electronic discourse and refashioned virtual selfhood needs to be thoroughly *deflated*. People's uses and conceptions of new technology and
its transformative possibilities are predominantly local and practical,
heterogeneous, subculturally specific and socially stratified. Our own
experience as academic users should also tell us something about the
frustrations and the hokum of the new machinic spirit, and about how,
for every indication of the effervescent mindspace of high-tech passion,
there is an instance of failure, crash, commodification, disappointment
and waste.

Traumatic revelations

Alexander's attachment to the idea of 'cultural trauma' post-dates the
previous forms of analysis, and adds depth to the workings of his
basic tools of analysis. Attributions of good and evil, after all, are not
static – they go through cycles of iteration and adaptation as groups and
societies face challenges to their practices and identities. When social
instability becomes deep *cultural* turbulence, Alexander argues, we are
in the territory of cultural trauma. This has its mundane side, because
experiences of fundamental challenge and recovery often take time, and

are related to the ebbs and flows of collective memory, which might be piecemeal. Nevertheless, whether spectacular and sudden, or routine and drawn out, cultural trauma involves the societal enactment of sentiments of horror and alienation, reconciliation and redemption. Analysis along these lines needs to be discursively and psychically focused, not only because of the general tenets of the version of cultural sociology being defended, but because trauma can only be resolved 'by setting things right in the self' as well as 'setting things right in the world' (2004a: 5). At the same time, cultural trauma is constructed and negotiated through the *claims of injury and reparation* that are made by particular groups, through particular institutional means, and in relation to specific audience responses. Bearing in mind our earlier theoretical remarks, these represent the crucial causal and processual 'mechanisms' in virtue of which the societal-scale traumatic episodes can be held to pertain at all.

Alexander's most sustained instance of this paradigm looks at the way in which the Holocaust took a considerable time to emerge in its full traumatic status (Alexander 2003: Ch. 2, 2004b). He maintains that two competing discursive constructions of the Holocaust have been at work, one that plays down and one that points up its utter specialness as a permanent warning of social evil to humanity as a whole. At the time of the liberation of the camps, Alexander recounts, the predominant narrative was to emphasize the victory of freedom and progress. The characterization of Hitler and Nazism as representative of particularly appalling politics and personality had already been in place for a while, and for everyone, including the Jews, the sense of awfulness was already near saturation point. In this context, political and military elites thought it better to emphasize the positive role of the liberating troops, the bright future of Israel, and the camps' image as slave labour corrals rather than machines of genocide. In that way, a sense of typicality, not uniqueness, initially prevailed, and the distinctiveness of specific collective victimhood was minimized.

Steadily, of course, the Holocaust got separated out from even the direst other elements of its Nazi and War context, becoming endowed with truly primordial status as *the* locus, for all time and for all peoples, of our absolute responsibility for human good and evil. In the west, accordingly, collective and individual memories were unlocked, traumatic experiences rediscovered, public debates and memorials staged, and politics itself re-cast, in terms of this second narrative. Originally lacking widespread audience conditions for its relentlessly sombre message, the discursive and social conditions and the politics of claims-making became such that this gradually became the only possible construction of the events and their significance.

A number of issues about the 'trauma' paradigm can now be raised, other than noting, as we should, its stimulating and bold qualities. One issue is obvious enough: when socio-cultural theorists go into this vein of historical reconstruction, the question of empirical evidence and coherence is vital. What Alexander says about the competing narratives, the motivations behind them and 'audience' receptivity must therefore undergo proper scrutiny at that specialist level. However, a second point involves questioning the status and content of the model itself. Is the 'trauma' analysis supposed to be the *only*, or even the *main* way in which cultural sociology is to be conducted? There is, after all, something rather monolithic and unqualified in the terminology adopted, especially when it has such a transcendentally vicious 'case' at its apex. Are there not innumerable 'cases' of trauma that are more suited to treatment in terms of, say, 'unsettledness' or 'distraction'? And just to pose the issue of degrees of trauma, and the various terms we might concoct for them, highlights how *psychologistic* this metanarrative is. Psychologism inevitably opens up endless alternative constructions of the motivation and condition of the specified collective agent: socio-cultural envy, lack of self-esteem, Oedipality, aggressiveness, disappointment and so on. Even to be couching the significant history of a group or people or nation as that of a protagonist or 'self' in the first place, all kitted out with the personality tensions of a *person*, is a risky business, and arguably a 'pre-sociological' one.

Third, as before in our general theoretical critique, there is a sense in which the focus on mediating mechanisms *undercuts* the favoured culturalism of the general trauma scenario. Once you start looking at the social composition of claims-makers, their institutional locations and interests, and the complex, often malleable and indeterminate aspects of audience 'responses' to those claims, it becomes difficult to sustain any hugely 'effervescent' or univocal expression of the collective state of being. To take just one possible extension of the paradigm, it is plausible, at first sight, to think of *Scottish* culture and politics in Alexander's traumatic terms. Under that aspect, you could see the last three hundred years of English domination as the story of cultural trauma, only accepted as such late in the day, thanks to the dogged cultural work of various claims-makers. You could then conclude that having pragmatically 'forgotten' itself through large chunks of its modern history, cultural politics in Scotland subsequently released its repressed collective memory of the foundational 'traumatic' event (the Act of Union of 1707), proceeding, eventually, to redeem its better, long-repressed self through the establishment of the new Scottish Parliament of 1999.

However, this is a *protagonist's* story, and a specifically *nationalist* story at that, rather than a sociological story. It is told in psychodynamic terms as the reassemblage of a unified subject-position, an *a priori* collective 'we'. Yet, even sociologists and others who are supportive of Scottish devolution or independence have worked hard to rid history and politics of such an undifferentiated and quasi-romantic style of thinking. Moreover, to hark back to an earlier objection, such a storyline cannot be responsibly conducted in the *absence* of characterizations and observations about the nature of the Scottish economy and class formation, the structure of group life, and the competing interests and power relations among the different protagonists. It may be, of course, that Alexander just wants to offer the cultural sociology of trauma as a 'heuristic', something to be exemplified or discounted case by case. But why should this be the *first* analytical resource that we turn to? For all the enhanced emphasis upon episodic sensibilities, one suspects here that there is still a remnant of a kind of 'general law' sociology at work: particularities are important only as instances of a general social form, in this case the traumatic experience.

The final difficulty with Alexander's articulation of trauma theory relates to his new-found normative voice. This is an issue because when one takes up any rigorously social constructionist position, it is hard to break back into first-order substantive moral or sociological positions. Constructionism starts by bracketing off naturalism in all areas except perhaps as a minimum species characterization – for example, 'human beings are storytelling animals' (Alexander 2004b: 262). In that case, the most suitable subjectivity for the observing analyst is one of sensitive irony: we see how much particular stories mean to those concerned, but it is not appropriate to decide which are more solidly rooted in the social facts as such. This premise of narratological neutrality is at work in Alexander's account of the rival Holocaust constructions, for example – that is, until its later stages. At that point, as if from nowhere, Alexander launches into an impassioned plea that the stronger, tragic reading of the Holocaust, should prompt us all, across all four corners of our global world, to 'learn to share the experiences of one another's traumas and to take vicarious responsibility for the other's afflictions' (2004b: 262). The point here is not to directly engage with these humanistic, therapeutic portrayals of our moral situation, but simply to note that they do not particularly follow from, nor even sit comfortably with, the social constructionism which grounds the analysis in the first place.

The immanent utopia of civil society

How are the irreducible symbolic valuations that characterize modern social forces to be negotiated and institutionalized in a progressive way? Alexander's reworking of the concept of *civil society* and his advocacy, within this understanding, of *multiculturalism* address this question. Alexander argues against two common versions of the civil society concept. One stems from European Enlightenment discussions of the upside of commercial society, in which all manner of public and private association are orientated around the cultivation of polite, disciplined, responsible interaction between groups and persons. The second, the historical rejoinder to the first, conceives of civil society – part private realm, part public sphere – as dominated by the logic of the capitalist market and self-interest. The modern state, for its part, is necessarily involved in securing the conditions of existence of the competitive, capitalistic private sphere.

Unsurprisingly, Alexander counters these competing concepts of civil society with a third that emphasizes its *separation* as a social sphere from both market and state. Ideal-typically, civil society is to be depicted as the site where democratic public opinion and community solidarity are constructed out of the interaction of various sectional interests and narratives. Civil society is buffeted on all sides by 'anti-civil' forces that exist exterior to it: the personalized loyalties of the family, the acquisitive and competitive ethos of capitalist economics, the anti-egalitarian impulses of patriarchy, ethno-racial primordialism. But in spite of these 'crippling' pressures, the public civil sphere of modern societies requires genuine commitment to 'equality, solidarity and respect', forces that converge in a sufficiently potent symbolic regime to push back 'destructive intrusions' and thereby carry out 'civil repairs' (Alexander 1998b: 7–8, 2001b: 240–2).

Alexander anticipates the protest that is likely to arise at this point, namely that there is something rather *utopian* and unreal about all this. On the one hand, he insists on its solid basis in current, mainstream, American reality (Smelser and Alexander 1999). Far from being a hopelessly unfulfilled ideal, pluralism and inclusive democracy in the USA have been largely *successful* in ameliorating the social conditions of, and granting full recognition to, previously marginalized people and subcultures. For radicals to continue to complain, against the evidence, that contemporary democratic civil society is intrinsically *incapable* of working towards progressive change amounts to whingeing negativity for its own sake.

As for utopianism, the whole issue needs to be re-thought (Alexander 2001a). For the Left, 'critical theory' is an honorific tag that only ever seems to be bestowed upon the kind of totalizing critique that points in the direction of wholesale social transformation, completely new ways of being in society. But these are dangerous constructions, disrespectful negations of many of the things that real people in actual societies have endowed with effort and value. Instead of experiencing the 'inspiring and disciplining tension' between the 'is' and the 'ought', all the emphasis amongst Leftist utopians is on the latter. They even seem to think that the more radically 'other' the 'ought' is, the better (2001a: 581). And if anyone dares to question this appeal to total otherness, they are greeted, for example by Russell Jacoby (1999), with yet another bout of sentimental lamentation, this time about the decline of utopian thinking itself.

For Alexander, by contrast, critical thinking is an 'actually existing' practice of utopia, since every aspiration to greater levels of equality and respect within civil society implies consciousness of a better ordering of identities and relations. Utopia is thus implicit in every particularist-group claim that is couched in the languages of inclusion, justice, or aspiration. Even theoretical constructions – from Plato's republic to Rawls's 'original position', Habermas's 'ideal speech situation', and 'post-modernity' – provide utopian glimpses in relation to the present. Importantly, however, these sphere-specific openings do not result in a holistic institutional and cultural template for change. The new vision is rather one of 'self-limiting civil utopia', a 'robust' and 'mundane' conception of pluralistic coexistence and mutual understanding.

There is much to agree with in Alexander's thinking about civil society. In fact, although he unfairly caricatures and stigmatizes the Left's credentials on these matters, the broad tenor of his claim that civil society has the potential to counteract the worst ravages of capitalism and other 'non-civil' social forces has been the staple diet of neo- and post-Marxist discourse since the mid-1970s. The theoretical note that Alexander strikes so as to avoid any easy convergence is a familiar one: that neo-Marxists *reduce* the autonomy of the sphere of civil society to that of the workings of the socio-economic realm. But the matter of *degree* of explanatory and evaluative priority cannot properly be embraced in a one-line flourish of this sort. Take the question of 'genetic' explanation in science and society, for example. Counting genetic make-up as a relevant causal factor cannot be boiled down to a straightforward reductionism-autonomism choice, either at the theoretical or the moral level. There are politico-scientific reductionists, no doubt, for whom social and cultural phenomena are entirely a matter of individuals' genetic predispositions. But others legitimately qualify this: genetic endowments and configurations may play some kind of significant constraining role, but not a determining one. Others again might hold that the balance of determination and autonomy may not be open to formulaic general expression, but instead varies contingently. Now, why should the complexity and variation of the relationship between 'civil society' and its capitalist socio-economic context be treated in a radically different way – especially since Alexander accepts that the different social spheres are separate only 'analytically', so that civil society's autonomy can only be 'relative', because it is 'dependent' on the other spheres for 'inputs and resources' (Alexander 1998c: 97)?

The difficulty is, however, that in Alexander, partly because of his obsession with (avoiding) reductionism, capitalism and civil society are envisaged more in the way of *dual systems* than as parts of a complex interwoven matrix. Rather like Habermas's posited relationship between 'system' and 'lifeworld', Alexander's two ideal-types thrust and parry at one another, engaged as they are in 'boundary maintenance' and 'destructive intrusions'. And as in Parsons, what fundamentally drives civil society as a system-type is the attachment of its posited subjects to core *values*, whereas the state and economy take their place in the societal pattern according to the (different) rationalities by which *they* are governed – respectively, Darwinian-adaptive and instrumental rationality. Such a mode of theorizing remains today, as it was in the heyday of functionalism, suggestive but mechanical, systemic but undialectical, comprehensive but lacking in historical density. There is no sustained effort to ascertain causal primacy or social hierarchies within the matrix, and this is partly because, underneath, the pursuit of core values is given decisive normative and analytical priority.

Turning now to Alexander's comments on utopia and utopianism, again, some firm common ground opens up. For many years, on the Left the concept of utopia has been actively debated. If its credibility and popularity are now waning to the point, indeed, where the idea has become rather 'elusive' (Levitas 2003), this is due as much to internal complexity as to external critique. Utopian commentators have thus been intensely aware of movement and pluralization in the very understanding of utopia: from 'content' to 'process', from blueprint to desire, and from a heralding of total transformation to critical heuristic in the present. Things get additionally interesting here, for it then has to be ascertained whether 'critique' as such, however radical and 'utopistic' (Wallerstein 1999b), represents a legitimate *broadening out* of utopian thinking, or instead represents a signal *retreat* from it (Levitas 2000: 26). Taking the latter stance seems to be the stronger intellectual option, for there can be little doubt that including the 'utopian realism' of Anthony Giddens (1990: 154–8), or the (pragmatic) 'romantic utopianism' of Richard Rorty (1998), thins the concept out beyond the bounds of coherent integrity. And yet: when someone like Fredric Jameson (2004) disqualifies programmatic utopianism because we can no longer feasibly contemplate the *annulment* of our current personalities and situatedness; or when someone like Zygmunt Bauman (2003) is prepared to accept fleeting moments of happiness in the present as the only remnant of utopia today, the demise of the concept, rather than its modification and pluralization, seems at hand.

In this context, Alexander's notion that utopia is immanent within existing social practices of many different sorts is challenging. He suggests that a wide range of social movements involve critiquing the present order with a view to substantial reform, and a qualitative upgrading of the delivery of civil society values – equality, trust, and respect. But why does Alexander call such critical thinking *utopian* as such, rather than honourable liberal reformism? Indeed, what does Alexander mean, exactly, when he states that 'adversarial social thought is inspired by utopian reference' (2001a: 580)? By itself, adversarialism – whether exemplified in court, on the picket lines, or through claims for equal treatment against specific rights-deniers – can hardly be considered utopian or transformative, though it will surely involve being critical. Much depends, of course, on the way in which *particularistic* claims relate to *universal* aspirations, as Alexander readily accepts. But very often, and understandably, particularistic cultural claims are *not* presented in relation to universality; they are stand-alone demands about *we, this group*. And this need bear no necessary relation to the question of a principled desirable future for everyone.

Alexander's case for immanent utopianism takes it as read that the connotations of transformation and universalism in the idea of utopia have to be abandoned. But even if 'blueprint' utopianism has had its day, Jameson (2004) puts forward a plausible intermediate proposal in its place: even if utopia in the sense of a totally alternative organization of human life is to be demoted or rejected, radical critics of society should be able to specify some fundamental and substantive aspect of collective possibility that is *currently absent*, the achievement of which would require massive transformative, cross-sectional effort. Taking his cue from Adorno's stipulation in this mould – that no one should go hungry – he adds his own candidate: that there should be global full employment. No realistic vision of contemporary capitalism, Jameson argues, could accommodate this demand, which thus turns out to be remarkably revolutionary without being other-worldly in the slightest. Whether or not this particular framing of 'utopian' aspiration could command widespread agreement, the point is that Alexander has no equivalent touchstone. Meanwhile, the characterization of various expressions of particularistic adversarialism as immanently utopian stretches the basic nomenclature beyond useful limits.

Pure multiculturalism

For Alexander, the agenda for cultural politics that best approaches the recommended utopian scenario, that is to say, an actually-existing and 'stitched together' (2001a: 586) one – is *multiculturalism*. Multiculturalism as he reads it is to be distinguished from two similar-sounding but defective alternative conceptions of societal 'integration'. The first of these rivals is 'assimilation', according to which out-groups enter civil life 'by shedding their polluted primordial identities' (2001b: 243). But it is wrong, Alexander maintains, that persons are honoured in the civic sphere only by effectively ridding them of many of the *concrete cultural attributes* that make them what they are. Assimilationism, furthermore, is 'culture blind' when it comes to the specificities of the in-group itself, which are taken for granted as 'universal'. In the second scenario, integration as 'hyphenation', out-groups are encouraged to sustain their specific cultural markers, but these are legitimated in and through their *relationship* with certain core values (African–American, British Muslim, and so on). In this model, *persons* are 'purified' and included, but *qualities* are only, at best, half-recognized.

Multiculturalism is supposed to improve radically on these modes by 'purifying' both persons *and* qualities. The forms of cultural identity (being a woman, black, disabled, Muslim etc) become 'variants on civil and utopian themes', to be valued in themselves. Of course, differences and conflicts continue to exist, but in the democratic civil sphere so constituted, the goal is genuine understanding and not merely pragmatic acceptance, so that 'notions of particularity and universality become much more thoroughly intertwined' (2001b: 246). Thus, 'noncore primordialities . . . are folded into the culture of authenticity' and more and more 'outsider' qualities 'begin to be embraced by core group members themselves' (2001b: 247). Once again, Alexander accepts that the three forms of integration are 'ideal types' and that in reality they blend into one another. But still, multiculturalism is to be seen as having a distinctive logic and pull, organized as it is around 'inclusion and solidarity' rather than 'separation and difference' (2001b: 248). As such, it represents the best current expression of the 'utopian promise of civil society' as it exists in 'real history' (2001b: 241).

Once again, it can be agreed that what Alexander is sketching here represents a positive approach to democratic pluralist politics. We can also agree that assimilationism is a deeply conservative alternative. Moreover, even though we should strenuously question Alexander's *a priori* equation of civil society with the 'authentic' realm of 'inclusion and solidarity', we might nevertheless accept that this has normative appeal and critical leverage. But the proposition that *multiculturalism* is the right label for the nearest feasible approximation to the realization of ideal civil society values is a different matter. For one thing, and uncharacteristically, Alexander does not venture into any vigorous conceptual exercise concerning the possible definitions and varieties of multiculturalism, except to assert the fact of its categorical difference from hyphenation and assimilation in his construction. This is a pivotal matter, because as we saw in Chapter 6, some 'classic' issues are by now well-rehearsed in the various 'multiculturalism' literatures. Are the component cultures of the multicultural spectrum, for example, to be conceived in a 'primordial', essentialist fashion, or as 'socially constructed'? Are multicultural identities to be regarded as preeminently *ethno-cultural* in character, or will any ascribed or elected principle of group membership suffice from national identification to micro-level subcultural affiliation? How 'saturated' are we to understand the participating *selves* to be by the cultural community within which they are set? Can identities be overlapping and multiple, porous and changeable? Must primary cultural identifications reveal some kind of *long-term* unity and resilience if they are to act as the kind of social bond between the particular and universal, or do we take every perceived identity claim at current *face value*? No robust conception of multiculturalism can get going at all without these issues being taken up in some detail: but such a discussion is absent in Alexander's presentation.

In any case, here I would wish to reiterate my sense that there is a profound *paradox* at the heart of the very idea of multiculturalism. On the one hand, cultural identities and loyalties have to exhibit considerable depth and distinctiveness if they are to earn recognition and representation in the democractic civil sphere, and for the polity and ethos of the latter to be reorganized around them. Yet, on the other hand, people brought up within, and motivated to advocate for, just that kind of deep particularity will be entirely sceptical about, if not hostile to, multiculturalism *itself* in any strong normative sense. This is because the latter involves commitment to the idea that all deep cultures are of roughly equal worth and as such require protection and advancement, an 'even handedness' that participant cultures would not endorse, at least from within the perspective of their own norms and practices.

So multiculturalism itself can only become deep and distinctive when it works *against*, not *for*, strong expressions of cultural difference and distinctiveness. It is thus theoretically logical and politically reasonable to think that once 'folded into' the general civil society discourse, 'primordial' particularities would *not* thereafter have to be embraced, as Alexander implies it would, in full and without considerable dilution. But at that point, we would seem to be back with 'hyphenation' as the main game currently in town, supplemented by a future conceived firmly in terms of greater neo-humanist universalism, whether this is couched in terms of cosmopolitan democracy, or deep democratic citizenship, or even socialism. Interestingly, in one of his best and most reproduced essays, Alexander states that 'it is wise to acknowledge that it is a renewed sense of involvement in the project of universalism rather than some limpid sense of its concrete forms that marks the character of the new age in which we live' (Alexander 2003: 228). But in speaking up for the kind of multiculturalism that requires the determined demotion of that project, he has rather failed to heed his own advice. In doing so, he has also increasingly lost some of his sociological, multidimensional bearings. As Seyla Benhabib (1999) points out in her contribution to a volume edited by Alexander, if some of the difficult political dilemmas around multiculturalism are to be resolved, we need to evince greater 'sociological scepticism' about all manner of group-differentiated rights and identities claims, and to re-connect issues of cultural recognition with questions of material and social (re)distribution. Alexander may still have a point: that exercises in sociological scepticism fall far short of the moral and cultural *envisioning* that public intellectuals must aspire to. But even if this is right enough, this does not make sociological materialism any less *necessary* in understanding the contemporary matrix of cultural and political motivation.

Conclusion

In the new American cultural sociology, Alexander has developed an ambitious, multi-levelled, and politically challenging project. And he has been impressively traversing the hard-earned path from academic scholar to public intellectual, with useful things to say about a number of vital contemporary matters. Nevertheless, I have been arguing that in each sector of his theoretical and normative argumentation, there are definite problems and deficits. In particular, I hope to have shown that Alexander does not convincingly establish the crucial fault line that is supposed to separate his preferred framework of cultural sociology from the allegedly superseded 'sociology of culture'; that the substantive practice of the new cultural sociology is excessively binaristic and psychologistic in register; and that Alexander's arguments about contemporary politics and civil society involve both an implausible 'practical utopianism' and a naive multiculturalism. Overall, Alexander's tendentially 'idealist' inclinations continually stall his otherwise commendable aspiration to multidimensional social theory. Terry Eagleton has observed, ironically, that many formally anti-foundationalist cultural theorists have gone on to endorse nothing less than a *new* foundationalism, one that privileges 'culture, rather than God or Nation' – or, we might add, 'society' – as the essentialist basis for all social analysis (Eagleton 2003: 58). The purpose of this chapter has been to include Alexander in the ranks of such theorists. And I want to draw from this engagement a message that transfers to a number of strands of thought within cultural studies and cultural sociology alike: the problem is *not* the importance of culture, but rather the elevation of 'Culture' to a near-sacred interpretative status.

8
The Turn to Complexity

In the final two chapters, I return to some of the central 'methodo-logical' issues that bestride contemporary discussion about the nature of the human sciences. The notions of complexity and reflexivity are especially pivotal and omnipresent in that regard, and how we under-stand and prescribe these desiderata significantly affects the prospects of a more integrated cultural studies and sociology. Ever since Comte envisaged sociology as the culmination of all scientific endeavour, and ever since Durkheim's resounding instruction that social facts be treated as things, sociology has had trouble convincing sceptical onlookers that it is not essentially positivistic or mechanically reductive in character. Cultural studies has had to face charges of reductionism and mechan-icism too, but only at those times when cultural studies has seemed at its most sociologistic. Post-Birmingham, the job of social understanding has been assumed to require emphasizing rather than minimizing the elements of contingency and indeterminacy in social and cultural life. Whether justly attributed or not, the persistent feeling is that sociology is unreceptive to these aspects of cultural existence, and that the onus is thus specifically on sociology, and not its successor discourses, to shake off its ambitions to achieve simplicity and reduction, so that it can finally make the 'turn to complexity' that others have already taken.

In this chapter, I develop some considerations on the way that complexity theory is being 'taken on board' in social theory today, and to consider the ways in which complexity theory allows us to re-think the 'rules of sociological method'. I do this by examining the way in which John Urry in particular has sought to re-orientate sociology around complexity. A leading sociologist whose work on 'disorganized capitalism' and 'economies of sign and space' has been widely taken up in cultural studies, Urry's sense of the imperative of complexity presents one of the most productive theoretical openings for inter- and trans-disciplinary thinking, the methodological horizon within which the two traditions can best coalesce. In fact, it is just because I support this latter prospect that I seek to temper aspects of Urry's enthusiasm for complexity theory, because the last thing we need is for complexity jargon to be taken up for interdisciplinary purposes in the form of a craze, or as a sign of nothing more than one's possession of the right kind of symbolic capital. The idea behind this chapter, then, is that you do not have to 'talk complexity' to be properly engaged in complex matters. In the first section of the chapter, I introduce the imperative of complexity, Urry style, especially in relation to his understanding of the fluid global context within which we are all nowadays situated. In the next part, I pick out four complications of a more general sort that arise in considering complexity theory as the latest manual for theoretical revolution in the social disciplines, and I go on to identify three dangers that can be witnessed in exemplifications of complexity theory in social scientific writing. Two overall conclusions emerge with some force: that sociology is not as deeply threatened by complexity discourse as is often imagined, and that we need to be very careful not to fall into a kind of hype around complexity. This is because 'complexity' itself is too complex, or at least too abstract, to underwrite any particular strategy or style of enquiry.

Complexity rules?

How might the 'rules of sociological method' be brought into alignment with the turn to complexity? John Urry (2000a,b, 2003, 2005) has been particularly exercised in this task, and his case for complexity opens with the proposal that two of sociology's core concepts since the time of Durkheim – 'society' and 'the social' – must be jettisoned. These ideas, he maintains, prevent sociology becoming decisively more flexible in its explanatory modality, something it has to do if it wants to comprehend the new forms and foci of social life in the global age, namely mobilities, flows, scapes, and networks.

The first aspect of Urry's complexity campaign involves pointing out that an internal logical connection has held in sociology between 'society' imagined as a general theoretical entity, and its substantive reference point as marked by the boundaries of modern *nation states*. But now that we are in a situation of thoroughly global social relations, this simple idea of (national) society becomes glaringly inadequate. However, this initial criticism of sociology – exposing what Urry terms its 'vernacular nationalism' – whilst salutary, is overstated, as plenty of sociologists have been well aware of the 'inter-societal' character of modernity, and of the profound global tendencies at work in its transformation. More importantly, conceptually speaking, it appears to involve a straight *non sequitur*, because the source of the trouble seems to lie in the idea of a *national* society, rather than that of a national *society*. So if the complaint is to have any weight, a further argument is needed to the effect that the global situation we have now entered exhibits none of the generic (structural, determinate) *qualities* that sociologists once thought could be identified in national and inter-national societies.

Urry does want to take that further step, insisting that global complexity is not to be understood as merely a larger form of spatially bounded totality (the world, etc). Rather, societies have become 'unbounded' in some more fundamental way. Today, there are 'global fluids' which have no necessary end or purpose, and which display distinctive 'viscosities', directions, speeds and temporalities that are quite unlike the more static social processes of past times, and these are ungraspable in terminologies oriented to conceptual and material finality (Urry 2000a: 194). Thus, when we talk about global *movements*, we are not just referring to movements of *people*, or to *institutional* spread, but to the virtualities and uncanny pathways of objects, images, media and wastes – for example global communications, the Internet, money, climate change, health hazards, worldwide protest, automobility, the oceans, and so on (2000a: 186, 2003: 14). Organizational *networks* are thus more varied and interactive, *products* are manifold in form and content (hardware, software, 'social-ware'), and a routine state of *non-equilibrium* prevails (2003: 31–2). Regimes of social *regulation*, too, are changing to fit this new scenario, from a 'gardening' form of governmentality to a 'gamekeeping' mode. The first of these – the terms are taken from Bauman – 'presumes exceptional concern with pattern, regularity and ordering', whereas the latter is a matter of 'regulating mobilities' (Urry 2000a: 186). Clearly, if all this is so, we must hurry to upgrade our menu of conceptual resources. Instead of an approach to globalization that is 'linear', or that sees it as a 'unified process' driven by an acting *subject* in its engine room, we need to regard globalization not as something like a super-region, but more like a 'co-constitutive fluid' (2003: 44).

A number of observations can be made of this attempt to lodge complexity at the very heart of the contemporary understanding of the global. One is to notice, with some irony, the classically 'modernist' way in which *the past* is constructed as static and simple when compared to the ever-moving, exciting present. And we might ask in this regard: are we really to think that current ways of regulating global mobilities involve *zero* concern with pattern, regularity and ordering? Or that the 'gardening' model itself did not represent, in its time, a profound coming-to-terms with what were then unprecedented *movements*, movements not only of people – from villages to cities, from fields to factories, from settled stations in life to a swirling maelstrom of more mobile practices and mentalities – but also of various sorts of 'objects' and 'information' too, that is, the fashions, commerce, ideas, fellowship, violence and association that have been empirically observable since humans first went on the move? In other words, if the discourse of networks and fluids is good to work with conceptually, then there is no reason why it should not apply across the board and over all time. Indeed, complexity theory itself *requires* us to treat *all* human systems as complex. The relative simplicity and fixity of the past, we might insist, is simply a function of the *distance* we have gained from it, and so our understanding of the present too might fully be expected, in due course, to be just as comprehensible, that is to say just as complex, overall. This point wholly undercuts, however, the suggestion of some basic *epistemological break* between our understanding of the 'national' past and our grip on the global present.

Moreover, when Urry comes to exemplify his post-social networks and flows, contrary to his headlines, they seem eminently trackable and analysable in the usual ways: the products of transnational corporations, for instance, are described as requiring 'predictable, calculable, routinized, and standardized environments' (2000a: 193). Or again, the processes by which people travel around the world for various purposes (work, slavery, tourism, sex, academic conferences), and the ways that they encounter or pass each other by in global 'non-spaces' like airports – these 'complex intersections' remain entirely determinate and observable. Actually, after the initial flourishes, Urry does *not* want to say that everything is 'liquid, moving' because 'immobilities' and 'moorings' exist – necessarily – as well (2003: 62, 126).

Perhaps all that Urry is really getting at is that sociology cannot afford to approach the global present in any kind of *simplistic* or *necessitarian* way. That is why he talks of the figure of 'glocalization' as a 'strange attractor', and the global predicament as involving all manner of 'chaotic spill-overs' of systems, impelling the prospect of 'spiraling global disequilibrium' and 'constant disorder'. But if we can agree with the thoughts behind most of this discourse, we should not get carried away with its *energetics*. For example, when Urry talks about the way in which global fluids of whatever sort exhibit distinctive viscosities, speeds and directions, we have to ask, how does he *know* these things?

There is good reason, let us agree, for sociologists to get excited about complexity theory, partly because, *at last*, it seems to give us the kind of philosophical overview that allows *social* knowledge as well as the hard sciences an exemplary status. For example, Mitchell Waldrop uses the collapse of the Soviet bloc as the opening module in his celebrated introduction to the science of complexity, and he goes on to invoke the 'punctuated equilibrium' of historical causality as emblematic of its explanatory mode (Waldrop 1992: 9, 320). But we need to note here that these things are portrayed as neither *inexplicable*, nor do they constitute testimony to the kind of 'spiraling disequilibrium' that would defy understanding. Indeed, we can find important elements of the complexity paradigm in the thinking of the classical sociologists. Urry himself cites Marx's understanding of capitalism as an illustration of thinking about *dynamic systems* and their driving, but contradictory, tendencies, whilst David Byrne (1998: 47–9) thinks that the concept of *emergent properties* that is so important for the new science 'corresponds exactly to Durkheim's conception of social facts'. Even Herbert Spencer might be cited as having a rudimentary inkling of emergence, if the latter is posed as the idea of 'much coming from little' in situations of complex interaction (Waldrop 1992: 297).

Complexity's complexity

Further complications arise in any transfer of complexity concepts to the social sciences from the natural sciences, which is where the technicalities of the jargon, after all, originate. Indeed there is already a complication or paradox in the fact that those who reach for complexity jargon include many who have long been suspicious of scientism and naturalism in the social disciplines. So a first major concern is the extent to which complexity terminology is to be taken *literally*. The fact that social events and processes *involve* natural events and process as part of their constitution is one reason for thinking that they should be. Further confirmation arrives if we consider that social events or processes, in themselves and not just by way of analogy, consistently reveal complex overdetermined networks of causality and feedback, and possess the quality and trajectory of a multiply structured whole that is more than the sum of its component parts.

The making and breaking of a labour strike, for example, will reveal a tight combination of necessary ingredients and contingent variation; will be triggered by sensitivity to initial conditions; and will show a self-organizing criticality that takes it, probably more than once, to 'the edge of chaos' and back, before a resolution is obtained. Indeed, resolution is *never* obtained: the outcomes and effects of strikes, whether successful or not, change things forever, and only arbitrarily can a firm line be drawn under our list and observations of its consequences. There was no 'equilibrium' to begin with, and none comes at the end. Throughout, there is a rampant disparity between causes and effects, and plenty of the 'path dependence' that Urry emphasizes as central to complexity explanation. So, clearly, we might think, complexity terms apply directly to social phenomena.

On the other hand, the technical discourse of complexity theory is primarily scientific, and specifically mathematical, and this makes its application to social things destined to mislead in certain ways. For example, the talk about 'self-organizing criticality' in the context of a labour strike will immediately connote things to do with the way in which the strike was consciously organized, the self-understanding of the agents involved, and the nature of internal criticism of the leadership, employers and so on. And we will be inclined to connect these factors, reasonably enough, to thoughts about *other* ways that the dispute might have been conducted and concluded. (This example is fairly arbitrary, but almost any other example will serve the point, due to the omnipresence of organization, criticism and consciousness in human affairs.) However, that is not, strictly speaking, what 'self-organizing criticality' means in the natural sciences. Take that standard illustration of this principle, namely the way in which the addition of just one grain sends a whole pile of sand into avalanche, only for the latter to settle down again so that the process begins afresh. Urry uses this example for the purpose of re-orientating *social theory*, and one could even suppose that this discursive purpose enters, so to speak, into the very explication of the example itself, just as it certainly enters into the social science reader's response. Because of Urry's concern to over-turn mechanical ways of thinking in sociology, and even to intimate the inexplicably ethereal, the implication in such instances is that in its self-organizing criticality the sand pile 'knows what it is doing' and that the outcome is remarkably 'uncanny' because of this. What this overlooks, though, is that the sand event is, in purely physical terms, perfectly *deterministic*; indeed some scientists do not regard it even as complex in any interesting sense (Ellis 2004: 608).

Another way of getting at this question of literal translation is by noting how frequently social theorists use the term 'non-linear' to describe what social understanding must become if it is to be complex. It appears countless times, for example, throughout the pages of *Global Complexity*. However, most of these uses have little directly to do with the mathematical meaning of 'non-linear', which refers to a particular type of equation, the formidable explorations of which by mathematicians are beyond the ken of the vast majority of social scientists. Yet social theorists do not hesitate to borrow the *aura* and *gravitas* of complexity mathematics in their sometimes worryingly woolly usages, as in the statement: 'the social science of globalization has taken the global for granted and then shown how localities, regions, nation-states, environments and cultures are transformed in linear fashion by this all-powerful "globalization"' (Urry 2005: 58). But 'linear' here, together with the 'non-linearity' that is marked connotatively as its superior form of reasoning, is *not* being used here in its proper mathematical or complexity sense. Rather, what is meant is something more like 'unilineal' and 'non-unilineal', a significantly different matter (though one that is no less contestable). In any case, for most purposes, sociological thinking is *not* 'linear' at all. Linearity has to do both with scale (if you double the input, you double the output) and addition (if you mix two inputs, the result is what you get just by adding each output). According to that formula, if the number of police officers is doubled, the crime rate will be halved. But no sociologist asserts such things, nor have sociologists ever thought of explaining social life in general in that linear way.

A final example: Urry makes a strong recommendation that we see 'glocalization' as the crucial 'attractor' of our times, because it is 'developing on a progressively worldwide basis and drawing more and more sets of relationships into its awesome power' (Urry 2003: 86). Actually, Urry hesitates to characterize globalization, or global society, as a system of *any* kind, even a dissipative one, but attractors do need systems to operate within because what they do is yield a formula which abstractly condenses the bundles of possible trajectories of a system. *Strange* attractors are those relevant to *very* complex or chaotic systems, giving them some kind of coherence such that 'an unstable and unpredictable patterned disorder develops that can be mathematically modeled' (Urry 2003: 27). Now if all that is so, once again it is hard to see how glocalization *can* be taken literally as an attractor. Its description is not nearly precise enough for it to play this role, nor is there any way to decide whether it is of the 'strange' or the 'normal' sort. Not only does any current notion of the social or global system lack the kind of 'force laws' that are elementary requirements for comprehending and calculating physical complexity, it is not clear how, abstractly or empirically, glocalization could be established as being *the* attractor within the system rather than other plausible alternatives, both real *and* possible. Urry's case for glocalization, then, which we should note still stands as an interesting proposition in social-theoretical terms, is only very remotely anything to do with attractors in the scientific sense, even though it comes across as a straight transfer of authority.

But perhaps the truly important thing about complexity theory is precisely that it underlines the necessity and value of *analogical* thinking in *all* explanations and descriptions? This is what Urry seems to maintain in his later statements of the complexity turn. He asks, 'Can complexity theory generate productive metaphors for analysing various "post-material" worlds that unpredictably and dramatically smashed into each other on September 11th?' And again, 'special focus will be directed to those metaphors appropriate for examining the "material worlds" implicated in the apparent "globalization" of economic, social, political, cultural and environmental relationships' (Urry 2005: 58). This withdrawal from the literalness of complexity theory at least seems more intellectually honest than claiming real scientific expertise in the matter, but it can still be questioned. One point would be simply that the scientists from whom the terminology is gratefully borrowed have little doubt about the 'materiality' of the worlds to which complexity theory applies. Second, whilst metaphors and analogies have long been accepted as crucial in the process of scientific understanding, there is a sense in which no knowledge can be affirmed just, as it were, in the process of metaphorical elaboration itself. Rather, there must be ways in which we can judge the respects in which metaphors are indeed *appropriate* for describing particular systems. Otherwise, we could just as well replace complexity metaphors with fancies of turtles standing on elephants in our story of 'post-material' social worlds.

In considering the difficulty of interpreting chaos and complexity in a literal sense for sociological purposes, we should also note that there is no consensus amongst mathematical experts themselves about whether their work on systems of non-linear equations and fractals ever could really 'apply' to empirical reality, at least for explanatory purposes. This is because, in a twist that should give social scientific enthusiasts pause for thought, the mathematical modeling of chaos is very radically *simplifying* and (largely) deterministically *predictive* (Smith 1998).

The second general complication I want to mention concerns the relationship *between* complexity and chaos. Partly, 'chaos' summons up complexity itself, and might be thought of as 'monstrous complexity' (Smith 1998: 46). But this monstrous complexity triggers off ideas of instability, randomness, indeterminacy and unpredictability, and these connotations work *against* the notion of complexity. A complex system might be unpredictable, but it is not by that token indeterminate or merely random. Rather, it might only be 'order masquerading as randomness' (Gleick 1998: 22). Indeed 'chaos' – moving away now from its mathematical sense – might be taken to signal *epistemic* limitation rather than the actual indeterminacy of real systems (Eve *et al.* 1997: xiii, Holland 1998: 43–4). This means that the uncertainty generated by apprehension of chaos need not at all be taken as 'an admission of defeat' for explanatory endeavour (Prigogine and Stengers 1997: 183). So for every emphasis in the science journalism on 'spiraling disequilibrium' and 'out of control-ness', there is a more than counterbalancing emphasis on 'islands of structure amidst the disorder' (Gleick 1998: 56). Santa Fe complexity doyen Doyne Farmer, for example, is reported as having quickly gotten 'bored with chaos', because it did not address 'the inexorable growth of order and structure in the universe' (Waldrop 1992: 288).

This has led to a situation in which chaos is dropping out of the picture, and the main connection being asserted is that between complexity and *emergence* (Cilliers 1998: xi). After all, what happens at 'the edge of chaos' is self-organized dynamic re-stabilization. And fascination with the famous 'butterfly effect' has subsided too, because nothing so particularistic prevents us developing accounts of the 'emergent macro-patterns that depend on shifting micropatterns' (Holland 1998: 7), in this case the interaction of the larger 'building blocks' of weather patterns. So, at this more general level of abstraction, 'chaos has little relevance' (Holland 1998: 44).

The complexity of complexity, it turns out, is that it is always a matter of chaos *and* structure, order *and* disorder, complexity *and* simplicity. Indeed, it is a matter of 'simplexity' and 'complicity' as well:

Simplexity is the tendency of simple rules to emerge from underlying disorder and complexity, in systems whose large-scale structure is independent of the fine details of their substructure. Complicity is the tendency of interacting systems to coevolve in a manner that changes both, leading to a growth of complexity from simple beginnings – complexity that is unpredictable in detail, but whose general course is comprehensible and foreseeable (Cohen and Stewart 1995: 3).

The third complication to register is that there are different *types* of complexity and emergence. Distinctions can be made, for example, between organized complexity and disorganized complexity, and between weak emergence and strong emergence. The latter refers to situations in which the complex conditions prevalent in the newly emerged larger system do not, as it were, leave behind its original component elements or systems in an unchanged state – that would only be 'weak' emergence. Rather, in strong emergence, these original contributing elements are causally altered in fundamental ways in the formation and stabilization of the new configuration (Clayton 2004: 598). As for complexity, one philosopher of biology distinguishes three main forms in the biological context – *compositional* complexity, *processual* complexity, and contingently evolved *population diversity* (Mitchell 2003: 167–9). This interesting classification would seem productive to think with in social science too, as long as we remember that compositional and processual complexity amongst social relations will have their own irreducible, but still 'structural', substantive characteristics (Jackson and Pettit 1992, Cilliers 1998: 104–6).

The fourth complication is that although we might look to complexity theory to help resolve long-standing philosophical or meta-methodological questions in the social sciences, it is more likely that those questions will turn out to subsume the new solution itself. One question in this vein is about whether categorical thinking about the variants of emergence and complexity is ultimately itself a scientific, or a philosophical, matter. Clearly, there is a sense in which the key general questions of complexity and emergence – when and how do complex systems '*get* to the edge, how do they *keep* themselves there, and what do they *do* there?' (Waldrop 1992: 295); 'How can the interactions of agents produce an aggregated entity that is more flexible and adaptive than its component agents?' (Holland 1998: 248) – can only be answered in relation to the identified structures and relations of particular sciences (biology, economics, psychology, and so on). But another (valid) sense of emergence is clearly more metaphysical, namely the view that the natural world is such that it 'produces continually more complex reality in a process of ongoing creativity' (Clayton 2004: 603). Other super-general articulations of complexity look slightly different again – *methodological* rather than metaphysical – as in Prigogine and Stengers' (1997: 189) advice that we must tread the 'narrow path' between 'pure determinism' and 'pure chance' if we are to produce real insights into 'the concrete world around us'. But if this is indeed sage advice, it hardly comes as news from the scientific frontier, because sociologists have known it all along.

Another philosophical question that complexity theory probably leaves unresolved is that of realism and anti-realism. In some ways, complexity and emergence, and perhaps even chaos too, are quite obviously properties of real systems. Indeed, there is an understandable temptation to say complexity theory simply makes no sense *unless* it is regarded as an update of critical realism itself, and that theorists who take a 'postmodern' view of complexity simply do not fully understand what they have got themselves involved in (Byrne 1998, 1999). Yet there is an irrealist line of some force to be pressed, according to which chaos, complexity and indeterminateness characterize the *observers*, their positions, identities and reflections, as well as the things they are (supposedly) observing or filtering. Of course, as with irrealism of any interesting sort, this version would seem to be finally underwritten by some kind of basement-level realism about the existence of persons and worlds. But that kind of realism would be very general indeed, hardly mattering when it came to what we are to understand as complexity in any given domain. For that reason, some social scientists take a third path between or beyond realism and irrealism, rather than engaging directly in this potentially endless philosophical dispute. They prefer to take as their object of enquiry not the validity and applicability of the complexity package as such, but rather the circuitry of complexity *discourse* itself, the social assemblages that it enables, and the social effectivity of its metaphors, modulations and uptake. The idea behind this third way with complexity is productive, and its results, to date, are suitably circumscribed (Thrift 1999), except where they are glossed with the aura of having some kind of secret epistemological specialness all of their own (Mackenzie 2005).

The variations and dilemmas picked out in this section, then, should guard us against taking up complexity in anything other than a socially specific way (Medd and Haynes 1998), and to be confident in the thought that it is not compulsory to use complexity discourse in order to advance a suitably complex social account. Yet there is still a paradox overall: if complexity talk is to be regarded as valid and useful in social science, even for very specific phenomena and purposes, then this must be through the power of generality that it possesses. And indeed, many complexity scientists see its full potential in terms of providing a new kind of positivistic 'unity of science' programme, in which *laws* of complexity might emerge, thus enabling a final integration of all the sciences under one comprehensive system, each occupying its relevant level (Ellis 2004: 608). Auguste Comte, inventor of 'sociology' and perhaps not the most complex of thinkers, may thus have been right all along.

Exemplifying complexity in social science

That itemization of complications around the understanding of complexity should encourage us to be extremely watchful when bringing it to bear on social scientific research. There are *three dangers* that I particularly want to draw attention to in that regard. The first danger is to think that complexity theory is something that can simply be *applied* in producing works of social research. Just as there was a glut of books in the 1980s and 1990s having the obligatory 'social construction of . . . ' locution in their titles and framings, so we are beginning to see a headlong rush of people eager to describe their assorted investigations and findings as coming courtesy of complexity theory itself.

To take just one example out of this trend, in her book *Education and Conflict: Complexity and Chaos* (2004), Lynn Davies understands complexity theory as 'a way of seeing connections and possibilities', and describes her specific way of developing complexity theory as 'an eclectic mix of feminist theory, deviance theory, management theory and development theory' (2004: 7, 19). Davies proceeds to examine her focus on global influences on curriculum changes through a kind of complexity checklist, seeking to demonstrate how her project and findings can be seen as exemplifying, in sequence: non-linearity, sensitivity to initial conditions, self-organization, attractors, information and the edge of chaos. As if this mechanical and derivative 'approach' were not problematical enough, some of the things that are said in the name of complexity are wholly banal where they are not seriously misleading. Thus, not only are all education systems said to be 'complex nested' ones, pulled between 'ossification and disintegration', but there are different kinds of 'fitness for purpose' in educational leadership models, and we must see children's classroom interaction as involving 'the creative recognition of new order', pushing teachers to get a balance between 'directiveness and connectivity' (Davies 2004: 21–5). Although Davies is manifestly impressed by complexity theory, she confides to her readers that she had some doubts, being 'concerned initially that complexity theory did not contain a theory of power'. But this qualm passes, enabling her to develop such propositions as: 'in complexity terms, it is better to ask forgiveness than to ask permission' (2004: 33–4). No doubt it is unfair to single out one scholar in this way, but the point is that such alarming vacuity, in the name of complexity science, is becoming all too common. This is unfortunate, not least because Davies' *substantive thesis* – that there are 'grave omissions' in the educational curricula of both stable and conflictual societies today that contribute to the acceptance of war (2004: 5) – might well have a specific character and importance that we need to know about. But this only underscores further the mistake in thinking that complexity theory is 'useful', something to be *deployed* in social science. On the contrary, if we are doing our explanatory and descriptive job well, our accounts, in their own terms, will turn out to be perfectly complexity-adequate.

A related danger is that of seeking to *spot* complexity theory as a virtue in social science writings, especially by way of surface complexity *talk* rather than in the deeper structure of the *argument*. In this light, let us recall Manuel Castells's ideas about the information age and network society, not least because John Urry spots Castells as a complexity person on the basis that he 'breaks with the idea that the global is a finished and completed totality' (2003: 10). Now it is certainly the case that Castells's terminology is akin to Urry's own account of global complexity, and some of this in turn appears to break with typically modernist sociological categories. Thus, informationalism is held to constitute 'a new social structure', introducing 'a pattern of discontinuity in the material basis of economy, society, and culture' (Castells 1996: 14, 30). 'For the first time in history', Castells avers, 'the human mind is a direct productive force', and social development is governed by a distinctive 'networking logic' attuned to complexity, unpredictability, and creative power (1996: 32, 60). Virtual flows and network modalities inaugurate new trends towards flattened and mobile organizational forms. Conventional notions of time and space consequently come under severe pressure, making for a profoundly new sort of cultural experience, based on 'timeless time' and a 'space of flows', the culture of 'real virtuality' (1996: 372–5, 464–7). Moreover, the quest for identity is 'becoming the main, and sometimes the only, source of meaning' in a novel drama enacted between 'the Net and the Self' (1996: 3).

If this is Castells at his most complexity-driven, we might note that he does not posit timeless time as *replacing* 'biological time' and 'industrial clock time', but rather it comes as an *addition to* those familiar forms. In any case, 'timeless time' is an exaggeration: what he thinks is going on is an unprecedented *speeding-up* of processes and information transfer. Castells does go on to assert that time becomes 'de-sequenced', and claims that we can now witness 'past, present and future occurring in random sequence'. However, we should take this as a case of

complexity overkill, a near-mystical thought that gets no support at all
from its supposed exemplification in 'electronic hypertext' and 'the blur-
ring of life-cycle patterns' (Castells 2000: 13–14). Another misty passage
finds Castells talking of 'organizing the simultaneity of social practices
without geographical contiguity'. But still, it is not exactly 'spaceless
space' that is being proposed here, because Castells goes on to acknowledge the inescapability of 'territorial dimensions' and the locatedness
of the technological infrastructures that enable these transformations
(2000: 14). And on the question of virtuality, Castells seems on the
whole quite critical of this, especially where it might imply that energy
and resource production do not require *material* work and disposal.

There are other long stretches of his analysis in which Castells – to
his credit – seems to break *no* new conceptual ground. The mode of
information, for example, turns out not to be a self-standing novel
social structure, but a new structural variant of capitalism. Moreover,
most of the examples of complex *networks* that Castells instances are
acknowledged to be very familiar *social* networks – families, neigh-
bourhoods, social movements – rather than radically different sorts of
informational conduits. Castells talks of the information society having
transformed *work*, but this by no means signals the 'end of work' as
we know it. Neither is global informationalism so fluid that we cannot
detect its class divisive tendencies, most notably the gulf between elite
'self-programmable' labour and mass 'generic' labour. Indeed, these new
forms of stratification are accepted by Castells to build directly on
existing patterns of capital accumulation or its absence.

As to how the network society has come about, Castells develops an
account of the timing of the appearance of these forms of interaction
and regulation, in which the important ingredients are the deregula-
tion of capitalism on a planetary scale, the further 'depersonalization'
of ownership and control of capital, counter-cultural movements, the
resurgence of neo-liberalism, the media-fication of exchange and understanding, and the failure of statist forms to contain the growth of technology. *Methodologically*, all this is entirely conventional. It is a form of
factorialism, based on systematic 'observation' and governed by a pluralistic approach to theory in which the latter gets framed as providing
'suggesting hypotheses' rather than 'preconceived answers' (1996: 26–7).
For convenience, Castells groups all the relevant elements into a classic
threefold division of social spheres – the economic, the political and
the cultural – in terms of each of which he then examines the current
shape of global social life. There is no ultimate and absolute causal
hierarchy amongst these spheres, partly because the network form is

a kind of cultural cipher through which innovation within economic organizations expresses itself. But overall, network culture is generated by something like a prime mover, in that communications *technology* marks something awesomely 'value-neutral' (2000: 10).

In sum, the burden of my reading of Castells is that, far from the classical rules of sociological method being overturned, they appear to have been consolidated. I can be much briefer with the *third danger* that remains to be identified: the tendency to think of complexity theorists as necessarily – like Castells himself – *progressive* in some ideological or quasi-political sense. I can be briefer with this thanks to an exhaustive examination of Kevin Kelly's (1994, 1998) work already conducted by Steven Best and Douglas Kellner (1999). Best and Kellner point to the many ways in which Kelly's methodology of 'countercybernetics' and his substantive focus on global post-industrial networks show the hallmarks not only of Castellsian informationalism, but also of edgy critical postmodernism. For example, in his proposal to re-perceive social interaction in terms of 'vivisystems', and in his insistence that the world of the *born* and the world of the *made* are becoming as *one*, Kelly's discourse echoes, variously, the revival of vitalism in social theory, 'posthuman' cultural studies, postfeminist manifestos for cyborg culture, and actor network theory. Intent upon 'overthrowing modern paradigms', just as Urry and others might recommend, Kelly puts together in an 'impressive synthesis' all those elements that are being touted as being as exciting as they are necessary for social science renewal: 'chaos and complexity theory, evolutionary theory, information theory and discussions of new technologies' (Best and Kellner 1999: 141–2). The result is, without question, even in the eyes of these sceptical reviewers, 'substantive' and 'stimulating', the kind of 'broad, novel and bold theorizing' that we would hope, and possibly expect, that complexity theory could offer the social disciplines (1999: 143–4, 159).

The trouble is, however, that Kelly has a 'crypto-libertarian political philosophy', being 'wholly uncritical' of the new capitalism, vehemently anti-statist, and unapologetically pro-Bush or 'Reaganesque' in his populist forays into the political implications of his thinking. The 'new rules of the new economy', indeed, are projected by Kelly as nothing other than the 'Laws of God'. Now, Best and Kellner rightly forestall any surprise in all this by recalling that Friedrich von Hayek was one of the most able proponents of the spontaneously self-organizing character of social life (following Adam Smith). But this rather compounds the problem: we can no more say of Hayek than of Kelly that because he has the wrong *ideology*, his thinking is inadequately *complex*. This may or may not be true, and must stand or fall by the attention to detail that Best and Kellner provide in Kelly's case. But the wider point stands, that there is no *direct* connection between a vocabulary of complexity and substantive explanatory adequacy, or between either of these things and progressive politics. Unfortunately for those that see complexity theory as improving on *realism* in the social sciences, we can no more guarantee the success of social analysis by reference to its credentials in complexity talk than we could by insisting that realism was an intrinsically 'critical' philosophy for social science. If complexity theory undoubtedly brings stimulating and deeper understanding of the work of social science, then it might be better regarded as providing an explication of what good knowledge, when successful, captures and stands for, rather than being a *recipe* for how to obtain that knowledge.

Conclusion

Whilst in no sense seeking to minimize the significance of complexity theory, I have been emphasizing some weaknesses and dilemmas in the appeal to complexity within the social sciences. One point is that adopting the *discourse* does not, in itself, generate good theory or research, and another is that the message of contemporary manifesto statements for complexity theory is not exactly new, or always very accurate. In that regard, when complexity talk is in the air, sociology tends to be figured as the very paradigm of non-complex or 'linear' reasoning, with all the failings that that seems to imply. But these associations are misleading and unfair. John Urry closes one of his own manifestos by praising the high degree of intellectual flexibility and fluidity within the sociological culture of enquiry, noting its relatively unpoliced and non-hierarchical qualities, attributes that give it a certain post-disciplinary advantage over other discourses (2000a: 200–1). And others who have worked through some of the consequences of the new complexity science for sociology similarly come up with the conclusion that it 'supplements' previous conceptions and knowledges rather than 'overthrowing' them (Eve *et al.* 1997: 274–5). David Byrne goes as far as to insist that complexity theory altogether vindicates 'unregenerate progressive modernism' (Byrne 2005: 98). I would not go quite as far as that because to seek to *prove* that sociological progressive modernism and complexity theory run along together entirely hand in hand risks falling into some of the 'dangers' outlined in the later part of this chapter. But the main line of argument in this chapter is compatible with most of what Byrne says, especially in its denial that the turn to complexity suddenly and decisively leaves the sociological imagination looking debilitated and about to expire. Perhaps it is 'complexity' that will expire first, at least in its faddish versions. In any case, many experts and analogists alike now see that part of the complexity of complexity, and its beauty, is that simplicity is one of its components at the start, and one of its surprises at the end.

9
Reflexivity and Positivity

Since the run-up to the Millennium, yet another 'turn' seems to have been underway in social and cultural theory. It has not quite materialized even now, and it may not even come to receive a commonly agreed name, but something like a 'turn to positivity' is going on across the human sciences. And the turn to positivity is a slow one because unlike all the other turns of recent decades, positivity signals a definite *corrective* to the previously dominant mood of sceptical, pluralistic multiplicity in intellectual life. The need for such a corrective has been apparent for some time. In *Spectres of Marx*, for example, Jacques Derrida declared that there had been quite enough 'interminable self-critique', and he proposed that we should 'never be ready to denounce' that 'messianic affirmation' and 'spirit of Enlightenment' that were evident in the *Communist Manifesto* (Derrida 1994: 88–9). Richard Rorty went on to name Derrida himself as one of the chief instigators of 'principled, theorized, philosophical hopelessness' (Rorty 1998: 36–7), just as Rorty's own conversational postmodernism has often been the target of exactly the same charge.

In some ways, the question of positivity is simply a matter of intellectuals becoming more *politically engaged*. The later years of Pierre Bourdieu and Edward Said were memorably distinguished in just that way. Yet truly to inspire, political engagement cannot only rest in (entirely legitimate) fury about the state of the world. It needs to be coupled with positivity and affirmation *in thought*, and that has been found hard to sustain. Symptomatically, McRobbie (2005: 3–5) observes that theoretical leaders in cultural studies appear to be caught in a circle of 'tactical retreat', 'jaded spirits' and generalized 'melancholia'. In recommending positivity as a way forward from intellectual negativity, or as a way of breaking that sense of 'impasse' that exists in relation to many important issues, a number of hazards immediately arise. One is that 'positivity' is so general that it might be thought to be nothing more than mood-music, an aid to self-help counselling for the jaded. Another drawback is that, promising an end to pluralism and negativity, positivity is bound to be self-defeating, because strongly opposed accounts will quickly emerge concerning *what* we are to be positive about, and *why*. On top of that, there is the risk that in playing up positivity, we might be bringing back *positivism* itself.

Unexpectedly, none of these arguments is effective. If positivity's upbeat surface affect disguises a vacuous lack of content, exactly the same can be said of those constant ritual invocations of generalized *pluralism* as something that is self-evidently good, and of the therapy that is assumed to come with appeals to *reflexivity*. As for the charge of 'positivism', this might be something to productively *explore* rather than unthinkingly repeat. Just as we saw in Chapter 1 that postpositivism is a capacious umbrella within which different sorts of theorizing shelter, so too is positivism. One thing that critical social thought, in fact, *shares* with positivism, once we understand that few positivists support inductive empiricism, is the centrality of *theory*. And some of those who are still inexplicably listed as positivists by social theorists – Popper for example – were among the first to insist that scientific theorizing above all exercises the *creative*, imaginative faculties.

Moreover, the positivists were not necessarily 'rationalist' or 'reductionist' in every sense. Amongst the classical sociological positivists, Comte viewed the unity of science not as a matter of different domains having the same basic laws of operation, but in terms of the necessary interconnectedness of the various sciences. And while Pareto was certainly methodologically positivist, he thought that the driving underlying forces in social life (his 'residues' and 'derivations') were essentially non-rational, and even unrepresentable. Add to this the way in which Victorian positivists like Frederic Harrison framed their project, not so much in terms of disinterested scientism, but rather as a determined *synthesis* of the persistent binaries within modern intellectual culture – theory/fact, science/faith, sociology/other disciplines (Vogeler 1984). Then, in the twentieth century, a line of 'emotivists' came to the fore in moral theory, essentially developing Hume's dictum that reason is the slave of the passions. The Vienna Circle of logical positivists for their part took a radically eliminative approach to all metaphysical essentialism. Circle convener Moritz Schlick ended up in the deconstructionist-like position of regarding all claims to know reality 'in itself' to be undecideable (Hanfling 1981: 55), and leading theorist Rudolph Carnap took the view that to be real was 'to be part of the system', that is, part of the system of preferred scientific *categories*. Marxist Otto Neurath, it seems, persuaded Carnap to couch those categories in strictly *phys-icalist* terms, because Neurath thought that this was the politically progressive thing to do at a time of fascistic mysticism. Carnap went along with this, but his main motivation was his view that science's goal was to achieve theoretical coherence and inter-subjective agreement, not necessarily to designate the nature of the world in itself (Neurath 1973: 44–5). From this rather different image of the varieties of positivism, any easy contrast between positivism and postmodernist relativism is firmly blocked (Laudan 1996).

If that begins to dent our sense that positivism is obviously monolithic and naively realist, appeals to long-standing *alternatives* to positivism are hardly convincing either. Habermas's effort to show that hermeneutic interpretivism carries within it an intrinsically conservative moment remains decisive, no matter how much we would like to recruit Gadamer and others to the critical wing of social understanding. But of course 'critical theory' itself now stretches far beyond any association with the Frankfurt School, and is invoked so often and so harmlessly that we might wonder why this label itself persists. Countless textbooks and PhD theses in every social science discipline are adorned with the tag that they represent a 'critical' approach, when often this usually only means that some aspect of social complexity is being descriptively registered. Craig Calhoun (1995: 35) described the core ingredients of critical theory as: a critical engagement with the contemporary social world; a crit-ical awareness of the historico-cultural conditions in which theory is produced; a self-critical re-examination of one's own theoretical under-standing; and a critical confrontation with other works of social explan-ation. Whilst this is all entirely supportable, it seems compatible with a large number of substantive or political consequences. Above all, this idea of critical theory is not *self-sufficient* because it requires some positive knowledge of the world to be critical *about*. For all these reasons, perhaps we need to pay greater heed to the warning of neo-positivist sociologist Jonathan Turner (1992: 167): if the search for general social laws and indubitable accounts is to be abandoned, we had better be careful not to end up with a veritable ragbag of second-rate philosophy, commentary on events, vague conceptual schemes, militant relativism, and historical and empirical description.

Bearing in mind our discussion of explanation in Chapter 3, we should note here, *apropos* Turner's warning, that many of the key issues in philosophy raised by positivists are still ongoing. Realists tend to believe that explanation is mainly (if very broadly) *causal* because causal information tells us about, and stems from, the fundamental *dispositions* of things and relations. But it is not easy to say what is fundamental and what is not in the 'essential' way that things are, so we have to infer generative invariance in the way things are from invariance and generality in our observations – a basically positivistic emphasis, and one that is still sufficiently strong to make updated Humean and nomological perspectives 'serious philosophical contenders' on the matter of scientific explanation (Psillos 2002: 6). According to James Woodward (2003), even if we think broadly of causal understanding as operating in many ways at many levels, and as involving not laws but generality, the basic motivation for explanation and investigation into causes is control, intervention and *manipulation*. Now whilst some would regard even this important contemporary statement of explanatory logic as a positivist conception, no convincing alternative exists within the various anti-positivist frameworks. Habermas (1972) famously tried to counterbalance the instrumental 'knowledge-constitutive' interest with communicational and emancipatory ones. But not only was Habermas, at the time, unwilling entirely to exclude instrumental knowledge from his scheme, his 1990s work on the connection between facts and norms has never involved simply subsuming the former under the latter.

We also saw in our handling of explanation in Chapter 3 that Bruno Latour took a suspicious attitude towards both control and facticity. And that attitude is entirely fitting, we might think, for someone who has been portrayed repeatedly as a radical constructivist. But we noted how Latour conceded that explanation for purposes of control was *inescapable*, and he now wonders, in addition, whether he might have been 'foolishly mistaken' in taking science studies all the way down the constructivist track. This is because Latour has discovered a new-found regard for the facts, expressing grave concern about the routine assumption today 'that there is no such thing as natural, unmediated, unbiased access to truth, that we are always the prisoners of language', and holding that critical theory has suffered from 'an excessive confidence in *distrust* of good matters of fact disguised as bad ideological biases!' (Latour 2003). As always, Latour remains reflexive – he is *wondering* about these things. But emphatically, for Latour and for others, reflexivity alone will no longer do.

Practical methodological reflexivity

The idea that reflexivity is the best intermediate station between sceptical deconstructionism and positivism remains strong, however, and there are three main ways in which reflexivity has been taken to provide a *methodological* platform for the cultural disciplines. The first of these regards reflexivity as part of an overarching ethos of inter- or trans-disciplinary research practice. In *The Practice of Cultural Studies*, Richard Johnson and his colleagues operate in the conviction that methodological reflexivity represents a 'whole philosophy or approach' and not a toolbox of techniques (Johnson *et al.* 2004: 1–3). This study re-builds bridges between cultural studies and sociology (and other disciplines), seeking to establish a comprehensive map of the entire 'circuit' of the contemporary human sciences. A strong ethical and philosophical centerpiece is clearly required for such a large task, and reflexivity is part of that core, because it enables cultural studies 'to strongly align with an anti-objectivist view of knowledge' (2004: 17). The 'primary methodological task' in this anti-objectivism is 'not to correct for bias in our research procedures', because partiality and situatedness are inevitable and even *desirable* in engaged social and cultural research. With 'thoroughgoing reflexivity' in command, then, 'belief in objectivity seems inconsistent with cultural understanding and sociological insight' (2004: 17, 52).

Let me note other key values at work in this text before pinpointing what is wrong with this notion of reflexivity. Johnson *et al.* are not methodological pluralists, in fact they are rather fed up with sheer eclecticism in cultural studies. If we do need a plurality of methods, they argue, this is because of the complexity of real processes, not because of the existence of multiple realities according to perspective. They also feel that postmodernist fragmentation has diminished our 'seriousness about intellectual work'. They want a stronger approach to classification in cultural theory, because the social world is a 'system of connections and relations'. And while standpoint epistemology is part of their own reflexive positionality, they are well aware that 'subjugated or marginalized points of view do not automatically carry superior knowledge' (2004: 27, 37, 42, 49). In short, these sentiments are similar to the ones I have adopted throughout this book, except that Johnson *et al.* draw the line at objectivity.

However, this is inconsistent on their part because, in fact, their notion of reflexivity is not 'anti-objectivist' at all. Johnson *et al.* think that 'self-consciousness' is paramount because it reminds us of 'who we are and why we ask the questions that we do and what our prior relations might be to our objects of study' (2004: 17). And *that* is important because we need certain 'forms of distancing, estrangement or depersonalization' in our work (2004: 52). Otherwise, *presumably* – though this is never explicitly said – our research activity will be nothing more than the projection of our unthinking opinions. Since research activity is *never* a mere projection of our opinions or standpoints, reflexivity serves to check our predispositions as well as to develop them. But reflexivity's distancing role here is quite apparently nothing other than a form of 'correcting for bias', the very thing that was supposed to constitute the objectivist fallacy. As I argued in Chapter 1, just because our knowledge, *all* knowledge, is partial does not mean it is 'subjective'. Johnson *et al.* agree with this, because they stress that reflection is about 'society, culture and history' and not (only) biography. But here we are fully in the territory of explanation and evidence, where every partiality requires critical interrogation and not just receptive understanding. This is why Johnson says that standpoints are not valid in themselves, but only as 'starting points for creativity, insight, or even a new kind of "objectivity"' (2004: 50–2). However, the scare quotes around 'objectivity' here should be removed, for it is only the misconceived equation between reflexivity and *anti*-objectivism that keeps them there.

Pragmatist methodological reflexivity

The second variant of methodological reflexivity involves, as a matter of principle, setting the 'social' against the 'science' in the concept of 'social science'. Bent Flyvbjerg exemplifies this approach in his book *Making Social Science Matter*, which seeks to offer a route out of the science wars through the adoption of 'concrete practical rationality' (2001: 29). Flyvbjerg thinks that the scientistic ideal of 'expertise', which involves a mechanical application of abstract, value-neutral rules and universal principles, is wrong, signalling mere 'competence' at best (2001: 9). True expertise is more a matter of virtuosity, specificity, holism, intuition and commitment, all of which require liberation from analytical rationality. Flyvbjerg develops this initial distinction into a deeper contrast between the Aristotelian notions of *episteme* (rationalistic cognition, knowing-*why*) and *phronesis* (ethical reflection, public engagement, knowing *how*), and urges us to adopt the latter mode at the expense of the former. Whenever Socrates asked for a principle, Flyvbjerg reminds us, he got only *cases*, yet we are still bent, apparently, on figuring out what social *rules* our cases exemplify, instead of treating cases as primary constellations of information and reflection in their own right.

There appears to be much to commend in this reflexive-pragmatist conception of social science and why it matters. Unfortunately, the discourse is thoroughly inconsistent. For example, in order to make the point about intuition and non-mechanical expertise in social science, Flyvbjerg applies nothing less than a *general model* of learning and intellectual temperament (that of Hubert Dreyfus) to ground it. But this is *just* the sort of procedure that is categorized as second rate in the adopted schema itself. The irony is that if we apply the rules of the schema mechanically, so that intuition and virtuosity always trump analysis, we seem to be engaged only in dull competence. Conversely, if, in order to progress an issue, we introduce a stringent dose of analytical schematizing to get *past* the existing cacophony of intuitions, we appear, paradoxically, to have exercised the virtuoso in us.

This kind of antinomial quality pervades the appeal to *phronesis* too. Flyvbjerg tells us that we must not use 'cases' in a generalizing fashion, but he singles out Foucault as the perfect case of how to think about power. We are told to interpret authors in terms of their practical and public wisdom rather than to mark them against scientist or carefully ordered criteria, but then Habermas is condemned both for not being Foucault and for failing 'to stand up to historical–empirical test' (2001: 105). And although the phronetic approach should not really result in the production of anything so directive as a set of 'methodological guidelines', this is exactly what Flybjerg offers – to notably innocuous effect ('get closer to reality', 'join agency and structure', 'emphasize little things', 'do narrative'). Finally, when Flyvbjerg immodestly proffers his own research studies on urban planning initiatives as exemplifying the phronetic and reflexive approach, again things backfire. Essentially, behind some apparently technical and liberally benign proposals for transport change in Aalborg, commercial interests were all the while driving the policy agenda. To 'make social science matter' in this case thus requires not contestable, reflexive interpretation, but positive and objectivist understandings, in order to underpin a 'revelatory' rhetoric and better alternative strategies. The 'reflexive' methodologist's dilemma is apparent here: in spite of onslaughts against rationalist analytical schemes, they are working with just such schemes, necessarily, all the time.

Pluralist methodological reflexivity

Things might have turned out better for the pragmatic methodological reflexivist had it been argued less militantly that some styles of research theory and practice are closer to an ideal model than others. What we need to develop instead, perhaps, is a more systematically theorized *pluralist* perspective on methodology, one that could include positivistic and generalizing models, amongst many others, in the reflexive order of things. This is the sort of project that John R. Hall sets out to build in his *Cultures of Enquiry: From Epistemology to Discourse in Sociohistorical Research* (1999). Hall begins by establishing four 'formative discourses' – value discourse, narrative, social theory and explanation/interpretation – each of which is conceived as internally variable and externally contestable, with different mixtures and weightings of the various elementary schemas being put to work in particular sociohistorical investigations. From the combinations of the core discourses emerge eight 'practices of inquiry', four of which are of a 'generalizing' sort, with another four couched as 'particularizing'. The matrix of social thought as a whole is thus portrayed as having definite positions within it, but a hybrid and emergent texture too, because a steadily increasing attitude of post-positivist awareness enters into particular projects of explanation as they come to acknowledge the wider grid of possibilities. Hall then proceeds to usher a huge range of positions and theorists – Weber to Harding, Hempel to Rorty – to their allotted places within the matrix, identifying carefully the different degrees of objectivity and generality that mark the various social science traditions. Many further distinctions and sub-distinctions are made, but overall the central argument is that socio-historical accounts *co-constitute* the 'worlds' they describe, and they do so because of the very different *values* that enter directly into their distinctive analytical operations. This is where Hall's subtitle matters: socio-historical perspectives are distinctive *cultures* of enquiry, not just models to be ranked according to a purely epistemological notion of representational adequacy.

For all the subtlety and interest of this project, crucial ambiguities emerge. Hall's attitude to the various discourses that he describes, for example, is geared to favour relatively reflexive over relatively realist ones. But this preference is problematical because he is also committed to presenting them not in terms of adequacy but as *equally* driven by the value element that all possess. This ambiguity is reproduced in Hall's discussion of *social theory*. Theory is the name we give to those presentations of a field that identify 'fundamental phenomena' on the basis of 'a coordinated set of concepts'. Soon after, however, a different definition is provided: theory is really about 'nuanced interpretation drawing on multiple perspectives' (1999: 149). Yet these definitions clash in central ways, because the characteristic will to truth captured in the first is simply withdrawn in the second.

We can approach the status of Hall's overarching classificatory matrix in the same way. In one sense, he has tried to totalize an object of his own, namely *the field of social enquiry*. However, following poststructur-alist warnings against totalization, he conceives his grid as yielding only one possible interpretation, a 'heuristic' rather than any foundational 'system of correspondences' (1999: 232). But this is not right, because Hall clearly wants to persuade us that in spite of innumerable disparities among levels of abstraction, value-orientations and interpretive styles, 'deep affinities' within his field of enquiry reveal it to be significantly integrated after all (1999: 229–30). So the matrix is not merely 'optional'; it is the very condition of intelligibility. Hall wants to have it both ways: an appreciative 'history of values' *and* a 'theory of theorizations' (1999: 5); a nominal anti-realism, but a little bit of realism as well – just because discourses are 'constructed and unstable . . . does not mean that concepts bear no relation to their referents in the world' (1999: 255). The trouble is that reflexivity alone will not deliver both halves of this programme.

Against reflexivity?

I am underlining the contradictions in ambitious efforts to theorize reflexively, because the ambition always outruns reflexivity's concep-tual capacity. The same is true of pluralism, to which reflexivity closely relates. Somehow the drama and worth of a *monistic* understanding of the purpose of social science has come to seem 'totalitarian' or 'coercive'. Accordingly, assertions abound to the effect that there are always multiple perspectives to be considered and that having a range of theories to consult – the more the better – captures what we are all about. I want to contest this presumption of pluralism (McLennan 1995a). Pluralism can certainly be acknowledged to be an inescapable *fact*, and indeed the very *vehicle* through which social theory is formu-lated and debated. But this does not mean that pluralism – to be left with many different and contrary ways of looking at things – is the proper or inevitable *goal* of enquiry. On the contrary, it is only because some views have to be *excluded* from the final plurality, and because that plurality is constantly refigured as an integrated *whole*, that we are animated by the very existence of many particular perspectives.

As for reflexivity itself, this cannot generate a substantial *methodolo-gical strategy*. The basic problem, put simply, is that we can never tell if we are being reflexive *enough*. To see this, let us think of reflexivity in three ways. *Sociological reflexivity* requires that when presenting our own, or understanding someone else's, scholarly position, we need always to remember that it is a product of its time, place, culture, class, gender and other sectional interests. So the advice is that when assessing theoretical ideas or empirical findings, we do it with sociological reflexivity in mind. But is this reflexive move meant to result in a *cancellation* of the theoretical or substantive commitment? Once we see the sort of 'point of view' that is motivating the research, how exactly are we to bring this to bear on our appreciative judgement? Are we supposed to presume that the sociological standpoint *determines* the intellectual product, or not? It is impossible to say.

Next there is *rhetorical reflexivity*. This is the requirement, discussed in Chapter 3, that we see all explanatory argumentation as having a pragmatic and communicational dimension, such that the credibility of the claims being made is acknowledged as being dependent, at least in part, on its performative and rhetorical *form*. Realists, in particular, are strongly advised to watch out for their own particular sleight of hand – the 'rhetoric of no rhetoric'. However, once we have come to see the place of rhetoric in all forms of argumentation, what then? Does a reductionist or realist form *disqualify* all aspects of whatever discourse is under consideration from being taken seriously? And does the contrary rhetorical style, a hyper-conscious presentation – for example, writing social theory as though you might be a poet of some kind – make a given account any more attractive or insightful or 'clever'? As with many of the ingenious exercises in the 'New Literary Forms' genre of science studies in the 1980s (Ashmore 1989), the probability is that this strategy will succeed only in making a 'clever-clever' impression.

In spite of efforts to distinguish both sociological and rhetorical reflexivity from something more humdrum and 'uncritical', namely *liberal reflexivity*, this separation cannot easily be achieved. In liberal-minded reflexivity, we are meant to bear in mind that there will always be other legitimate *questions* than the ones we ask, and other legitimate *answers* to the ones we do ask. Reflexivity in this sense involves being very aware that our opinions may be ours alone, and may in addition be wrong, inconsistent, unfair, one-sided or inconclusive. Liberal intellectual culture then requires us to try to give 'balance' to our discussions as a safeguard against hasty dogmatism or egoism. But the same problem that confronts the other types of reflexivity surfaces here too – either we are propelled into a paralysis of ambivalence and uncertainty about stating *anything* as a result of our reflexive predicament, or we press ahead and say what we can in the best way that we can. Reflexivity here signals nothing more – and also nothing *less* – than *reflection* itself. But to try to make something 'methodological' out of this generic quality of thought is wrongheaded.

It bears repetition, finally, that reflexivity is *parasitic* upon positivity in the business of creating knowledge, and not the other way round. The primary goal of social understanding is to generate substantive grasp and creative ideas, a pairing that certainly *includes* giving attention to our process of reflection and reflexivity, but that is by no means reducible to it. So rather than reflexively focusing on difference, standpoint and partiality, perhaps what is needed now is a stronger sense that social and cultural understanding is a coherent and *cumulative* enterprise, something that, in fact, Johnson *et al.* bring out particularly well. To assist with that, we need to entertain more positively a term that has brought a curl to the lip of all good radicals since the 1960s, namely *consensus*. Consensus here does not always mean coming to *cosy agreement* about everything, though the importance of *that* in a public culture, and with a student body, that are genuinely sceptical about the achievements of social theory, should not be underestimated. But the kind of consensus I have in mind will often be appropriately more complex, signalling something like agreement about the state of *agreement and difference* in a particular field, or across a number of them. To illustrate how this kind of complex consensus can develop, to positive effect, I will try to summarize something of the state of play within and about *feminist* thought today. To keep this manageable, I concentrate on questions of feminism and disciplinarity (philosophy and sociology), and on issues already broached concerning objectivity and reflexivity, not least because feminist thinking on these topics has been very influential.

Feminism mainstreamed?

The two sets of questions (disciplinarity/objectivity) are of course closely bound up with one another. This is because the revolutionary feminist challenge was to insist not only that women had been left out – left out of the profession, left out of the profession's subject matter – but also that the dominant normative images and philosophies of scientific knowledge themselves were profoundly *masculinist*. Modern epistemology, its very will to truth, was encapsulated in the figure of the disembodied rational knower of truth and justice, the ideal public man. A creative, driven search then ensued to find a radically alternative model of feminist knowing, one in which commitments of a personal and social kind could not only fully be acknowledged, but could be in command. This, however, did not materialize, partly because of the almost impossible complications and binds that enveloped the very idea of a counter-epistemology. These complications were particularly relevant to feminist sociology. This is because the claim that the form and content of knowledge is reducible to the social and political interests of its wielders (men) is a starkly *sociologistic* claim. So at least one kind of general, scientific, un-complex knowledge, namely knowledge about the relation between social interests and knowledge, must be held to be legitimate. But this seems to reaffirm, not challenge, the traditionalist conception of sociological knowledge, which in *form* as well as in content was supposed to have been patriarchal from top to bottom. From that core contradiction – a *productive* one, it has to be said – developed the profound and still-unresolved tension between those who willingly accept that sociological feminism is 'modernist' in its logic and political temperament, and those *postmodernist* feminists who question the whole idea of an epistemologically based feminism, from the assumption of 'women' as the singular knowing subject, to the supposed 'experiential validity' upon which the specificity and normativity of women's knowing was based.

For those developing standpoint epistemology, the bind between objectivity and whatever objectivity was not (experience, reflexivity, commitment etc.) became difficult (Holmwood 1995, McLennan 1995c). On the one hand, the argument is that knowledge is never neutral, and that no 'better' knowledge is conceivable other than from the inside of wholly situated and value-saturated standpoints. On the other hand, the claim is that feminist standpoint epistemology is not just a better meta-theory *for women*, but, as an account of the way knowledges work, it is altogether more *adequate* – in *some* sense, therefore, more 'objective'. In the 1990s, a series of sophisticated philosophical hybrids and compromises were hammered out to try to arrive at the right kind of objectivity, notably Sandra Harding's (1993) 'strong objectivity' and Helen Longino's (1993) 'socially constituted objectivity'. These epistemological constructions must be recognized as *compromises*, not only because it proved impossible for serious women thinkers to give up on the 'progressivist' and 'rationalist' idea of improving our knowledge about knowledge, but also because as the philosophical mainstream itself came to be better *known*, and became in turn more *receptive* to feminist ideas, the idea that it stood for some notion of absolute rational objectivity became dramatically less credible.

Lorraine Code, for example, sought to rehabilitate relativism, with strong feminist reasons in mind. Her case for relativism hardly gets started, however, before the author acknowledges that she is, of course, just as much against 'extreme relativism' as realists are (Code 1995: 196–8). Indeed, relativism itself must not be seen to exclude a certain *aspect* of objectivism; the point is rather that whatever objectivity we arrive at should be regarded as having been *dialogically* rather than monologically produced. In that case, relativism is not so much a denial of the existence of concept-independent real structures as an acceptance that knowledge of these structures is a matter of negotiation between different explanations, to the point where we can actually be *certain* of very little. But as we have seen several times already, there is nothing here for an objectivist or a realist to flatly disagree with. The only thing that draws readers to that conclusion is Code's determination to portray the objectivist or universalist in a thoroughly overstated way: 'a universalist presumably believes that there is an unchanging reality, of which human beings can gain better and better knowledge, until near perfection is achieved; and that truths established now will be true for all time'. Similarly, Code's final summation – that 'naturalism provides moorings, not foundations' (1995: 231) – keeps both the debate, and the steadily emerging *consensus*, rolling along. It does not settle anything.

Postmodernist feminists were not so eager to participate in any consensus of that kind. Subject-fragmentation, in every sense, was to be more seriously entertained. This meant destabilizing notions of the self as constituted in the sociological imagination, to be at least supplemented, if not replaced, by whatever semblance of identity the psychoanalytical imagination allows. And it also meant destabilizing epistemology *in toto*. It was not a matter of replacing epistemological objectivity by subjectivity, but rather the whole *epistemological* paradigm had to go. Whether it was to be considered specifically masculinist or not, epistemology was not sufficiently rich or creative to serve as the right kind of medium for understanding the important things: desire, sensibility and being. Such thinking has led many feminist theorists who were neither familiar with nor interested in analytical philosophizing about science to leave every remnant of standpoint theory behind in order to build alternative perspectives on consciousness. Judith Butler is perhaps the most prominent feminist thinker that this kind of trajectory encompasses.

Once again, it is important to acknowledge that none of this remains in the past tense, because the viability of such trajectories is still very much under consideration. If feminist postmodernists resort, for example, to *psychoanalysis*, instead of epistemology, then that only raises the stakes about whether the alternative perspective requires or dissembles a *foundationalist* explanatory grounding of its own. If resort is made to social or discursive *constructionism*, as in Butler's (1990, 1993) efforts to show that both sex and gender are repeatedly 'done' and 'undone' *discursively* and *performatively*, then the heavy reliance of this theoretical move on that most unlikely of companions for feminism, J. L. Austin, needs to be worked through, just as Butler's development of phenomenological themes via the definitive influence of Merleau-Ponty is significant (Butler 2005). Another current interest that feminists are involved in is the post-Deleuzian revival of *vitalism* (*Theory, Culture & Society* 2005) – this once again being a highly metaphysical way to bypass epistemology.

In other words, in none of these lines of flight from the rationalist medium of epistemology is there any relief from conceptualization and argument of a general kind, and in no case can that argument be exclusively feminist. Meanwhile in discussions occurring in the epistemological register itself, feminists are used to aligning themselves with theorists and traditions around which there is not likely to be any spontaneous agreement just on the basis of feminism alone. Thus, some individual authors follow a pragmatist line (Seigfried 1996), whilst others display a relativist but *anti*-standpoint inclination (Hekman 1997), or they continue, ever more carefully, to take the line that runs between rationalism, empiricism and social realism (Longino 2002).

What is going on here across the piece, then, is that feminist thought is no longer providing, or seeking, a uniquely *feminist* philosophical universe. Rather, it is distinctively inhabiting, and seeking to mould, the wider philosophical universe. With this more negotiatory attitude comes a guarded, but unmistakeble, recovery of positivity too. Thus, Donna Haraway, for example, makes the idea of science as *culture* entirely compatible with her proposal that the way to transcend the objectivism/subjectivism duality is to produce 'better accounts of the world, that is, "science"' (1996a: 258). After the Millennium, after postpositivism, and after complexity theory, some feminists want to go further, feeling that all remaining guardedness about mainstreaming, and all remaining scare quotes, need to be completely removed. For Sylvia Walby, who takes this stance, feminism's 'retreat from modernism, rationality, and science is mistaken' (2001: 489).

Today, in the mainstream tradition of analytical philosophy, even the official tomes that summarize the state of play in the specialist domains of the discipline feature a large and growing number of women contributors. The contributor of the 'feminist philosophy' section of one of these volumes, consequently, observes an 'easy going state of partial uncomfortableness' between mainstream philosophers and feminists (Langton 2005: 232). This may sound complacent – it *sounds* complacent – but the scope for reconstructive creativity that a more positive attitude harbours can tangibly be seen in the interesting way in which the canon is being raked over, not (only) for confirmation of mysogeny and the absence of women, but for unexpected intellectual affinities – between feminism and Hume for example (Baier 2002, Nye 2004).

As for feminism and sociology, a similar state of partial uncomfortableness is exuded from the current overviews. On the one hand, the 'imaginative architecture of the social... both presumes and erases the masculine', and 'the canon and core problematics are still moot points'. On the other hand, there has been 'mutual growth and accommodation of feminist and sociological methodological procedures over the past 30 years', as sociology has come fully to accept that gender represents a 'fundamental dimension of social life' (Marshall and Witz 2004: 1, 8). Gender has now become so taken for granted, indeed, that it can easily be forgotten 'how it once went against the grain of the mainstream' (Jackson and Scott 2002: 1). Of course, guarding against complacency, these established sociologists continue to insist that the right attitude for feminists to adopt is that of 'critical interrogation' (Marshall and Witz 2004: 10), and they press beyond a sociology of gender towards a fully gendered sociology (Jackson and Scott 2002: 21).

Yet, what a 'gendered sociology' might be, precisely, is not exactly clear, except as consciousness of the pervasive role of gender in all behaviour, thinking, and institutions – something that seemed to have been granted to the sociological mainstream. And such a conception necessarily takes the form of 'the social' itself: the way in which structural influences come to define behaviours and thoughts in a certain typical way. So just why it is thought that the 'imaginative architecture of the social' is specifically male remains puzzling. Of course, if we give some *content* to the 'social', for example by designating it as 'modernity', then there is a way that 'the social' can be seen as masculinist, (a) if modernity is patriarchal, and (b) if sociology as the discipline which seeks to understand modernity takes on the values of modernity. In certain respects, of course, both those things hold, or at least arguably did, until relatively recently. But still, this does not entail that the *concept of the social*, as such, is masculinist, partly because feminists themselves absolutely rely on such a concept in order to *show* that modernity is masculinist. The air of paradox into which this train of reasoning drifts is no doubt part of sociology's 'ambivalent legacy' that feminists still 'grapple with'. Ultimately, though, the imperative is not completely to dispose of the social, but in a positive spirit to 'rethink' it, 'reworking it to make it more inclusive' (Witz and Marshall 2004: 33–4).

Post- and trans-disciplinarity

Beyond the fact that feminists have found it easier to feel uncomfortably at home in their disciplines, there are other reasons to be quite positive about disciplinarity. Throughout the book, I have been defending the idea of sociology, but sometimes this seems like a very uphill task, given the amount of internal as well as external repudiation that is still encountered. Let me rehearse one or two 'millennial' episodes of that negative kind, and then see where we get to on this whole question of disciplinarity. Around the year 2000, Immanuel Wallerstein repeatedly suggested that it was time to 'unthink' the modernist culture of sociology (Wallerstein 1999a), so that the 'two cultures' divide can finally be overcome in favour of a 'reunited' structure of social knowledge (Wallerstein 2000).

Wallerstein's complaint is that sociology has just stood by and watched, defensively, as complexity studies from one side, and cultural studies from another, have jointly conducted a devastating 'pincer movement' against the two ruling ideologies of social science – intrinsic cultural value on the 'appreciative' side, and linear scientific determinism on the other (Wallerstein 2000: 30–1). Much battle-hardened folklore and pedagogical convenience are packed into these summative assessments, so their half-truths need to be qualified. It should surely no longer need pointing out, for example, that, leaving aside the technocratic mid-century American phase of the discipline, sociologists have time and again consciously refused to conform to any strictly positivistic model. Notoriously, the forward march of scientism has regularly halted over its inapplicability to social scientific explanatory practice. In any case, the kind of cultural studies that Wallerstein cites approvingly – 'Birmingham', in the terms of my first chapter – is the tradition that is most obviously *continuous* with sociology, rather than that variant – postmodern conjuncturalism – that would swiftly consign Wallerstein's own project in world systems theory to the linear and rationalist category.

In more conceptual vein, Wallerstein identifies the persistence of the distinction between nomothetic and ideographic understandings as the main obstacle to productive cross-disciplinary moves, believing that the former dimension remains, regrettably, sociology's disciplinary redoubt. This is very debatable. Recalling Chapter 3, we can say that if sociology is relatively more committed to explanatory reasoning, and cultural studies to description and evaluation, it is not as if the kind of generality sociology is after is *law-like* generality, nor does the evocation of cultural life and experience come into being lacking theoretical context or go away again resistant to generalization. Any approximate division of labour between the two disciplines is best regarded heuristically or ideal-typically.

Mention of ideal types brings the canonical figure of Max Weber to mind, and whilst Wallerstein approves of certain Weberian notions (especially 'substantive rationality') to signal the kind of orientation that he thinks is now required, he fails to note Weber's definitive problematization of the nomothetic/ideographic distinction. In a compelling analysis, Fritz Ringer (1998) has clarified how best to read Weber's epistemological strategy, and were we to follow Ringer, we would see that this classic sociologist pre-empted by about hundred years the sort of approach Wallerstein thinks remains undeveloped. Ringer depicts Weber both as hostile to the naturalism and positivism of his day (with its focus on the nomothetic), and as highly suspicious of culturalist descriptivism (the ideographic). Undoubtedly, Weber regarded the world as constituted by concrete particulars, but rather than only interpretatively appreciating these, Weber saw the job of social scientists as grasping the 'adequate causation' amongst them, and this specifically involves what Ringer calls 'singular causal analysis'. Singular causal analysis is pursued by means of counterfactual reasoning and subsequent generalization about the ways in which certain sorts of actions and events make a *difference* to the causal networks within which they are enmeshed. Weber's ideal types come into play here as those abstract projections of what social reality would be like if singular causal 'lines' were allowed to go all their own way, that is to say, unimpeded by cross-cutting causal processes. Weber's conception implies that if, without doubt, the complexity of the social world makes prediction and certainty impossible, judgements of 'objective probability' can legitimately be made, if framed in the right methodological way.

Given that Weber has been the single most important sociologist in terms of both influence in the discipline and dialectical finesse, it is a bit rich for sociologists to be lectured by Wallerstein about their inability to get past the nomothetic/ideographic distinction in order to enter the world of complexity and reflexivity. Yet there might still be aspects of sociology's disciplinarity that stand as strong institutional constraints on truly exploratory knowledge. The case for *post-disciplinarity* would be that it decisively removes these constraints. Andrew Sayer develops this position in his contribution to the British Sociological Association's millennial collection *For Sociology*. Sayer's attack on disciplinary parochialism has three prongs. One point is that the academic training, hiring, funding and ranking mechanisms over several decades – decidedly heightened by, in the UK, periodic 'research assessment exercises' – have pushed social scientists into being more, rather than less, narrowly disciplinary. The second point construes any perceived movement towards inter-disciplinarity within the fabric of the disciplines themselves as being no more than exercises in disciplinary imperialism. Pretending to be more outgoing, sociologists (and other disciplinarians) are really only interested in widening the market for their own goods. And the third thrust is that whilst sociology frequently claims to be intrinsically more supra-disciplinary than other academic specialisms because of its concern with 'the social', from whose remit, tautologically, nothing can be excluded, this self-appointed status is high-handed and arbitrary. After all, if anything has location, it falls under geography's aegis; if it has duration, it becomes history's object; and if it costs, then economics accounts for it. In short, all the disciplines are 'universal' in scope, but only from their own limited point of view.

None of these arguments is wholly convincing, because they are cast, rather ironically, in an overly reductionist way. After all, if functional and material factors help explain the solidification of disciplines and the interest groups that form around them, inter-disciplinarity too has an eminently functional rationale, one that is increasingly to the fore in the demand for, and rhetoric about, generic and mobile professional skills, knowledge society advantages, large-scale team-based empirical research, inter- and intra-institutional cooperation and 'synergy', joined-up governance, boundary crossing innovation and creativity, thinking out of the box, and much else culled from the lexicon of new educational managerialism. Moreover, even if disciplinary entrenchment does have its interest-driven aspect, still the intrinsic intellectual trend within sociological teaching and research itself is consistently to expand rather than restrict the scope of its enquiry. So it cannot be right here to imply, as Sayer does, that if sociology remains traditionalist in topics and methods, it stands condemned as parochially narrow; but if it becomes more expansive, then this is to be seen as duplicitous. Any glance at the contemporary university curriculum reveals the very considerable overlaps and borrowings that have developed across the gamut of humanities and social sciences. To put this down to the positional interests of the institutional groups involved would seem, ironically, to be committing the same kind of 'sociologism' that Sayer (2000b: 88) spends time exposing in Bourdieu.

What about sociology's claims to be more residually encompassing of the social universe than other disciplines? This could simply be a matter of historical precedence, and it can be put in an ironic rather than an 'imperialist' way: now that geography, history and so on have become so vague, so meta-theoretical, and so over-stretched they resemble nothing other than dear old sociology itself. Also, if all disciplines approach universality, but only from their own side, it remains hard to define exactly what sociology's 'side' is. While it makes sense to say that time, space and exchange values are partial aspects of the social, 'the social' itself is a trickier kind of aspect. Durkheim amongst the classics, and Parsons amongst the moderns, tried to make something special of the social – though Parsons could pursue this only by shunting this object out of his sociology department and into the more expansive field of 'social relations'. But on the whole, sociology has not managed to make any decisive move from the generic to the specific. This infernal indeterminateness has long been something of an embarrassment, and a source of utter frustration for those inclined to 'positivism'. But now, surprisingly perhaps, sociology's very instability appears a signal advantage in a flexible, fuzzy-logic intellectual culture, that is to say, the culture of 'complexity'. Thus, despite the efforts of Sayer and others to re-educate sociology, we have to wonder just how its traditional, capacious, disciplinary self-image differs exactly from his own preferred conception of the goal of social science, that is, 'achieving a more coherent understanding of the social world' (Sayer 2000b: 90).

For Sayer, post-disciplinarity is superior to inter-disciplinarity because the latter tends to leave the disciplines intact, and is thereby able to resist fundamental change. And he gets a good purchase on post-disciplinarity by recalling that *pre*-disciplinary thinkers like Smith and Marx were simultaneously scientific and free-thinking, substantive and normative. If that kind of role model can be summoned up again, and a renewed definition of the intellectual agenda as 'problem-oriented' rather than discipline-defensive, then this constitutes a signal epistemic gain, because our *modus vivendi* would be to follow the intrinsic features of our explanatory situation wherever it happened to lead.

But there are some complications here too. One is that we do not have to be outright constructionists to appreciate that historically established discourses not only track objects of enquiry, but in some sense constitute them. Explanatory domains do not have a wholly pre-conceptual essence that calls into being the most appropriate mode of enquiry.

This makes it difficult to assess in any definitive sense what is lost and what is gained after disciplinarity. Moreover, post-disciplinarity would only fully thrive under a process of dissolution of the established academic departments and professional associations, a prospect that runs up against Sayer's own point about institutionally entrenched loyalties. The formidable logistical difficulties that would crowd into view in such conditions of dissolution are not to be brushed aside. And very likely, what would happen as a result of having to regroup large groups of researchers, teachers and students is that the new problem-centred areas of investigation would tend steadily to develop their own meta-theoretical norms and quasi-disciplinary sectarianism in order to deflect the constant danger of ephemerality and marginalization. This is precisely what has occurred in the solidification of 'problem-oriented' fields such as cultural studies, media studies, and social policy.

Conclusion

Andrew Abbott has made the point that without core disciplines to challenge and transgress, no exciting new marginal knowledge gets articulated. Indeed, the standing arrangement has long been that 'a structure of flexibly stable disciplines' is 'surrounded by a perpetual hazy buzz of inter-disciplinarity' (Abbott 2001: 136). Disciplines remain defensible because they simultaneously preserve coherence whilst, as a matter of necessity, continually reaching outward in order to produce 'richer and richer knowledge of our world' (Abbott 2001: 153). All this, in my view, counts against post-disciplinarity, and to some extent plays down inter-disciplinarity too. But *trans*-disciplinarity might be rather different, especially amongst those disciplines that, being more 'interstitial' than others, lack a clear and distinct 'axis of cohesion' (2001: 6, 140). I have been proposing that the 'idea of sociology' supplies the kind of axis of cohesion that makes for flexible or minimal disciplinarity. Its remit being very broad, it propels sociology into trans-disciplinary dialogues and problematics, whilst acting as a centre of gravity for other interstitial discourses such as cultural studies. But the thrust of the chapter as a whole has not been restricted to talking up the positivity of particular disciplines or trans-disciplinary potential. Indeed, such considerations, just on their own, would remain in the realm of reflexivity itself, because they take as their object the *form* of knowledge and academic self-awareness rather than the positive research and ideas that such platforms make possible.

Conclusion

Writing in the early 1770s, John Millar wrote the following:

> When we contemplate the amazing diversity to be found in the laws of different countries, and even of the same country at different periods, our curiosity is naturally excited to enquire in what manner mankind have been led to embrace such different rules of conduct... In searching for the causes of those peculiar systems of law and government which have appeared in the world, we must undoubtedly resort, first of all, to the differences of situation which have suggested different views and motives of action to the inhabitants of particular countries... The variety that frequently occurs in these and such other particulars, must have a prodigious influence upon the great body of a people; as, by giving a peculiar direction to their inclinations and pursuits, it must be productive of correspondent habits, dispositions, and ways of thinking. (Millar, in Lehmann 1960: 175)

Exhibiting many of the classic features of the Scottish Enlightenment, Millar's discourse could straight away be construed as fundamentally Eurocentric. Millar happened to be a strong abolitionist, but in a way that only European liberal-minded folk could be. And without much ado at all, we could also characterize the epistemological and sociological imagination of this (relatively) privileged man as typically and problematically gendered. Millar happened to think that commercial society had demeaned the status of women, but his alternative view of the kind of dignity and equality that he perceived in earlier social formations quite likely expressed a variant of 'separate spheres' patriarchy. But such critical observations, we might note, are themselves dependent on the very principles of social enquiry that Millar is articulating. And it is not a *simple* message. Millar is saying that we need to establish *both* the uniformities *and* the differences that characterize a huge variety of situations, systems of rules, popular views and motives. Following this statement in *Observations Concerning the Distinction of Ranks*, Millar went on to itemize the complex *layering* that compounds any social situation: natural environments, types of labour/subsistence, demography, 'proficiency in arts', advantages of 'mutual transaction', and the innumerable forms of 'intimate correspondence' between social subjects.

In reflecting on his project, we should also note that Millar presents the relation between situation and motives as only the *first step* in a larger strategy of understanding, and that he avoids any element of *determinism* in the way that situations 'influence' and 'give direction to' people's cultural 'inclinations'. The great merits of Millar's programme are that it is explanatory but not reductive, naturalistic but recognizing the specificities of the social, and positive about the task of comprehending a level of variety and difference across situation that could easily overwhelm any project of understanding. Is Millar's statement universalist, causalist, and scientific? Of course it is – anything less would signal a failure of intellectual nerve. Would we wish to cross its priorities with a greater emphasis on matters of culture, embodiment, and affect? Probably – though it is not obvious that Millar's statement does minimise these dimensions. Undoubtedly, Millar is coming, as we all are, from a particular place and time, and his thought is unmistakeably marked by that context. But overall, what is remarkable is how easy it is to recognize in Millar's statement the logic and promise of sociological cultural studies. In this book I have been trying to show why this project is an enduring one, and arguing, for more than the sake of sociology, that it deserves to be re-energized in our own day.

Bibliography

Abbott, A. (2001). *Chaos of Disciplines*. Chicago: University of Chicago Press.
Abrams, P. (ed.) (1981). *Practice and Progress: British Sociology 1950–1980*. London: Allen & Unwin.
Achinstein, P. (1983). *The Nature of Explanation*. Oxford: Oxford University Press.
Agger, B. (1992). *Cultural Studies as Critical Theory*. London: Falmer Press.
Ahmad, A. (1992). *In Theory*. London: Verso.
Ahmad, A. (1997). 'Post-Colonial Theory and the "Post-" Condition', *Socialist Register 1997*: 353–81. London: Merlin Press.
Alasuutari, P. (1995). *Researching Culture: Qualitative Method and Cultural Studies*. London: Sage.
Alexander, J. C. (1988). 'The New Theoretical Movement', in Smelser, N. (ed.) *Handbook of Sociology*. Newbury Park: Sage.
Alexander, J. C. (1989). 'Durkheimian Sociology and Cultural Studies Today', in Alexander, J. C. (ed.) *Structure and Meaning: Relinking Classical Sociology*. New York: Columbia University Press.
Alexander, J. C. (1990). 'Analytic Debates: Understanding the Relative Autonomy of Culture', in Alexander, J. C. and Seidman, S. (eds) *Culture and Society: Contemporary Debates*. Cambridge: Cambridge University Press.
Alexander, J. C. (1998a). *Neo-functionalism and after*. Oxford: Blackwell.
Alexander, J. C. (1998b). 'Civil Society I, II, III: Constructing an Empirical Concept from Normative Controversies and Historical Transformations', in Alexander, J. C. (ed.) *Real Civil Societies: Dilemmas of Institutionalization*. London: Sage.
Alexander, J. C. (1998c). 'Citizen and Enemy as Symbolic Classifications: On the Polarizing Discourse of Civil Society', in Alexander, J. C. (ed.) *Real Civil Societies: Dilemmas of Institutionalization*. London: Sage.
Alexander, J. C. (2001a). 'Robust Utopias and Civil Repairs', *International Sociology* 16(4): 579–91.
Alexander, J. C. (2001b). 'Theorizing the "Modes of Incorporation": Assimilation, Hyphenation, and Multiculturalism as Varieties of Civil Participation', *Sociological Theory* 19(3): 237–49.
Alexander, J. C. (2003). *The Meanings of Social Life: A Cultural Sociology*. Oxford: Oxford University Press.
Alexander, J. C. (2004a). 'Toward a Theory of Cultural Trauma', in Alexander, J. C., Eyerman, R., Smelser, N. J., and Sztompka, P. (eds) *Cultural Trauma and Collective Identity*. Berkeley: University of California Press.
Alexander, J. C. (2004b). 'On the Social Construction of Moral Universals', in Alexander, J. C., Eyerman, R., Smelser, N. J., and Sztompka, P. (eds) *Cultural Trauma and Collective Identity*. Berkeley: University of California Press.
Alexander, J. C. and Seidman, S. (1990). *Culture and Society: Contemporary Debates*. Cambridge: Cambridge University Press.
Alexander, J. C. and Smith, P. (1993). 'The Discourse of American Civil Society: A New Proposal for Cultural Studies', *Theory & Society* 22(2): 151–207.
Amin, S. (1989). *Eurocentrism*. London: Zed Books.

Anderson, P. (1969). 'Components of the National Culture', in Cockburn, A. (ed.) *Student Power*. Harmondsworth: Penguin.

Archer, M. S., Collier, A., and Porpora, D. V. (2004). *Transcendence: Critical Realism and God*. London: Routledge.

Arnason, J. P. (1993). *The Future that Failed: Origins and Destinies of the Soviet Model*. London: Routledge.

Arnason, J. P. (1997). *Social Theory and the Japanese Experience: The Dual Civilization*. London: Kegan Paul International.

Ashcroft, B., Tiffin, H., and Griffiths, G. (eds) (1995). *The Post-colonial Studies Reader*. London: Routledge.

Ashmore, M. (1989). *The Reflexive Thesis: Wrighting Sociology of Scientific Knowledge*. London: University of Chicago Press.

Assiter, A. (2003). *Revisiting Universalism*. Basingstoke: Palgrave Macmillan.

Baetens, J. (2005). 'Cultural Studies after the Cultural Studies Paradigm', *Cultural Studies* 19(1): 1–13.

Baier, A. (2002). 'Hume, the Woman's Moral Theorist', in Lloyd, G. (ed.) *Feminism and History of Philosophy*. Oxford: Oxford University Press.

Baldwin, E., Longhurst, B., McCracken, S., Ogburn, M., and Smith, G. (2004). *Introducing Cultural Studies*, 2nd ed. London: Prentice Hall.

Barker, C. (2003). *Cultural Studies: Theory and Practice*, 2nd ed. London: Sage.

Barrett, M. (1991). *The Politics of Truth: From Marx to Foucault*. Cambridge: Polity Press.

Barrett, M. (1999). *Imagination in Theory: Essays on Writing and Culture*. Cambridge: Polity Press.

Barrett, M. (2000). 'Sociology and the Metaphorical Tiger', in Gilroy, P., Grossberg, L., and McRobbie, A. (eds) *Without Guarantees: In Honour of Stuart Hall*. London: Verso.

Bass, A. (2002). 'Translator's Introduction', in Derrida, J. *Writing and Difference*. London: Routledge.

Bauman, Z. (1987). *Legislators and Interpreters: On Modernity, Post-modernity and Intellectuals*. Cambridge: Polity Press.

Bauman, Z. (1992). *Intimations of Postmodernity*. London: Routledge.

Bauman, Z. (2003). 'Utopia with no Topos', *History of the Human Sciences* 16(1): 11–26.

Becker, H. S. and McCall, M. M. (eds) (1990). *Symbolic Interaction and Cultural Studies*. Chicago: University of Chicago Press.

Belghazi, T. (1995). 'Cultural Studies, the University and the Question of Borders', in Adam, B. and Allan, S. (eds) *Theorizing Culture: An Interdisciplinary Critique After Postmodernism*. London: UCL Press.

Benhabib, S. (1999). 'Civil Society and the Politics of Identity and Difference in a Global Context', in Smelser, N. J. and Alexander, J. C. (eds) *Diversity and its Discontents*. Princeton: Princeton University Press.

Bennett, T. (1998). *Culture: A Reformer's Science*. London: Sage.

Benton, T. (1991). 'Biology and Social Science: Why the Return of the Repressed Should Be Given a (Cautious) Welcome', *Sociology* 25(1): 1–29.

Berthold-Bond, D. (1989). *Hegel's Grand Synthesis*. Albany NY: SUNY Press.

Best, S. and Kellner, D. (1999). 'Kevin Kelly's Complexity Theory: The Politics and Ideology of Self-organizing Systems', *Organizations and Environment* 12(2): 141–62.

Bevir, M. (1998). *The Logic of the History of Ideas*. Cambridge: Cambridge University Press.

Bhabha, H. (1994). *The Location of Culture*. London: Routledge.

Bhaskar, R. (1978). *A Realist Theory of Science*, 2nd ed. Hassocks: Harvester Press.

Bhaskar, R. (1979). *The Possibility of Naturalism*. Brighton: Harvester Press.

Bhaskar, R. (2000). *From East to West: Odyssey of a Soul*. London: Routledge.

Bhatt, C. (1997). *Liberation and Purity: Race, New Religious Movements and the Ethics of Postmodernity*. London: UCL Press.

Bird, A. (1998). *Philosophy of Science*. London: UCL Press.

Blackburn, R. (1969). 'A Brief Guide to Bourgeois Ideology', in Cockburn, A. (ed.) *Student Power*. Harmondsworth: Penguin.

Bland, L., Brunsdon, C., Hobson, D., and Winship, J. (1978a). 'Women "Inside and Outside" the Relations of Production', in Women's Studies Group CCCS, *Women Take Issue: Aspects of Women's Subordination*. London: CCCS/Hutchinson.

Bland, L., Harrison, R., Mort, F., and Weedon, C. (1978b). 'Relations of Reproduction: Approaches Through Anthropology', in Women's Studies Group CCCS, *Women Take Issue: Aspects of Women's Subordination*. London: CCCS/Hutchinson.

Blaut, J. M. (1993). *The Coloniser's Model of the World: Geographical Diffusionism and Eurocentric History*. London: The Guildford Press.

Bocock, R. and Thompson, K. (1992). 'Introduction', in Bocock, R. and Thompson, K. (eds) *Social and Cultural Forms of Modernity*. Cambridge: Polity Press/Open University.

Bourdieu, P. and Wacquant, L. (1999). 'On the Cunning of Imperial Reason', *Theory, Culture & Society*, 16(1), 41–58.

Brantlinger, P. (1990). *Crusoe's Footprints: Cultural Studies in Britain and America*. London: Routledge.

Brook, E. and Finn, D. (1978). 'Working Class Images of Society and Community Studies', in *On Ideology*. London: CCCS/Hutchinson.

Butler, J. (1990). *Gender Trouble*. London: Routledge.

Butler, J. (1993). *Bodies that Matter*. London: Routledge.

Butler, J. (2005). 'Merleau-Ponty and the Touch of Malebranche', in Carman, T. and Hansen, M. (eds) *The Cambridge Companion to Merleau-Ponty*. Cambridge: Cambridge University Press.

Butters, S. (1976). 'The Logic of Enquiry of Participant Observation: A Critical Review', in Hall, S. and Jefferson, T. (eds) *Resistance Through Rituals: Youth Subcultures in Post-war Britain*. London: CCCS/Unwin Hyman.

Byrne, D. (1998). *Complexity Theory and the Social Sciences*. London: Routledge.

Byrne, D. (1999). 'Complexity and Postmodernism', *Journal of Artificial Societies and Social Simulation* 2(2).

Byrne, D. (2005). 'Complexity, Configurations and Cases', *Theory, Culture & Society* 22(5): 95–111.

Calhoun, C. (1995). *Critical Social Theory*. Oxford: Blackwell.

Carter, B. and New, C. (2004). 'Introduction: Realist Social Theory and Empirical Research', in Carter, B. and New, C. (eds) *Making Realism Work*. London: Routledge.

Castells, M. (1996). *The Rise of the Network Society*, Vol. 1 of *The Information Age*. Oxford: Blackwell.

Castells, M. (2000). 'Materials for an Exploratory Theory of the Network Society', *British Journal of Sociology*, 51(1): 5–24.

Caws, P. (1994). 'Identity: Cultural, Transcultural and Multicultural', in Goldberg, D. T. (ed.) *Multiculturalism: A Critical Reader*. Oxford: Blackwell.

CCCS (1973). 'Literature/Society: Mapping the Field', in *Culture Studies 4 Literature-Society*. Birmingham: CCCS.

CCCS (1981). *Unpopular Education: Schooling and Social Democracy in England since 1944*. London: Hutchinson.

Chaney, D. (1994). *The Cultural Turn: Scene Setting Essays on Contemporary Cultural History*. London: Routledge.

Cilliers, P. (1998). *Complexity and Postmodernism*. London: Routledge.

Clarke, J., Hall, S., Jefferson, T., and Roberts, B. (1976). 'Subcultures, Cultures and Class', in Hall, S. and Jefferson, T. (eds) *Resistance Through Rituals: Youth Subcultures in Post-war Britain*. London: CCCS/ Unwin Hyman.

Clayton, P. D. (2004). 'Emergence: Us from It', in Barrow, J. D., Davies, P. C. W., and Harper, C. L. (eds) *Science and Ultimate Reality: Quantum Theory, Cosmology, and Complexity*. Cambridge: Cambridge University Press.

CMEB (2000). *The Future of Multi-ethnic Britain*. London: Profile Books.

Code, L. (1995). *Rhetorical Spaces: Essays on Gendered Locations*. London: Routledge.

Cohen, J. and Stewart, P. (1995). *The Collapse of Chaos*. Harmondsworth: Penguin.

Couldry, N. (2000). *Inside Culture: Re-imagining the Method of Cultural Studies*. London: Sage.

Craib, I. (1992). *Modern Social Theory*, 2nd ed. Hemel Hempstead: Harvester/ Wheatsheaf.

Craib, I. (1997). *Classical Social Theory*. Oxford: Oxford University Press.

Crane, D. (1994). 'Introduction: The Challenge of the Sociology of Culture to Sociology as a Discipline', in Crane, D. (ed.) *The Sociology of Culture: Emerging Theoretical Perspectives*. Oxford: Blackwell.

Critcher, C. (1979). 'Sociology, Cultural Studies and the Post-war Working Class', in Clarke, J., Critcher, C., and Johnson, R. (eds) *Working Class Culture: Studies in History and Theory*. London: CCCS/Hutchinson.

Danermark, B., Ekstrom, M., Jakobsen, L., and Karlsson, J. (2002). *Explaining Society: Critical Realism in the Social Sciences*. London: Routledge.

Davies, L. (2004). *Education and Conflict: Chaos and Complexity*. London: Routledge Falmer.

De Lillo, D. (1997). *Underworld*. New York: Simon & Schuster.

Dennett, D. (2006). *Breaking the Spell: Religion as a Natural Phenomenon*. London: Allen Lane.

Denzin, N. K. (1992). *Symbolic Interactionism and Cultural Studies: The Problem of Interpretation*. Oxford: Blackwell.

Derrida, J. (1994). *Specters of Marx: The State of the Debt, the Work of Mourning, the New International*. London: Routledge.

Derrida, J. (2002). 'Structure, Sign and Play in the Discourse of the Human Sciences', in *Writing and Difference*. London: Routledge.

Devine, F., Savage, M., Scott, J., and Crompton, R. (eds) (2004). *Rethinking Class: Cultures, Identities and Lifestyles*. Basingstoke: Palgrave Macmillan.

Du Gay, P. (1997). 'Introduction', in Du Gay, P., *et al.* (eds) *Doing Cultural Studies: The Story of the Sony Walkman*. London: Sage/Open University.

During, S. (1993). 'Introduction', *The Cultural Studies Reader*. Cambridge: Polity Press.

During, S. (1995). 'Postmodernism or Post-colonialism Today?' in Ashcroft, B., Tiffin, H., and Griffiths, G. (eds) *The Post-colonial Studies Reader*. London: Routledge.

During, S. (2005). *Cultural Studies: A Critical Introduction*. London: Routledge.

Eagleton, T. (2003). *After Theory*. London: Allen Lane.

Editorial Group (1978). 'Women's Studies Group: Trying to do Feminist Intellectual Work', in Women's Studies Group CCCS, *Women Take Issue: Aspects of Women's Subordination*. London: CCCS/Hutchinson.

Edmondson, R. (1984). *Rhetoric in Sociology*. Basingstoke: Macmillan.

Edwards, D., Ashmore, M., and Potter, J. (1995). 'On Death and Furniture', *History of the Human Sciences* 8(2): 25–49.

Eisenstadt, S. N. (1973). *Tradition, Change and Modernity*. New York: John Wiley.

Eisenstadt, S. N. (1985). 'Macro-societal Analysis – Background, Development and Indications', in Eisenstadt, S. N. and Helle, H. J. (eds) *Macro-Sociological Theory*. Beverly Hills, Calif.: Sage.

Eisenstadt, S. N. (1986). *Origin and Diversity of Axial Age Civilizations*. New York: John Wiley.

Eisenstadt, S. N. (1987a). *European Civilization in a Comparative Perspective: A Study in the Relations between Culture and Social Structure*. London: Norwegian University Press.

Eisenstadt, S. N. (1987b). 'Introduction', in Eisenstadt, S. N. (ed.) *Patterns of Modernity, Vol. I. The West*. London: Frances Pinter.

Elliott, A. (ed.) (1999). *The Blackwell Reader in Contemporary Social Theory*. Oxford: Blackwell.

Ellis, G. F. R. (2004). 'True Complexity and its Associated Ontology', in Barrow, J. D., Davies, P. C. W., and Harper, C. L. (eds) *Science and Ultimate Reality: Quantum Theory, Cosmology, and Complexity*. Cambridge: Cambridge University Press.

Eve, R. A., Horsfall, S., and Lee, M. E. (eds) (1997). *Chaos, Complexity, and Sociology: Myths, Models and Theories*. Beverley Hills: Sage.

Ferguson, M. and Golding, P. (eds) (1997). *Cultural Studies in Question*. London: Sage.

Fine, A. (1984). 'The Natural Ontological Attitude', in Leplin, J. (ed.) *Scientific Realism*. Berkeley: University of California Press.

Flyvbjerg, B. (2001). *Making Social Science Matter: Why Social Inquiry Fails and How It Can Succeed Again*. Cambridge: Cambridge University Press.

Frankfurt, H. G. (2005). *On Bullshit*. Princeton, NJ: Princeton University Press.

Friedman, J. (1997). 'Global Crises, the Struggle for Cultural Identity and Intellectual Porkbarrelling', in Werbner, P. and Modood, T. (eds) *Debating Cultural Hybridity*. London: Zed Books.

Fulcher, J. and Scott, J. (2004). *Sociology*, 2nd ed. Oxford: Oxford University Press.

Game, A. (1991). *Undoing the Social: Towards a Deconstructive Sociology*. Milton Keynes: Open University Press.

Game, A. and Metcalfe, A. (1996). *Passionate Sociology*. London: Sage.

Garfinkel, A. (1981). *Forms of Explanation*. New Haven: Yale University Press.

Gasper, P. (1990). 'Explanation and Scientific Realism', in Knowles, D. (ed.) *Explanation and Its Limits*. Cambridge: Cambridge University Press.

Gates, H. L., Jr. (1994). 'Goodbye Columbus? Notes on the Culture of Criticism', in Goldberg, D. T. (ed.) *Multiculturalism: A Critical Reader*. Oxford: Blackwell.

Gellner, E. (1988a). *Plough, Sword, Book: The Structure of Human History.* London: Collins.

Gellner, E. (1988b). 'Introduction', in Baechler, J., *et al.* (eds) *Europe and the Rise of Capitalism.* Oxford: Blackwell.

Gellner, E. (1992). *Postmodernism, Reason and Religion.* London: Routledge.

Giddens, A. (1984). *The Constitution of Society.* Cambridge: Polity Press.

Giddens, A. (1990). *The Consequences of Modernity.* Cambridge: Polity Press.

Gilbert, J. (2000). 'In Defence of Discourse Analysis', in Bewes, T. and Gilbert, J. (eds) *Cultural Capitalism: Politics After New Labour.* London: Lawrence & Wishart.

Gills, B. K. (1995). 'Capitalism and Power in the Processes of World History', in Sanderson, S. K. (ed.) *Civilizations and World Systems: Studying World-Historical Change.* Walnut Creek, Calif.: AltiMira Press.

Gilroy, P. (1982). 'Steppin' Out of Babylon – Race, Class and Autonomy', in CCCS, *The Empire Strikes Back: Race and Racism in 70s Britain.* London: CCCS/Hutchinson.

Gilroy, P. (2000). *Between Camps: Nations, Cultures and the Allure of Race.* London: Allen Lane, The Penguin Press.

Gilroy, P., Grossberg, L., and McRobbie, A. (eds) (2000). *Without Guarantees: In Honour of Stuart Hall.* London: Verso.

Giroux, H. A. (1994). 'Insurgent Multiculturalism and the Promise of Pedagogy', in Goldberg, D. T. (ed.) *Multiculturalism: A Critical Reader.* Oxford: Blackwell.

Giroux, H. A. (1995). 'The Politics of Insurgent Multiculturalism in the Era of the Los Angeles Uprising', in Kanpol, B. and McLaren, P. (eds) *Critical Multiculturalism: Uncommon Voices in a Common Struggle.* Westport, Conn.: Bergin and Garvey.

Gleick, J. (1998). *Chaos: The Amazing Science of the Unpredictable.* London: Vintage.

Goldberg, D. T. (1994). 'Introduction: Multicultural Conditions', in Goldberg, D. T. (ed.) *Multiculturalism: A Critical Reader.* Oxford: Blackwell.

Goldthorpe, J. E. (2000). *On Sociology.* Oxford: Oxford University Press.

Grant, C. A. and Sachs, J. M. (1995). 'Multicultural Education and Postmodernism: Movement Towards a Dialogue', in Kanpol, B. and McLaren, P. (eds) *Critical Multiculturalism: Uncommon Voices in a Common Struggle.* Westport, Conn.: Bergin and Garvey.

Gray, A. (2003). *Research Practice for Cultural Studies.* London: Sage.

Grimshaw, R., Hobson, D., and Willis, P. (1980). 'Introduction to Ethnography and the Centre', in Hall, S., Hobson, D., Lowe, A., and Willis, P. (eds) *Culture, Media, Language.* London: CCCS/Hutchinson.

Grossberg, L. (1993). 'The Formation of Cultural Studies: An American in Birmingham', in Blundell, V., Shepherd, J., and Taylor, I. (eds) *Relocating Cultural Studies: Developments in Theory and Research.* London: Routledge.

Grossberg, L., Nelson, C., and Treichler, P. A. (eds) (1992). *Cultural Studies.* London: Routledge.

Habermas, J. (1972). *Knowledge and Human Interests.* London: Heinemann Education.

Hall, J. A. (1986). *Powers and Liberties: The Causes and Consequences of the Rise of the West.* Harmondsworth: Penguin Books.

Hall, J. A. (1988). 'States and Societies: The Miracle in Comparative Perspective', in Baechler, J., *et al.* (eds) *Europe and the Rise of Capitalism.* Oxford: Blackwell.

Hall, J. R. (1999). *Cultures of Inquiry: From Epistemology to Discourse in Sociohistorical Research*. Cambridge: Cambridge University Press.

Hall, S. (1977). 'The "Political" and the "Economic" in Marx's Theory of Classes', in Hunt, A. (ed.) *Class and Class Structure*. London: Lawrence and Wishart.

Hall, S. (1978). 'The Hinterland of Science: Ideology and the Sociology of Knowledge', in CCCS, *On Ideology*. London: CCCS/Hutchinson.

Hall, S. (1980). 'Cultural Studies and the Centre: Some Problematics and Problems', in Hall, S., Hobson, D., Lowe, A., and Willis, P. (eds) *Culture, Media, Language*. London: CCCS/Hutchinson.

Hall, S. (1988). 'New Ethnicities', in K. Mercer (ed.) *Black Film/British Cinema, FI/ICA Documents 7*: 27–31. London: Institute of Contemporary Arts.

Hall, S. (1996a). 'When was "the Post-colonial"? Thinking at the Limit', in Curti, L. and Chambers, I. (eds) *The Post-colonial Question: Common Skies, Divided Horizons*. London: Routledge.

Hall, S. (1996b). 'On Postmodernism and Articulation', in Morley, D. and Chen, K.-H. (eds) *Stuart Hall: Critical Dialogues in Cultural Studies*. London: Routledge.

Hall. S. (1997a). 'Introduction', in Hall, S. (ed.) *Representation: Cultural Representations and Signifying Practices*. London: Sage/Open University.

Hall, S. (1997b). 'The Centrality of Culture: Notes on the Cultural Revolutions of Our Time', in Thompson, K. (ed.) *Media and Cultural Regulation*. London: Sage/Open University.

Hall, S. (2000). 'Conclusion: The Multi-cultural Question', in Hesse, B. (ed.) *Un/settled Multiculturalisms*. London: Zed Press.

Hanfling, O. (1981). *Logical Positivism*. Oxford: Blackwell.

Haraway, D. (1996a). 'Situated Knowledges: The Science Question in Feminism and the Privilege of Partial Perspectives', in Fox Keller, E., and Longino, H. (eds) *Feminism and Science*. Oxford: Oxford University Press.

Haraway, D. (1996b). *Modest Witness @ Second Millennium*. London: Routledge.

Harding, S. E. (1993). 'Re-thinking Standpoint Epistemology', in Alcoff, L. and Potter, E. (eds) *Feminist Epistemologies*. London: Routledge.

Harding, S. E. (1994). 'Is Science Multicultural? Challenges, Resources, Opportunities, Uncertainties', in Goldberg, D. T. (ed.) *Multiculturalism: A Critical Reader*. Oxford: Blackwell.

Harris, D. (1992). *From Class Struggle to the Politics of Pleasure*. London: Routledge.

Hekman, S. J. (1997). 'Truth and Method: Feminist Standpoint Theory Revisited'. *Signs* 22(2): 141–65.

Hesse, B. (2000). 'Introduction: "Un/Settled Multiculturalisms" ', in Hesse, B. (ed.) *Un/settled Multiculturalisms: Diasporas, Entanglements, Transruptions,* London: Zed Press.

Hesse, M. B. (1966). *Models and Analogies in Science*. Notre Dame, Indiana: University of Notre Dame Press.

Higgs, P., Rees Jones, I., and Scambler, G. (2004). 'The Sociology of Health Inequalities', in Carter, B. and New, C. (eds) *Making Realism Work*. London: Routledge.

Hirst, P. Q. (1979). *On Law and Ideology*. London: Macmillan.

Holland, J. H. (1998). *Emergence: From Chaos to Order*. Oxford: Oxford University Press.

Hollinger, D. A. (1995). *Postethnic America: Beyond Multiculturalism*. New York: Basic Books.

Holmwood, J. (1995). 'Feminism and Epistemology: What Kind of Successor Science?', *Sociology* 29(3): 411–28.

Holmwood, J. (1996). *Founding Sociology: Talcott Parsons and the Idea of General Theory*. London: Longman.

Hostettler, N. (2004). 'The Dialectics of Realist Theory and the Eurocentric Problematic of Modern Discourse', in Joseph, J. and Roberts, J. M. (eds) *Realism, Discourse and Deconstruction*. London: Routledge.

Howe, S. (1998). *Afrocentrism: Mythical Pasts and Imagined Homes*. London: Verso.

Hughes, J. A., Sharrock, W. W. and Martin, P. J. (1995). *Understanding Classical Sociology*. London: Sage.

Inglis, F. (1993). *Cultural Studies*. Oxford: Blackwell.

Jackson, F. and Pettit, P. (1992). 'Structural Explanation in Social Theory', in Charles, D. and Lennon, K. (eds) *Reduction, Explanation and Realism*. Oxford: Clarendon Press.

Jackson, S. and Scott, S. (eds) (2002). 'The Gendering of Sociology', in *Gender: A Sociological Reader*. London: Routledge.

Jacoby, R. (1999). *The End of Utopia: Politics and Culture in an Age of Apathy*. New York: Basic Books.

Jameson, F. (2004). 'The Politics of Utopia', *New Left Review* 25: 35–54.

Johnson, P. (1994). *Feminism as Radical Humanism*. Boulder, Colo.: Westview Press.

Johnson, R. (1997). 'Reinventing Cultural Studies: Remembering for the Best Version', in Long, E. (ed.) *From Sociology to Cultural Studies*. Oxford: Blackwell.

Johnson, R., Chambers, D., Raghuram, P., and Ticknell, E. (2004). *The Practice of Cultural Studies*. London: Sage.

Joppke, C. and Lukes, S. (eds) (1999). *Multicultural Questions*. Oxford: Oxford University Press.

Joseph, J. and Roberts, J. M. (eds) (2004). *Realism, Discourse and Deconstruction*. London: Routledge.

Jutel, T. (2004). 'Lord of the Rings: Landscape, Transformation, and the Geography of the Virtual', in Bell, C. and Mathewman, S. (eds) *Cultural Studies in Aotearoa New Zealand*. Melbourne: Oxford University Press.

Kahn, J. S. (1995). *Culture, Multiculture, Postculture*. London: Sage.

Kanpol, B. (1995). 'Multiculturalism and Empathy: A Border Pedagogy of Solidarity', in Kanpol, B. and McLaren, P. (eds) *Critical Multiculturalism: Uncommon Voices in a Common Struggle*. Westport, Conn.: Bergin and Garvey.

Kanpol, B. and McLaren, P. (1995). 'Introduction: Resistance Multiculturalism and the Politics of Difference', in Kanpol, B. and McLaren, P. (eds) *Critical Multiculturalism: Uncommon Voices in a Common Struggle*. Westport, Conn.: Bergin and Garvey.

Kanth, R. (2004). 'Eurocentrism, Realism and the Anthropic Cartography of Emancipation', in Joseph, J. and Roberts, J. M. (eds) *Realism, Discourse and Deconstruction*. London: Routledge.

Kellner, D. (1995). *Media Culture: Cultural Studies, Identity, and Politics Between the Modern and the Postmodern*. London: Routledge.

Kelly, K. (1994). *Out of Control: The New Biology of Machines, Social Systems and the Economic World*. London: Fourth Estate.

Kelly, K. (1998). *New Rules for the New Economy*. New York: Viking.

Kemp, S. (2005). 'Critical Realism and the Limits of Philosophy', *European Journal of Social Theory* 8(2): 171–91.

Kemp, S. and Holmwood, J. (2003). 'Realism, Regularity and Social Explanation', *Journal for the Theory of Social Behaviour* 33(2): 165–87.

Kilminster, R. (1999). *The Sociological Revolution: From the Enlightenment to the Global Age*. London: Sage.

Kim, J. (1993). 'Explanatory Realism, Causal Realism and Explanatory Exclusion', in Ruben, D.-H. (ed.) *Explanation*. Oxford: Oxford University Press.

Kincheloe, J. L. and Steinberg, S. R. (1997). *Changing Multiculturalism*. Buckingham: Open University Press.

King, A. (2004). *The Structure of Social Theory*. London: Routledge.

Kinoshita, J. (1990). 'How do Scientific Explanations Explain?' in Knowles, D. (ed.) *Explanation and Its Limits*. Cambridge: Cambridge University Press.

Kitcher, P. (1988). 'Explanatory Unification' in Pitt, J. C. (ed.) *Theories of Explanation*. Oxford: Oxford University Press.

Laclau, E. (1990). 'The Impossibility of Society', in *New Reflections on the Revolutions of Our Times*. London: Verso.

Laclau, E. and Mouffe, C. (1985). *Hegemony and Socialist Strategy*. London: Verso.

Ladyman, J. (2002). *Understanding Philosophy of Science*. London: Routledge.

Langton, R. (2005). 'Feminism in Philosophy', in Jackson, F. and Smith, M. (eds) *Oxford Handbook of Contemporary Philosophy*. Oxford: Oxford University Press.

Lash, S. (2002). *Critique of Information*. London: Sage.

Latouche, S. (1996). *The Westernisation of the World*. Cambridge: Polity Press.

Latour, B. (1988). 'The Politics of Explanation: An Alternative', in Woolgar, S. (ed.) *Knowledge and Reflexivity: New Frontiers in the Sociology of Knowledge*, London: Sage.

Latour, B. (2003). 'Why Has Critique Run Out of Steam? From Matters of Fact to Matters of Concern', *Critical Inquiry* 30(2).

Laudan, L. (1996). *Beyond Positivism and Relativism*. Boulder, Colo.: Westview Press.

Lawrence, E. (1982). 'In the Abundance of Water the Fool is Thirsty: Sociology and Black "Pathology" ', in CCCS, *The Empire Strikes Back: Race and Racism in 70s Britain*. London: CCCS/Hutchinson.

Layder, D. (1997). *Modern Social Theory: Key Debates and New Directions*. London: UCL Press.

Lazarus, N. (1999). *Nationalism and Cultural Practice in the Postcolonial World*. Cambridge: Cambridge University Press.

Leadbeater, C. (1999). *Living on Thin Air: The New Economy*. London: Viking.

Lehmann, W. C. (1960). *John Millar of Glasgow 1735–1801*. Cambridge: Cambridge University Press.

Lemert, C. (1993). *Social Theory: The Multicultural and Classic Readings*. Boulder, Colo.: Westview Press.

Lemert, C. (1995). *Sociology: After the Crisis*. Boulder: Westview Press.

Levitas, R. (2000). 'For Utopia: The (Limits of the) Utopian Function in Late Capitalist Society', *Critical Review of International Social and Political Philosophy* 3(1): 25–43.

Levitas, R. (2003). 'Introduction: The Elusive Idea of Utopia', *History of the Human Sciences* 16(1): 1–10.

Lewis, J. (2003). *Cultural Studies: The Basics*. London: Sage.

Lipton, P. (2004). *Inference to the Best Explanation*, 2nd ed. London: Routledge.

Long, E. (1997). 'Introduction. Engaging Sociology and Cultural Studies: Disciplinarity and Social Change', in Long, E. (ed.) *From Sociology to Cultural Studies*. Oxford: Blackwell.

Longino, H. (1993). 'Subjects, Power and Knowledge: Description and Prescription in Feminist Philosophy of Science', in Alcoff, L. and Potter, E. (eds) *Feminist Epistemologies*. London: Routledge.

Longino, H. (2002). *The Fate of Knowledge*. Oxford: Princeton University Press.

Lopez, J. (2003). *Society and its Metaphors*. London: Continuum.

Lopez, J. and Scott, J. (2000). *Social Structure*. Buckingham: Open University Press.

Lopreato, J. and Crippen, T. (1999). *Crisis in Sociology: The Need for Darwin*. New Brunswick: Transaction Publications.

Luhmann, N. (1995). *Social Systems*. Stanford: Stanford University Press.

Macionis, J. J. and Plummer, K. (2005). *Sociology: A Global Introduction*, 3rd ed. Harlow: Pearson Prentice Hall.

Mackenzie, A. (2005). 'The Problem of the Attractor', *Theory, Culture & Society* 22(5): 45–65.

Mann, M. (1986). *The Sources of Social Power, Vol. I: A History of Power from the Beginning to AD 1760*. Cambridge: Cambridge University Press.

Mann, M. (1988). 'European Development: Approaching a Historical Explanation', in Baechler, J., *et al.* (eds) *Europe and the Rise of Capitalism*, Oxford: Blackwell.

Mann, M. (1993). *The Sources of Social Power, Vol. II: The Rise of Classes and Nation States*, 1760–1914. Cambridge: Cambridge University Press.

Marshall, B. L. and Witz, A. (eds) (2004). 'Introduction: Feminist Encounters with Sociological Theory', in *Engendering the Social*. Buckingham: Open University Press.

May, S. (1999a). 'Introduction: Towards Critical May, S. (ed.) Multiculturalism', in May, S. (ed.) *Critical Multiculturalism: Rethinking Multicultural and Antiracist Education*. London: Falmer Press.

May, S. (1999b). 'Critical Multiculturalism and Cultural Difference: Avoiding Essentialism', in May, S. (ed.) *Critical Multiculturalism: Rethinking Multicultural and Antiracist Education*. London: Falmer Press.

May, T. (1996). *Situating Social Theory*. Milton Keynes: Open University Press.

Maynard, M. (1989). *Sociological Theory*. London: Longman.

McGuigan, J. (1992). *Cultural Populism*. London: Routledge.

McLaren, P. (1994). 'White Terror and Oppositional Agency: Towards a Critical Multiculturalism', in Goldberg, D. T. (ed.) *Multiculturalism: A Critical Reader*. Oxford: Blackwell.

McLaren, P. (1997a). 'Introduction', in Kincheloe, J. L. and Steinberg, S. R. (eds) *Changing Multiculturalism*. Buckingham: Open University Press.

McLaren, P. (1997b). *Revolutionary Multiculturalism: Pedagogies of Dissent for the New Millenium*. Boulder: Westview Press.

McLaren, P. (1999a). 'The Educational Researcher as Critical Social Agent', in Grant, C. A. (ed.) *Multicultural Research*. London: Falmer.

McLaren, P. (1999b). 'Critical Multiculturalism and the Globalisation of Capital', *Journal of Curriculum Theorising* Winter 1999: 27–46.

McLaren, P. (2000). *Che Guevara, Paulo Freire and the Pedagogy of Revolution*. Maryland: Rowman and Littlefield.

McLaren, P. (2001). 'Wayward Multiculturalists: A Reply to Gregor McLennan', *Ethnicities* 1(3): 408–19.

McLennan, G. (1991). 'Post-Marxism and Retro-Marxism: Theorising the Impasse of the Left', *Sites: A Journal for Radical Perspectives on Culture* 23.

McLennan, G. (1995a). *Pluralism*. Buckingham: Open University Press.

McLennan, G. (1995b). 'The Craft of Large-scale Theory: W. G. Runciman and the Neo-traditionalist Revival in Sociological Theory', *Australian and New Zealand Journal of Sociology* 31(2): 93–106.

McLennan, G. (1995c). 'Feminism, Postmodernism, and Epistemology: Reflections on Current Ambivalence', *Sociology* 29(3): 391–409.

McLennan, G. (1996). 'Post-Marxism and the "Four Sins" of Modernist Theorizing', *New Left Review* 218: 53–74.

McLennan, G. (1998). '*Fin de Sociologie?* The Dilemmas of Multidimensional Social Theory', *New Left Review* 230: 58–90.

McLennan, G. (1999). 'Re-Canonizing Marx', *Cultural Studies* 13(4): 555–76.

McLennan, G. (2001). ' "Thus": Reflections on Loughborough Relativism', *History of the Human Sciences* 14(3): 87–103.

McLennan, G. and Osborne, T. (2003). 'Contemporary "Vehicularity" and "Romanticism": Debating the Status of Ideas and Intellectuals', *Critical Review of International Social and Political Philosophy* 6(4): 51–66.

McLeod, J. (2000). *Beginning Postcolonialism*. Manchester: Manchester University Press.

McNeill, W. H. (1963). *The Rise of the West*. Chicago: University of Chicago Press.

McNeill, W. H. (1995). '*The Rise of the West* after Twenty-Five Years', in Sanderson, S. K. (ed.) *Civilizations and World Systems: Studying World-Historical Change*. Walnut Creek, Calif.: AltaMira Press.

McRobbie, A. (1992). 'Post-Marxism and Cultural Studies: A Post-script', in Grossberg, L., Nelson, C., and Treichler, P. A. (eds) *Cultural Studies*. London: Routledge.

McRobbie, A. (1997). *Back to Reality? Social Experience and Cultural Studies*. Manchester: Manchester University Press.

McRobbie, A. (2005). *The Uses of Cultural Studies*. London: Sage.

McRobbie, A. and Garber, J. (1976). 'Girls and Subcultures: An Exploration', in Hall, S. and Jefferson, T. (eds) *Resistance Through Rituals: Youth Subcultures in Post-war Britain*. London: CCCS/Unwin Hyman.

Medd, W. and Haynes, P. (1998). 'Complexity and the Social', paper for ESRC Complexity Workshop, Centre for Social Theory and Technology, Keele University.

Mitchell, S. D. (2003). *Biological Complexity and Integrative Pluralism*. Cambridge: Cambridge University Press.

Miller, R. W. (1987). *Fact and Method: Explanation, Confirmation and Reality in the Natural and Social Sciences*. Princeton: Princeton University Press.

Modood, T. (2005). *Multicultural Politics*. Edinburgh: Edinburgh University Press.

Mongia, P. (1996). 'Introduction', in Mongia, P. (ed.) *Contemporary Postcolonial Theory: A Reader*. London: Arnold.

Moore-Gilbert, B. (1997). *Postcolonial Theory: Contexts, Practices, Politics*. London: Verso.

Moore-Gilbert, B., Stanton, G. and Maley, W. (eds) (1997). *Postcolonial Criticism*. London: Longman.

Morland, I. and Willcox, A. (eds) (2005). *Queer Theory*. Houndmills: Palgrave Macmillan.

Morley, D. (1997). 'Theoretical Orthodoxies: Textualism, Constructivism and the "New Ethnography" in Cultural Studies', in Ferguson, M. and Golding, P. (eds) *Cultural Studies in Question*. London: Sage.

Morley, D. (2000). 'Cultural Studies and Common Sense', in Gilroy, P., Grossberg, L., and McRobbie, A. (eds) *Without Guarantees: In Honour of Stuart Hall*. London: Verso.

Morley, D. and Chen, K.-H. (eds) (1996). *Stuart Hall: Critical Dialogues in Cultural Studies*. London: Routledge.

Morley, D. and Robins, K. (eds) (2001). *British Cultural Studies*. Oxford: Oxford University Press.

Mouzelis, N. (1991). *Back to Sociological Theory*. Basingstoke: Macmillan.

Mouzelis, N. (1995). *Sociological Theory: What Went Wrong? Diagnosis and Remedies*. London: Routledge.

Mouzelis, N. (1997). 'In Defence of the Sociological Canon: A Reply to David Parker', *Sociological Review* 45(2): 244–53.

Mulhern, F. (2000). *Culture/Metaculture*. London: Routledge.

Mulkay, M. J. (1985). *The Word and the World: Explorations in the Form of Sociological Analysis*. London: George Allen and Unwin.

Munch, R. and Smelser, N. J. (eds) (1992). *Theory of Culture*. Berkeley: University of California Press.

Nagel, T. (1997). *The Last Word*. Oxford: Oxford University Press.

Neurath, O. (1973). *Empiricism and Sociology*. Dordrecht: Reidel.

Norman, R. (2004). *On Humanism*. London: Routledge.

Norris, C. (2002). *Truth Matters: Realism, Anti-realism, and Response-dependence*. Edinburgh: Edinburgh University Press.

Nye, A. (2004). *Feminism and Modern Philosophy: An Introduction*. London: Routledge.

Oakley, A. (2000). *Experiments in Knowing: Gender and Method in the Social Sciences*. Cambridge: Polity.

Osborne, P. (2000). *Philosophy in Cultural Theory*. London: Routledge.

Osborne, T. (2004). 'On Mediators: Ideas and the Ideas Trade in the Knowledge Society', *Economy & Society* 33(3): 430–47.

Outhwaite, W. (1987). *New Philosophies of Social Science: Realism, Hermeneutics and Critical Theory*. Basingstoke: Macmillan.

Parekh, B. (2000). *Rethinking Multiculturalism: Cultural Diversity and Political Theory*. Basingstoke: Macmillan.

Parker, D. (1997). 'Why Bother with Durkheim? Teaching Sociology in the 1990s', *Sociological Review* 45(1): 122–46.

Pearson, G. and Twohig, J. (1976). 'Ethnography Through the Looking Glass: The Case of Howard Becker', in Hall, S. and Jefferson, T. (eds) *Resistance Through Rituals: Youth Subcultures in Post-war Britain*. London: CCCS/Unwin Hyman.

Piaget, J. (1971). *Structuralism*. London: Routledge and Kegan Paul.

Prigogine, I. and Stengers, I. (1997). *The End of Certainty: Time, Chaos and the New Laws of Nature*. New York: Free Press.

Psillos, S. (1999). *Scientific Realism: How Science Tracks Truth*, London: Routledge.

Psillos, S. (2002). *Causation and Explanation*. Chesham, Bucks: Acumen.

Rattansi, A. (1997). 'Postcolonialism and its Discontents', *Economy & Society* 26(4).

Rattansi, A. (1999). ' "Postmodernism" and Reflexive Multiculturalism', in May, S. (ed.) *Critical Multiculturalism: Rethinking Multicultural and Antiracist Education*. London: Falmer Press.

Ringer, F. (1998). *Max Weber's Methodology: The Unification of the Cultural and Social Sciences*. Cambridge, Mass.: Harvard University Press.

Ritzer, G. (1996). *Modern Social Theory*, 6th ed. New York: Prentice Hall.

Roberts, B. (1976). 'Naturalistic Research into Subcultures and Deviance: An Account of a Sociological Tendency', in Hall, S. and Jefferson, T. (eds) *Resistance Through Rituals: Youth Subcultures in Post-war Britain*. London: CCCS/Unwin Hyman.

Rojek, C. (1985). *Capitalism and Leisure Theory*. London: Tavistock.

Rojek, C. (1992). 'The Field of Play in Sport and Leisure Studies', in Dunning, E. and Rojek, C. (eds) *Sport and Leisure in the Civilizing Process: Critique and Counter-Critique*. Basingstoke: Macmillan.

Rojek, C. (2003). *Stuart Hall*. Cambridge: Polity Press.

Rooney, E. (1989). *Seductive Reasoning*. Ithaca, N.Y.: Cornell University Press.

Rorty, R. (1998). *Achieving Our Country*. Cambridge, Mass./London: Harvard University Press.

Ruben, D.-H. (1990). *Explaining Explanation*. London: Routledge.

Runciman, W. G. (1983). *A Treatise on Social Theory, Vol. I: Methodology of Social Theory*. Cambridge: Cambridge University Press.

Runciman, W. G. (1989a). *Treatise on Social Theory, Vol. II: Substantive Social Theory*. Cambridge: Cambridge University Press.

Runciman, W. G. (1989b). *Confessions of a Reluctant Theorist*. London: Harvester/Wheatsheaf.

Runciman, W. G. (1998a). 'The Selectionist Paradigm and its Implications for Sociology', *Sociology* 32(1), 163–88.

Runciman, W. G. (1998b). *The Social Animal*. London: Harper-Collins.

Said, E. O. (1978). *Orientalism*. Harmondsworth: Penguin Books.

Sanderson. S. K. (1995). *Social Transformations: A General Theory of Historical Development*, Oxford: Blackwell.

San Juan, E. (1998). *Beyond Postcolonial Theory*. Basingstoke: Macmillan.

San Juan, E. (2002). *Racism and Cultural Studies: Critiques of Multiculturalist Ideology and the Politics of Difference*. Durham NC: Duke University Press.

Sayer, A. (2000a). *Realism and Social Science*. Sage: London.

Sayer, A. (2000b). 'For Postdisciplinary Studies: Sociology and the Curse of Disciplinary Parochialism and Imperialism', in Eldridge, J., *et al.* (eds) *For Sociology: Legacies and Prospects*. Durham: The Sociology Press.

Sayyid, B. S. (1997). *A Fundamental Fear: Eurocentrism and the Emergence of Islamism*. London: Zed Books.

Schwarz, B. (1996). 'Conquerors of Truth: Reflections on Postcolonial Theory', in Schwarz, B. (ed.) *The Expansion on England*. London: Routledge.

Schwarz, W. (2005). 'Stuart Hall' (review of Rojek), *Cultural Studies*, 19(2): 176–202.

Scott, J. (1995). *Sociological Theory: Contemporary Debates*. Aldershot: Edward Elgar.

Seidman, S. (1991). 'The End of Sociological Theory: The Postmodern Hope'. *Sociological Theory* 9(2): 131–46.

Seidman, S. (1994). *Contested Knowledge: Social Theory in the Postmodern Era*, Oxford: Blackwell.

Seidman, S. (ed.) (1996). *Queer Theory/Sociology*. Oxford: Blackwell.

Seidman, S. and Alexander, J. C. (2001). 'Introduction', in Seidman, S. and Alexander, J. C. (eds) *The New Social Theory Reader*. Oxford: Blackwell.

Seigfried, C. H. (1996). *Pragmatism and Feminism: Reweaving the Social Fabric*. Chicago: University of Chicago Press.

Shakespeare, T. (2002). *The Disability Reader: Social Science Perspectives*. London: Continuum.

Shohat, E. and Stam, R. (1994a). *Unthinking Eurocentrism: Multiculturalism and the Media*. London: Routledge.

Shohat, E. and Stam, R. (1994b). 'Contested Histories: Eurocentrism, Multiculturalism and the Media', in Goldberg, D. T. (ed.) *Multiculturalism: A Critical Reader*. Oxford: Blackwell.

Shohat, E. and Stam, R. (2003). 'Introduction', in Shohat, E. and Stam, R. (eds) *Multiculturalism, Postcoloniality and Transnational Media*. New Brunswick, N.J.: Rutgers University Press.

Slack, J. D. (1996). 'The Theory and Method of Articulation', in Morley, D. and Chen, K.-H. (eds) *Stuart Hall: Critical Dialogues in Cultural Studies*. London: Routledge.

Slemon, S. (1994). 'The Scramble for Post-colonialism', in Tiffin, C. and Lawson, H. (eds) *De-scribing Empire*. London: Routledge.

Smelser, N. (1992). 'Culture: Coherent or Incoherent?', in Munch, R. and Smelser, N. J. (eds) *Theory of Culture*. Berkeley: University of California Press.

Smelser, N. J. and Alexander, J. C. (1999). 'Introduction: The Ideological Discourses of Cultural Discontent: Paradoxes, Realities, and Alternative Ways of Thinking', in Smelser, N. J. and Alexander, J. C. (eds) *Diversity and Discontent: Cultural Conflict and Common Ground in Contemporary American Society*. Princeton, N.J.: Princeton University Press.

Smith, P. (2000). 'Looking Backwards and Forwards at Cultural Studies', in Bewes, T. and Gilbert, J. (eds) *Cultural Capitalism: Politics After New Labour*. London: Lawrence & Wishart.

Smith, P. (1998). *Explaining Chaos*. Cambridge: Cambridge University Press.

Smith, P. (ed.) (1998). *The New American Cultural Sociology*. Cambridge: Cambridge University Press.

Soper, K. (1986). *Humanism and Anti-Humanism*. London: Hutchinson.

Sorell, T. (1991). *Scientism: Philosophy and the Infatuation of Science*. London: Routledge.

Spivak, G. C. (1996). 'Explanation and Culture: Marginalia', in Landry, D. and MacLean, G. (eds) *The Spivak Reader*. London: Routledge.

Spivak, G. C. (1999). *A Critique of Postcolonial Reason*. Cambridge, Mass.: Harvard University Press.

Stehr, N. (2001). *The Fragility of Modern Societies: Knowledge and Risk in the Information Age*. London: Sage.

Stones, R. (2005). *Structuration Theory*. Basingstoke: Palgrave Macmillan.

Storey, J. (2001). *Cultural Theory and Popular Culture: An Introduction*. Harlow: Prentice Hall.

Stratton, J. and Ang, I. (1996). 'On the Impossibility of a Global Cultural Studies', in Morley, D. and Chen, K.-H. (eds) *Stuart Hall: Critical Dialogues in Cultural Studies*. London: Routledge.

Sullivan, N. (2003). *A Critical Introduction to Queer Theory*. Edinburgh: Edinburgh University Press.

Taylor, C. (1994). 'Multiculturalism and the "The Politics of Recognition"', in Guttman, A. (ed.) *Multiculturalism and the 'Politics of Recognition'*. Princeton N.J.: Princeton University Press.

Thompson, J. B. (1990). *Ideology and Modern Culture*. Cambridge: Polity Press.

Theory, Culture & Society (2005). Special Issue: *Inventive Life: Approaches to the New Vitalism* 22(1).

Thrift, N. (1999). 'The Place of Complexity', *Theory, Culture & Society* 16(3): 31–70.

Tester, K. (1994). *Media, Culture and Morality*. London: Routledge.

Touraine, A. (1995). *Critique of Modernity*. Oxford: Blackwell.

Turner, B. S. and Rojek, C. (2001). *Society and Culture: Principles of Scarcity and Solidarity*. London: Sage.

Turner, G. (1990). *British Cultural Studies*. Boston: Unwin Hyman.

Turner, G. (2002). *British Cultural Studies*, 3rd ed. London: Routledge.

Turner, J. (1992). 'The Promise of Positivism', in Seidman, S. and Wagner, D. (eds) *Postmodernism and Social Theory*. Oxford: Blackwell.

Urry, J. (2000a). 'Mobile Sociology', *British Journal of Sociology* 51(1): 185–203.

Urry, J. (2000b). *Beyond Societies: Mobilities for the Twenty-first Century*. London: Routledge.

Urry, J. (2003). *Global Complexity*. Cambridge: Polity Press.

Urry, J. (2005). 'The Complexity Turn', *Theory, Culture & Society* 22(5): 1–14.

Van Fraassen, B. (1980). *The Scientific Image*. Oxford: Oxford University Press.

Venn, C. (1996). 'History Lessons: Formations of Subjects, (Post) Colonialism, and an Other Project', in Schwarz, B. (ed.) *The Expansion of England*. London: Routledge.

Venn, C. (2000). *Occidentalism: Modernity and Subjectivity*. London: Sage.

Vogeler, M. S. (1984). *Frederic Harrison: The Vocations of a Positivist*. Oxford: Clarendon Press.

Walby, S. (2001). 'Against Epistemological Chasms: The Science Question in Feminism Revisited', *SIGNS* 26(2): 485–510.

Waldrop, M. M. (1992). *Complexity: The Emerging Science at the Edge of Order and Chaos*. Harmondsworth: Penguin.

Wallerstein, I. (1996). *Unthinking Social Science*. Oxford: Polity Press.

Wallerstein, I. (1997). 'Eurocentrism and its Avatars: The Dilemmas of Social Science', *New Left Review* 226: 93–108.

Wallerstein, I. (1999a). 'The Heritage of Sociology, the Promise of Social Science', *Current Sociology* 47(1).

Wallerstein, I. (1999b). *Utopistics*. New York: The New Press.

Wallerstein, I. (2000). 'From Sociology to Historical Science: Prospects and Obstacles'. *British Journal of Sociology* 51(1): 25–36.

Walsh, W. H. (1974). 'Colligatory Concepts in History', in Gardiner, P. (ed.) *The Philosophy of History*. Oxford: Oxford University Press.

Weeks, J. (1993). 'Rediscovering Values', in Squires, J. (ed.) *Principled Positions: Postmodernism and the Rediscovery of Value*. London: Lawrence & Wishart.

Werbner, P. and Modood, T. (eds) (1997). *Debating Cultural Hybridity: Multicultural Identities and the Politics of Anti-Racism*. London: Zed Books.

White, M. and Schwoch, J. (eds) (2006). 'Introduction', in *Questions of Method in Cultural Studies*. Oxford: Blackwell.

Williams, P. and Chrisman, L. (eds) (1993). *Colonial Discourse and Postcolonial Theory: A Reader*. London: Harvester/Wheatsheaf.

Willis, P. (1977). *Learning to Labour: How Working Class Kids get Working Class Jobs*. Farnborough: Saxon House.

Willis, P. (1980). 'Notes on Method', in Hall, S., Hobson, D., Lowe, A., and Willis, P. (eds) *Culture, Media, Language*. London: CCCS/Hutchinson.

Willis, P. (2003). 'Introduction', in Barker, C. (ed.) *Cultural Studies: Theory and Practice*, 2nd ed. London: Sage.

Witz, A. and Marshall, B. L. (eds) (2004). 'The Masculinity of the Social: Towards a Politics of Interrogation', in *Engendering the Social*. Buckingham: Open University Press.

Wolf, E. R. (1982). *Europe and the People Without History*. Berkeley: University of California Press.

Wolff, J. (1999). 'Cultural Studies and the Sociology of Culture', *Contemporary Sociology* 28(5): 499–507.

Wolff, K. (ed.) (1964). *The Sociology of Georg Simmel*. New York: Free Press.

Wood, B. A. (1998). 'Stuart Hall's Cultural Studies and the Problem of Hegemony', *British Journal of Sociology* 49(3): 399–414.

Woodiwiss, A. (2001). *The Visual in Social Theory*. London: The Athlone Press.

Woodward, J. (2003). *Making Things Happen: A Theory of Causal Explanation*. Oxford: Oxford University Press.

Woolgar, S. (ed.) (2002). *Virtual Society?* Oxford: Oxford University Press.

Young, R. J. C. (1991). *White Mythologies: History Writing and the West*. London: Routledge.

Young, R. J. C. (1995). *Colonial Desire: Hybridity in Theory, Culture and Race*. London: Routledge.

Young, R. J. C. (2001). *Postcolonialism: An Historical Introduction*. Oxford: Blackwell.

Young, R. J. C. (2003). *Postcolonialism: A Very Short Introduction*. Oxford: Oxford University Press.

Index